focusMATH

Intensive Intervention

Francis (Skip) Fennell • Jim Cummins

PEARSON

Glenview, Illinois   Boston, Massachusetts   Chandler, Arizona   Upper Saddle River, New Jersey

Cover Illustration: Judith Espino

ISBN-13: 978-0-328-56330-2
ISBN-10: 0-328-56330-7

PEARSON

1 2 3 4 5 6 7 8 9 10 V064 13 12 11 10 09

CONTENTS

RESPONSE TO INTERVENTION AND MATHEMATICS

Francis (Skip) Fennell, **focus**MATH Consultant

Professor of Education
McDaniel College
Westminster, MD

Understanding Intervention

Intervention and the Response to Intervention (RtI) have become interrelated topics of critical importance for teachers of mathematics. This is particularly true at the elementary school level. No Child Left Behind (NCLB) and the Individuals with Disabilities Education Act (IDEA) both include provisions which require school districts to provide support for students who have difficulty keeping up with day-to-day expectations, hence the need for intervention. RtI can be thought of as an early detection, prevention, and ongoing support system that identifies those students and provides them with the support they need *before* they fall behind. The IDEA Act (2004) encouraged states and school districts to use RtI to provide additional support for students with academic needs, regardless of disability classification.

Intervention provides the opportunity for *all* students to learn. It is a structured plan for providing instructional materials and activities to support student learning during class time, or in programs before school, after school, or during summer school.

Any response to intervention must assume high quality instruction for all students. RtI programs often engage a teaching-learning cycle. Diagnostic assessments screen for early detection of specific mathematics needs. Instructional actions are then provided to support students in need. The cycle then includes follow-up assessments to determine whether students have made adequate progress and no longer need intervention, continue to need some intervention, or need more intensive intervention.

The 3 Tiers

The levels of intervention are typically referred to as *tiers*. RtI is typically thought of as having three tiers, with each tier having specific characteristics (Fuchs, Fuchs, and Vaughn, 2008), although some settings include more than three tiers for the intervention support.

Tier 1: Classroom-based intervention assesses or screens all students. Particular interventions (e.g., more time on a concept, use of a particular model, more practice) are determined and typically implemented by the classroom teacher.

Tier 2: Targeted assistance in key mathematics concepts is designed for small-group settings in the classroom or as supplemental instruction provided by the classroom teacher, a mathematics specialist, or an instructional assistant. This additional time for mathematics will vary, but may range from 20 to 40 minutes, four to five times a week (Fuchs, et al, 2008).

Tier 3: Supplemental programs that occur outside of the daily mathematics lesson are for students requiring more intensive assistance. Special education services and professionals may be involved at this level. At this level, foundational mathematics topics must be central to the instructional activities delivered.

While RtI may be considered a by-product of NCLB and IDEA, it has become a "lifeline" for struggling mathematics learners and must be a carefully considered opportunity for students in need, regardless of instructional level or how tiers are defined and addressed within schools and school districts.

focusMATH

Consider the title *focusMATH*. This intervention-based program allows the classroom teacher or the interventionist to focus and assist students in capturing understanding, proficiency, and problem-solving success within particular mathematics topics. Students having access to these materials will be at Tiers 2, 3, or perhaps beyond. Teachers will find that *focusMATH* provides assessments for screening and determining specific needs among mathematics topics aligned with the Curriculum Focal Points (NCTM, 2006).

The Focal Points—three at each grade level—represent important mathematical topics that are presented as a framework for states and school districts to determine topics of emphasis at particular grade levels.

focusMATH directly aligns with the Curriculum Focal Points (NCTM, 2006) and is intended to address core mathematics topics. *focusMATH* for Grade 6 consists of three books.

Book A: Number and Operations 1
Topic 1: *Multiplying and Dividing Whole Numbers* is a foundational skills topic that prepares students for multiplying and dividing fractions, mixed numbers, and decimals. Although this topic covers content taught in earlier grades, multiplying and dividing whole numbers is often a stumbling block for many students. Topic 2: *Fraction Meanings and Concepts* offers a strong presentation of fractional amounts prior to students beginning their work with the on-level skills and concepts introduced in Topic 3: *Multiplying and Dividing Fractions and Mixed Numbers*. The book then applies students' knowledge of whole numbers, fractions, and mixed numbers to build important conceptual understandings with decimals in Topic 4: *Multiplying and Dividing Decimals*.

Book B: Number and Operations 2
Topic 1: *Multiplication and Division* in Book B is a foundational skills topic about multiplication and division of whole numbers. However, this topic also includes activities for dividing decimals and solving equations to prepare students for solving proportions. Topic 2: *Fractions* is an on-level topic that covers the foundational skills necessary for work with ratio, proportion, and rate. Topic 3: *Ratios and Proportions* addresses the conceptual understanding of ratios, equal ratios and proportion, and similar figures and proportion. In Topic 4: *Rates*, ratio and proportion is extended to activities involving rates, unit rates, comparing rates, and applications involving distance, rate, and time.

Book C: Algebra
Topic 1: *Addition and Subtraction* and Topic 2: *Multiplication and Division* reinforce earlier work with whole numbers. Algebra is the focus in Topic 3: *Variables and Algebraic Expressions*, as students complete activities involving input/output tables, expressions, and variables. Algebraic concepts are extended in Topic 4: *Equivalent Expressions* as students encounter activities involving the order of operations and properties of operations. Topic 5: *Equations* is a critical building block for later work in algebra.

Bibliography

Fuchs, Douglas, Lynn S. Fuchs, and Sharon Vaughn, eds. 2008. *Response to Intervention: A Framework for Reading Educators*. Newark, DE: International Reading Associations.

Fuchs, Lynn S., Douglas Fuchs, Caitlin Craddock, Kurstin N. Hollenbeck, Carol L. Hamlett, and Christopher Schatschneider. 2008. Effects of Small-Group Tutoring with and without Validated Classroom Instruction on At-Risk Students' Math Problem Solving: Are Two Tiers of Prevention Better than One? *Journal of Educational Psychology* 100 (3): 491–509.

National Council of Teachers of Mathematics (NCTM). 2006. *Curriculum Focal Points for Prekindergarten through Grade Eight: A Quest for Coherence*. Reston, VA: National Council of Teachers of Mathematics.

ENGLISH LANGUAGE LEARNERS AND MATHEMATICS

Jim Cummins, **focus**MATH Consultant

Professor
University of Toronto
Toronto, Canada

The Language of Mathematics

Language is central to the teaching of every school subject. The concepts embedded in the curriculum are inseparable from the language we use to teach these concepts to our students. This fusion of language and content across the curriculum presents both challenges and opportunities in teaching English Language Learners (ELL).

We sometimes think of mathematics as less dependent on language than other areas of the curriculum. However, the language of mathematics has its own characteristics that present significant challenges, as well as learning opportunities, for ELL students. Mathematics and language are interconnected at several levels.

As in other academic subjects, mathematics uses a specialized technical vocabulary to represent concepts and describe operations. As early as Grade 1, students are required to learn the meaning of words such as *addition*, *subtraction*, *sum*, and *addend* that are likely to be found only in mathematics discourse. Other terms have specific meanings in mathematics that differ from their meanings in everyday usage and in other subject areas. Examples include words such as *table*, *product*, *even*, and *odd*. Homophones may also be confusing for ELL students. How would they know the difference between *sum* and *some*? Primary grade students are required to learn concepts such as *number facts* and *addition sentences* at a time when many of them (and particularly ELL students) may not know the broader meanings of the words *facts* and *sentences*.

In addition to the technical vocabulary of mathematics, language intersects with mathematics at the broader level of general vocabulary, syntax, semantics, and discourse. Most mathematical word problems require students to understand propositions and logical relations that are expressed through language. Clearly, the language demands of the math curriculum increase as students progress through the grades and this can cause particular difficulties for ELL students.

The ELL Challenge

Content teachers are usually acutely aware of the challenges of teaching ELL students within the subject-matter classroom. However, they may be less aware of the *opportunities* that exist for extending students' knowledge of academic English as they learn academic content. For example, students who are learning mathematics are learning that there are predictable patterns in the ways in which we form the abstract nouns that describe mathematical operations. Many of these nouns are formed by adding the suffix *–tion* to the verb, as in *add/addition*, *subtract/subtraction*, *multiply/multiplication*.

Numerous research studies (see Cummins, 2000 for a review) have demonstrated that ELL students generally pick up everyday conversational fluency within a year or two. However, a much longer period (generally at least five years) is required for students to catch up to native speakers in academic language proficiency (e.g., reading and writing skills). In mathematics, ELL students often make good progress in acquiring basic computation skills in the early grades. They typically experience greater difficulty, however, in solving word problems, particularly as these problems become more complex linguistically in later grades.

Thus, ELL students may require extended language support within the classroom in order to continue to make grade-level progress in content areas like mathematics. Despite the fact that they have acquired conversational fluency in English together with basic mathematical vocabulary and computational skills, students may still experience gaps in their knowledge of more sophisticated vocabulary, syntax, and discourse features of mathematical language.

Instructional Strategies

The research on ELL students' language learning (e.g., Gibbons, 2002) can be summarized in terms of five essential principles that support ELL students in acquiring academic content and simultaneously extending their ability to understand and use language as a tool for cognitive and academic growth.

1. Identify and communicate language and content objectives. In planning and organizing a lesson, teachers must first identify what language and content objectives they will attempt to communicate to students. For example, *focusMATH* provides definitions, descriptions, examples, and visual supports when vocabulary terms are introduced for the first time as a means of simultaneously teaching both concepts and language. Essential vocabulary is reinforced across multiple lessons.

2. Frontload the lesson. Frontloading refers to the use of pre-reading or pre-instructional strategies that prepare ELL students to understand new academic content. Frontloading strategies used in *focusMATH* include activating prior knowledge, building background, previewing text, pre-teaching vocabulary, and making connections.

3. Provide comprehensible input. Language and content that students can understand is referred to as comprehensible input. Teachers make use of non-linguistic supports to enable students to understand language and content that would otherwise have been beyond their comprehension. *focusMATH* employs a wide range of visuals and manipulatives to enable students to understand math concepts and language.

4. Enable language production. Language production complements comprehensible input and is an essential element in developing expertise in academic language. Within *focusMATH*, use of both oral and written language enables students to solve problems, generate insights, and obtain feedback from teachers and peers.

5. Assess for content and language understanding. The instructional cycle flows into assessing what students have learned and then spirals upward into further development of students' content knowledge and language expertise. Within *focusMATH*, formal assessments include a Program Placement Test, Topic Tests, and a Program Exit Test. Also, opportunities for daily progress monitoring are given at point-of-use within each Step.

Bibliography

Cummins, J. 2000. *Language, Power, and Pedagogy: Bilingual Children in the Crossfire.* Clevedon, England: Multilingual Matters.

Gibbons, P. 2002. *Scaffolding Language, Scaffolding Learning: Teaching Second Language Learners in the Mainstream Classroom.* Portsmouth, NH: Heinemann.

ADDITIONAL RESEARCH

Intervention

Research says instruction during intervention should be explicit and systematic (What Works Clearinghouse, 2009).

focusMATH provides a balanced approach to mathematics instruction by blending interactive learning with explicit instruction to accelerate struggling students toward mastery of the grade-level Focal Point.

Concept Development

Research says problem-based instruction (before making math concepts explicit) enhances learning because it actively engages students in thinking about a problem and shows students that their thinking is valued (Mack, 1990).

focusMATH balances understanding concepts with procedural knowledge by linking the two through problem-based interactive learning activities in *Concept Development.*

ELL and Vocabulary

Research says mathematics is like a language and some techniques used to learn language can be used to learn the language of math (Paris and Cunningham, 1996).

ELL: Use Vocabulary allows teachers to check students' understanding of important mathematical terms and reinforces vocabulary.

Problem Solving

Research says understanding develops during the process of solving problems in which important math concepts and skills are embedded (Lester and Charles, 2003).

Problem solving is incorporated throughout the *focusMATH* Steps. In addition, there are Steps in each book dedicated to specific problem-solving strategies.

Progress Monitoring

Research says centering instruction decisions on the individual and tracking student progress enhances student learning (Fuchs and Fuchs, 2001).

focusMATH helps set measurable learning goals for individuals and groups, provides ongoing progress monitoring, and includes a way to exit the program.

Assessment

Research says assessment is a valuable tool for making instructional decisions. When teachers have useful information about what students are learning, they can support their students' progress toward significant mathematical goals (National Council of Teachers of Mathematics, 2000).

focusMATH identifies students' weaknesses with the Program Placement Test, monitors understanding using the results of the Topic Tests, and measures growth using the Program Exit Test.

Professional Development

Research says the quality of instruction depends on the teacher's knowledge of math content (Mathematics Learning Study Committee, 2001).

Math Background provides teachers with essential information about the mathematics presented in every *focusMATH* Step.

For complete bibliography, see page M52.

PROGRAM COMPONENTS

focusMATH

focusMATH provides districts and schools with a flexible program to meet any framework. This curriculum can be used in a variety of settings, including before- or after-school programs, summer school, pull-out or resource-room instruction, or tutoring programs.

focusMATH features concise Steps which target the NCTM Focal Points. Focusing on a smaller number of key skills allows the teacher to spend an extended amount of time on one concept. This strategy provides the student with a deeper understanding of the concept, better mathematical fluency, and the ability to transfer meaningful mathematics to different situations.

Teacher's Edition

There is **one Teacher's Edition** per grade, which contains support for all three student books, Teaching Tool Masters, Assessment Masters, and Answer Keys.

Student Books

There are **three consumable student books** per grade, one for each Focal Point. Students may be recommended for one or more of the books depending on the results of their Program Placement Test. Each student book can be completed in 4–6 weeks.

Manipulatives

The **manipulative kits** provide students with hands-on learning materials that support in-depth conceptual development.

Grade 6 Manipulatives

- Two-color counters
- Fraction strips
- Base-10 units
- Base-10 rods
- Base-10 flats

Student Placement

focusMATH provides teachers with easy-to-use assessments that evaluate student understanding of mathematics. The information from these assessments help tailor instruction, monitor student progress, and document student growth.

The **Program Placement Test** identifies weaknesses of individual students and determines entry points into *focusMATH*. You can give this assessment to an entire class or to students already identified as at-risk or requiring intensive instruction.

The Program Placement Test has 12 test items correlated to each of Books A, B, and C. In each book test, the first 8 items test foundational skills and the last 4 items test on-level skills. If you give the Program Placement Test during the school year, students must get 6 of the 12 test items correct to test out of that book. If you give the grade-level Program Placement Test during a summer school session, students must get 9 of the 12 test items correct to test out of that book.

Progress Monitoring

The **Quick Check** in every *focusMATH* Step provides a brief formative assessment of student understanding.

The **Topic Test** at the end of every *focusMATH* topic provides a summative assessment of student understanding of concepts taught in the topic. Based on topic test results, you may wish to reteach Steps as needed.

Use the **Individual Record Form** (Teaching Tool 1) to track student performance on the Program Placement Test, the Topic Tests, and the Program Exit Test that follows.

Use the **Student Progress Report** (Teaching Tool 2) to keep parents informed of their child's performance.

Student Exit

The **Program Exit Test** items parallel the Program Placement Test items. The Program Exit Test thus shows growth on the NCTM Focal Points and the foundational skills necessary for understanding them.

Administer the test section(s) for the Book(s) the students have completed. Students should get at least 9 of 12 items correct for each book they have completed. Teachers may need to recommend other instructional options for students who get fewer than 9 items correct in a section.

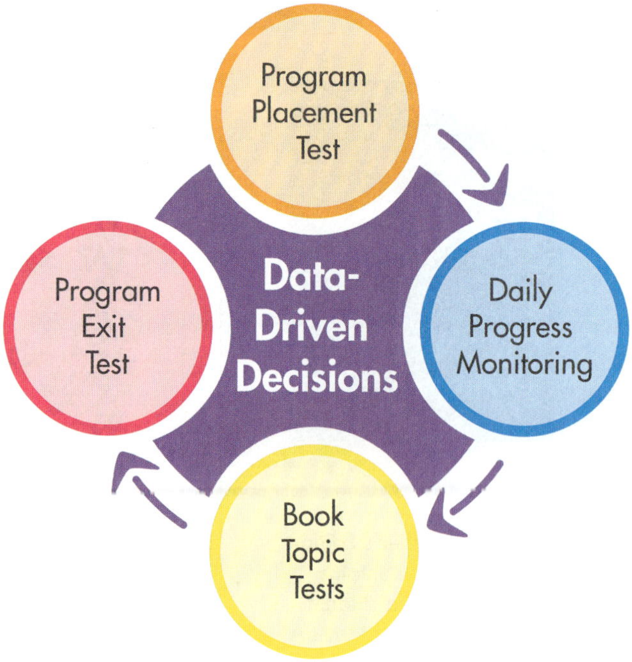

Flexible Implementation

focusMATH can be used **during the school year** or as a **summer school** program for students who struggled at their current grade. The chart below shows how to diagnose and place students in the appropriate *focusMATH* book. During the school year, students with scores of 6 or more on any section of the Program Placement Test may skip the corresponding student book. During summer school, students with scores of 9 or more on any section of the Program Placement Test may skip the corresponding student book.

Program Placement Test
Students take all sections to determine placement.

focusMATH Books
Students take Topic Tests to monitor progress.

Program Exit Test
Students take only the sections they have studied.

Book A Section
Items 1–12

School year
0–5 correct, student needs Book A

Summer school
0–8 correct, student needs Book A

Book A

Book A Section
Items 1–12

Book B Section
Items 13–24

School year
0–5 correct, student needs Book B

Summer school
0–8 correct, student needs Book B

Book B

Book B Section
Items 13–24

Book C Section
Items 25–36

School year
0–5 correct, student needs Book C

Summer school
0–8 correct, student needs Book C

Book C

Book C Section
Items 25–36

OVERVIEW OF A STEP

Steps

Each Step is designed to be covered in a single 30- to 40-minute session. This allows for a systematic approach to instruction and enables students to experience daily success. If needed, a Step can be covered over two days.

Math Background

Provides teachers with targeted information about the mathematics in the Step.

1 Concept Development

Provides teachers with problem-based instruction. This interactive activity engages students; makes meaningful connections to prior knowledge; and allows for important student-teacher and student-student interactions.

Strategic Questions

Help teachers make the mathematics explicit to students. Students verbalize what they have learned and the strategies they used.

Step **3-1**

Multiplying Two Fractions

Objective Students will multiply a fraction by a fraction.

Vocabulary Numerator, denominator

Materials Rectangular paper for folding, markers or colored pencils

Math Background

- The algorithm for multiplying fractions is simple: multiply the numerators and multiply the denominators. $\frac{a}{b} \times \frac{c}{d} = \frac{a \times c}{b \times d}$
- The multiplication of two fractions can be modeled as taking "a part of a part."

Name ____________________ Step **3-1**

Multiplying Two Fractions

Pablo's yard is $\frac{3}{4}$ of an acre. One-half of the yard is woods. What part of an acre is the wooded part of Pablo's yard?

Find $\frac{1}{2}$ of $\frac{3}{4}$ or $\frac{1}{2} \times \frac{3}{4}$ by answering 1 to 5.

1. Fold a sheet of paper into 4 equal parts, as shown at the right. Color 3 parts with slanted lines to show $\frac{3}{4}$. Color the rectangle at the right to show what you did.

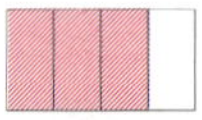

2. Now fold the paper in half the other way. Shade one half with lines slanted the opposite direction of the first set. Color the rectangle at the right to show what you did.

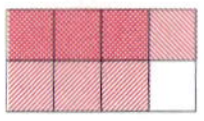

3. What fraction of the paper is shaded with crisscrossed lines? $\frac{3}{8}$
4. The part shaded with crisscrossed lines shows $\frac{1}{2}$ of $\frac{3}{4}$ or $\frac{1}{2} \times \frac{3}{4}$. So, what is $\frac{1}{2} \times \frac{3}{4}$? $\frac{3}{8}$
5. In Pablo's yard, what part of an acre is wooded? $\frac{3}{8}$ acre
6. To find $\frac{1}{2} \times \frac{3}{4}$, how many sections did you divide the paper into? 8
7. What is the product of the denominators in $\frac{1}{2} \times \frac{3}{4}$? $2 \times 4 =$ 8
8. To find $\frac{1}{2} \times \frac{3}{4}$, how many sections did you crisscross? 3
9. What is the product of the numerators in $\frac{1}{2} \times \frac{3}{4}$? $1 \times 3 =$ 3
10. Write the product of the numerators over the product of the denominators. $\frac{1 \times 3}{2 \times 4} = \frac{3}{8}$
11. Is your answer to item 10 the same as item 4? yes
12. Use paper folding to find $\frac{2}{3} \times \frac{3}{4}$. Color the rectangle at the right to show what you did. So, $\frac{2}{3} \times \frac{3}{4} =$ $\frac{6}{12}$.

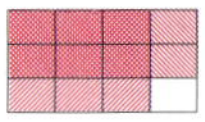

13. To find $\frac{2}{3} \times \frac{3}{4}$, how many sections did you divide the paper into? 12

24 Multiplying Two Fractions

1 Concept Development

Use with Exercises 1–11.

Purpose

You have learned how to multiply whole numbers. Today you will learn how to multiply fractions.

Pose the Problem

Pablo's yard is $\frac{3}{4}$ of an acre. One-half of the yard is woods. What part of an acre is the wooded part of Pablo's yard? Ask students to share their ideas about how to solve this problem. Explain that solving this problem requires finding the product of two fractions, $\frac{1}{2} \times \frac{3}{4}$.

Model

Distribute pieces of rectangular paper to students. *Let's say that your piece of paper represents an acre. What part of an acre is Pablo's yard?* [$\frac{3}{4}$] *How many equal parts do you have to divide the paper into to show $\frac{3}{4}$?* [4 equal parts] Ask students to complete Exercise 1 to show the part of an acre that is Pablo's yard.

A24 Multiplying and Dividing Fractions and Mixed Numbers | Topic 3

Name ______________________ Step 3-1

Multiplying Two Fractions (continued)

14. What is the product of the denominators in $\frac{2}{3} \times \frac{3}{4}$? $3 \times 4 =$ 12

15. To find $\frac{2}{3} \times \frac{3}{4}$ how many sections did you crisscross? 6

16. What is the product of the numerators in $\frac{2}{3} \times \frac{3}{4}$? $2 \times 3 =$ 6

17. Complete: $\frac{2}{3} \times \frac{3}{4} = \frac{2 \times 3}{3 \times 4} = \frac{6}{12}$

To multiply two fractions, you can multiply the numerators and then the denominators. Then simplify, if possible.

$\frac{2}{3} \times \frac{3}{4} = \frac{2 \times 3}{3 \times 4} = \frac{6}{12} = \frac{1}{2}$

18. **Reasoning** Shari found $\frac{3}{10} \times \frac{5}{9}$ as shown at the right. Why does Shari's method work?
She simplified before multiplying, instead of after.

$\frac{3}{10} \times \frac{5}{9} = \frac{\cancel{3}^{1} \times \cancel{5}^{1}}{\cancel{10}_{2} \times \cancel{9}_{3}} = \frac{1}{6}$

Multiply. Simplify, if possible.

19. $\frac{1}{8} \times \frac{2}{3} = \frac{1}{12}$ 20. $\frac{5}{6} \times \frac{1}{2} = \frac{5}{12}$ 21. $\frac{1}{4} \times \frac{3}{5} = \frac{3}{20}$

22. $\frac{6}{7} \times \frac{1}{3} = \frac{2}{7}$ 23. $\frac{3}{4} \times \frac{3}{8} = \frac{9}{32}$ 24. $\frac{1}{5} \times \frac{4}{5} = \frac{4}{25}$

25. $\frac{2}{3} \times \frac{4}{7} = \frac{8}{21}$ 26. $\frac{3}{7} \times \frac{3}{10} = \frac{9}{70}$ 27. $\frac{4}{9} \times \frac{3}{4} = \frac{1}{3}$

28. $\frac{5}{8} \times \frac{4}{5} = \frac{1}{2}$ 29. $\frac{7}{9} \times \frac{3}{5} = \frac{7}{15}$ 30. $\frac{1}{10} \times \frac{5}{7} = \frac{1}{14}$

31. $\frac{7}{8} \times \frac{5}{14} = \frac{5}{16}$ 32. $\frac{3}{11} \times \frac{1}{9} = \frac{1}{33}$ 33. $\frac{1}{12} \times \frac{4}{5} = \frac{1}{15}$

34. There are 45 tents at the summer camp. Girls will use $\frac{2}{3}$ of the tents. How many tents will the girls use? 30 tents

Multiplying Two Fractions 25

The three sections with slanted lines represent Pablo's yard. What part of Pablo's yard is woods? [$\frac{1}{2}$] *How can you use the paper to show the wooded part of Pablo's yard?* [Fold the paper in half so that each of the parts that represent Pablo's yard is folded in half.] Ask students to complete Exercise 2.

How many parts are shaded with crisscrossed lines? [3] *How many parts are there in all?* [8] Have students complete Exercises 3 and 4.

To multiply fractions, multiply the numerators and multiply the denominators. Simplify the fraction that is the product if possible. Have students complete Exercises 5 through 11. *So, what part of an acre is the wooded part of Pablo's yard?* [$\frac{3}{8}$ of an acre]

2 Guided Practice

Use with Exercises 12–18.

Allow students to continue to use paper for folding and coloring.

Exercise 18
Some students may prefer to simplify the problem before multiplying. Remind them to use the greatest common factor of one of the numerators and one of the denominators.

Error Intervention

If students have difficulty understanding why the product of two fractions that are less than 1 is less than either factor,

then say: *The paper model shows that the product of two fractions is "part of a part," so the product will be less than either factor.*

ELL Use Vocabulary

To check understanding, ask a student to repeat and complete this sentence: *The ______ is the bottom number of the fraction, and it tells the number of equal parts in the whole.* [Denominator]

Quick Check Formative Assessment

How do you find the product of two fractions? [Multiply the numerators, multiply the denominators, and simplify if possible.]

2 Independent Practice

Use with Exercises 19–34.

Point out to students that if 1 is the only common factor of the numerator and denominator in the product, that fraction is already in simplest form.

Exercise 34
Remind students that the whole number 45 can be written as the fraction $\frac{45}{1}$. *To find $\frac{2}{3}$ of 45, you multiply $\frac{2}{3} \times \frac{45}{1}$.*

Book A | Step 3-1 A25

2 Guided Practice

Allows students to begin working independently while providing corrective feedback to teachers.

Error Intervention

Helps teachers monitor understanding.

ELL: Use Vocabulary

Reinforces students' knowledge of essential vocabulary terms.

Quick Check

Provides a brief formative assessment of student understanding.

3 Independent Practice

Reinforces the concepts taught and leads students to develop automaticity with new skills.

Grade 6 NCTM Focal Point

Number and Operations 1: Developing an understanding of and fluency with multiplication and division of fractions and decimals

BOOK A

Number and Operations 1

Step 1-1

Multiplying by Two-Digit Numbers

Objective Students will multiply two-digit numbers by two-digit multipliers.

Vocabulary Ones, partial product, tens

Materials Multiplication Charts (Teaching Tool 4), red and blue pencils

Professional Development Math Background

- When the multiplier has two digits, first multiply the other factor by the ones, then by the tens, and then add the partial products.
- When multiplying by the tens, a zero is placed in the ones column of that partial product.

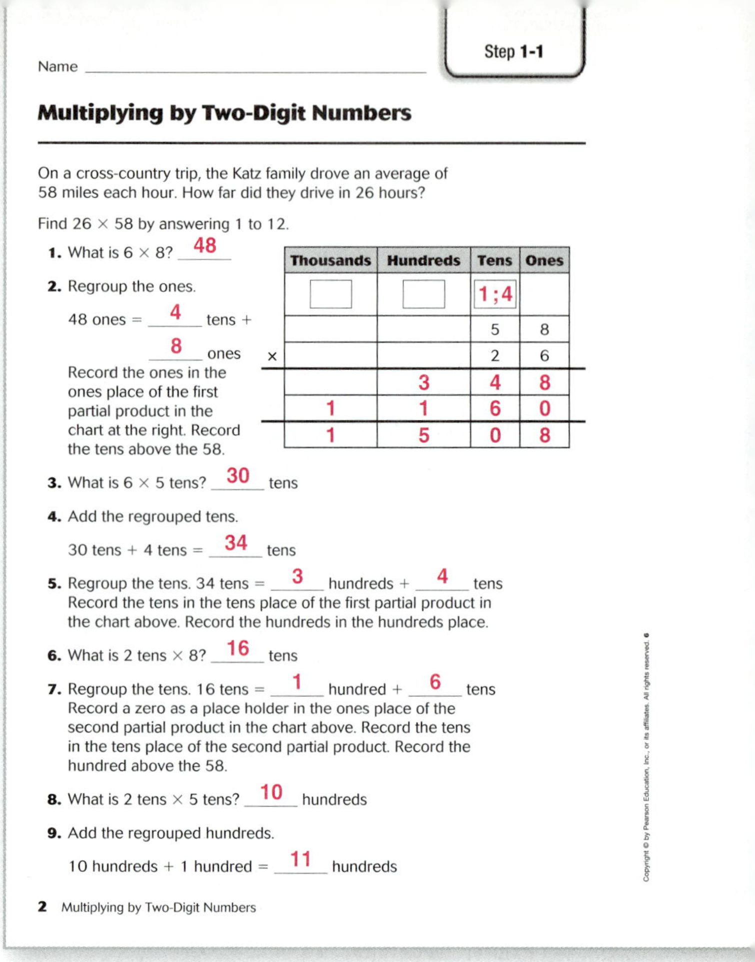

Name ____________ Step 1-1

Multiplying by Two-Digit Numbers

On a cross-country trip, the Katz family drove an average of 58 miles each hour. How far did they drive in 26 hours?

Find 26 × 58 by answering 1 to 12.

1. What is 6 × 8? 48

2. Regroup the ones.

48 ones = 4 tens + 8 ones

Record the ones in the ones place of the first partial product in the chart at the right. Record the tens above the 58.

	Thousands	Hundreds	Tens	Ones
	☐	☐	1;4	
			5	8
×			2	6
		3	4	8
	1	1	6	0
	1	5	0	8

3. What is 6 × 5 tens? 30 tens

4. Add the regrouped tens.

30 tens + 4 tens = 34 tens

5. Regroup the tens. 34 tens = 3 hundreds + 4 tens
Record the tens in the tens place of the first partial product in the chart above. Record the hundreds in the hundreds place.

6. What is 2 tens × 8? 16 tens

7. Regroup the tens. 16 tens = 1 hundred + 6 tens
Record a zero as a place holder in the ones place of the second partial product in the chart above. Record the tens in the tens place of the second partial product. Record the hundred above the 58.

8. What is 2 tens × 5 tens? 10 hundreds

9. Add the regrouped hundreds.

10 hundreds + 1 hundred = 11 hundreds

2 Multiplying by Two-Digit Numbers

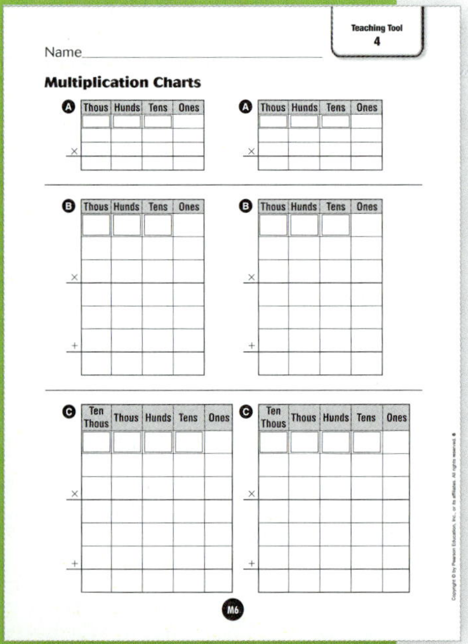

Name ____________ Teaching Tool 4

Multiplication Charts

1 Concept Development

Interactive Learning

Use with Teaching Tool 4.

Purpose

You know how to multiply a two-digit number by a one-digit number. Today you will learn how to multiply a two-digit number by a two-digit number.

Pose the Problem

Mrs. Leland bought 27 boxes of tile to cover her basement floor. Each box contains 64 tiles. How many tiles did she buy? Have students share their ideas about how to solve the problem. They should recognize that this is a multiplication problem.

Model

Distribute copies of Multiplication Charts (Teaching Tool 4). Write 27 × 64 in vertical form on the board. *Write this multiplication problem in a "B" chart.* Check that students have placed each digit in the correct column.

Name ______________________ Step 1-1

Multiplying by Two-Digit Numbers (continued)

10. Regroup the hundreds.

11 hundreds = 1 thousand + 1 hundred

Record the hundred in the hundreds place of the second partial product in the chart. Record the thousand in the thousands place of the second partial product in the chart.

11. Add the partial products. What is 26 × 58? 1,508

12. How far did the Katz family drive in 26 hours? 1,508 miles

Multiply.

13. 27 × 15 = 405	**14.** 25 × 13 = 325	**15.** 21 × 27 = 567	**16.** 34 × 24 = 816
17. 37 × 33 = 1,221	**18.** 81 × 46 = 3,726	**19.** 62 × 44 = 2,728	**20.** 32 × 65 = 2,080
21. 61 × 53 = 3,233	**22.** 84 × 42 = 3,528	**23.** 72 × 77 = 5,544	**24.** 84 × 34 = 2,856
25. 17 × 17 = 289	**26.** 21 × 14 = 294	**27.** 32 × 22 = 704	**28.** 27 × 35 = 945

29. Jason's dad's car can go 27 miles on each gallon of gasoline. When the tank is full, the car holds 21 gallons of gasoline. If the car is going 55 miles per hour, how far can it go on one full tank of gasoline? 567 miles

30. **Reasoning** How much greater is the product of 24 × 23 than the product of 24 × 21? Explain.

It is 2 × 24 or 48 greater since 23 is 2 more than 21.

Have students begin their work with a red pencil. *The first part of the problem is multiplying 27 by the ones in 64. Circle the 4. Multiply 27 × 4 and record the results in the row under the times sign.* Guide students as they multiply, regroup, and record the digits. *What is 27 × 4?* [108] *We call 108 a partial product because it is only part of the product of the original problem.*

Have students switch to a blue pencil. *The second part of the problem is multiplying 27 by the tens in 64. Circle the 6. When you multiply 27 × 6, write the results under the first partial product. Start by writing a zero in the ones place since you are multiplying by the tens.* Again, guide students as they multiply, regroup, and record the digits. Using a second color should help students keep track of the digits they write in the boxes as they regroup. *What is 27 × 6 tens?* [1,620] *This is the second partial product.*

Now add the two partial products. What is the product of 27 × 64? [1,728] *So, how many tiles did Mrs. Leland buy?* [1,728 tiles]

2 Guided Practice

Use with Exercises 1–12.

Have students continue to use a red pencil when they multiply by the ones, and a blue pencil when they multiply by the tens. Note that the top cell in the Tens column shows 2 regrouped numbers. The 4 represents the regrouped 4 tens from Exercise 2. The 1 represents the regrouped 1 hundred from Exercise 7.

Error Intervention

If students have trouble keeping track of multiple regroupings,

then have them cross out regroupings as they add them to the product before proceeding. Also remind students that they may need to regroup when adding the partial products.

ELL Use Vocabulary

To check understanding, ask a student to repeat and complete this sentence: *When you multiply by a two-digit number, you find two _____ and then add them to find the final product.* [Partial products]

Quick Check Formative Assessment

Find 53 × 46. [2,438]

3 Independent Practice

Use with Exercises 13–30.

Provide extra copies of Multiplication Charts (Teaching Tool 4) as needed. Have students use the "B" charts. Alternatively, students may do their work using Centimeter Grid Paper (Teaching Tool 10) to help them keep the digits correctly aligned.

Remind students to write zero as a place holder when they find the second partial product.

Exercise 29
Point out to students that this problem has extra information. *What information is not needed to solve the problem?* [The car is going 55 miles per hour.]

Step **1-2**

Multiplying Greater Numbers

Objective Students will multiply three-digit numbers by two-digit multipliers.

Vocabulary Ones, partial product, tens

Materials Multiplication Charts (Teaching Tool 4), red and blue pencils

Professional Development

Math Background

- The standard algorithm for multiplying greater numbers is just an extension of the algorithm for multiplying two-digit numbers to greater place values.

Name ______________________ Step **1-2**

Multiplying Greater Numbers

An airline company owns a plane that holds 267 passengers. How many passengers can the plane transport in 34 trips?

Find 34 × 267 by answering 1 to 17.

1. What is 4 × 7? __28__

2. Regroup the ones.

28 ones = __2__ tens + __8__ ones

Use the chart below. Record the ones in the ones place of the first partial product. Record the tens above the 267.

3. What is 4 × 6 tens? __24__ tens

4. Add the regrouped tens.

24 tens + 2 tens = __26__ tens

5. Regroup the tens.

26 tens = __2__ hundreds + __6__ tens

Record the tens in the tens place of the first partial product in the chart. Record the hundreds above the 267.

	Thousands	Hundreds	Tens	Ones
		2	2	
		2	6	7
×			3	4
	1	0	6	8

6. What is 4 × 2 hundreds? __8__ hundreds

7. Add the regrouped hundreds.

8 hundreds + 2 hundreds = __10__ hundreds

8. Regroup the hundreds.

10 hundreds = __1__ thousand + __0__ hundreds

Record the hundreds in the hundreds place of the first partial product above. Record the thousand in the thousands place.

9. What is 3 tens × 7? __21__ tens

10. Regroup the tens.

21 tens = __2__ hundreds + __1__ ten

4 Multiplying Greater Numbers

Interactive Learning

1 Concept Development

Use with Teaching Tool 4.

Purpose

You know how to multiply a two-digit number by another two-digit number. Today you will learn how to multiply a three-digit number by a two-digit number.

Pose the Problem

A skyscraper has 43 floors with 126 windows on each floor. How many windows are there in all? Have students share their ideas about how to solve the problem. They should recognize that this is a multiplication problem.

Model

Distribute copies of Multiplication Charts (Teaching Tool 4). Write 126 × 43 in vertical form on the board. *Write this multiplication problem in a "C" chart.* Check that students have placed each digit in the correct column.

Name ______________________ Teaching Tool 4

Multiplication Charts

A

	Thous	Hunds	Tens	Ones
×				

B

	Thous	Hunds	Tens	Ones
×				
+				

C

	Ten Thous	Thous	Hunds	Tens	Ones
×					
+					

M6

Name ______________________

Multiplying Greater Numbers (continued)

Record a zero as a place holder in the second partial product in the chart at the right. Record the 1 ten in the tens place of the second partial product. Record the 2 hundreds above the 267.

	Thousands	Hundreds	Tens	Ones
	☐	2 2	2 2	
		2	6	7
×			3	4
	1	0	6	8
	8	0	1	0
	9	0	7	8

11. What is 3 tens × 6 tens?
18 hundreds

12. Add the regrouped hundreds.
18 hundreds + 2 hundreds =
20 hundreds

13. Regroup the hundreds.
20 hundreds = 2 thousands + 0 hundreds
Record the hundreds in the hundreds place of the second partial product. Record the thousands above the 267.

14. What is 3 tens × 2 hundreds 6 thousands

15. Add the regrouped thousands.
6 thousands + 2 thousands = 8 thousands
Record the thousands in the thousands place of the second partial product in the chart.

16. Add the partial products. What is 34 × 267? 9,078

17. How many passengers can the plane transport? 9,078 passengers

Multiply.

18. 227 × 40 = 9,080

19. 425 × 13 = 5,525

20. 721 × 28 = 20,188

21. 534 × 24 = 12,816

22. Reasoning The school cafeteria prepares breakfast for 115 students each morning. In purchasing food for the week, they will need 2 apples and 35 ounces of juice for each student. How much juice will the cafeteria need for the week? 4,025 ounces

Have students begin their work with a red pencil. *The first part of the problem is multiplying 126 by the ones in 43. Circle the 3. Multiply 126 × 3 and record the results in the row under the times sign.* Guide students as they multiply, regroup, and record the digits. *What is 126 × 3?* [378] *Remember, we call 328 a partial product because it is only part of the product of the original problem.*

Have students switch to a blue pencil. *The second part of the problem is multiplying 126 by the tens in 43. Circle the 4. When you multiply 126 × 4, write the results under the first partial product. Start by writing a zero in the ones place since you are multiplying by the tens.* Again, guide students as they multiply, regroup, and record the digits. Using a second color should help students keep track of the digits they write in the boxes as they regroup. *How much is 126 × 4 tens?* [5,040] *This is the second partial product.*

The last thing you need to do is to add the two partial products. What is the product 126 × 43? [5,418] *So, how many windows are there in the skyscraper?* [5,418 windows]

2 Guided Practice

Use with Exercises 1–17.

Have students continue to use a red pencil when they multiply by the ones, and a blue pencil when they multiply by the tens.

Exercise 1
First, you will multiply 267 by the ones in 34. Circle the 4 in the ones place.

Exercise 9
Now you will multiply 267 by the tens in 34. Circle the 3 in the tens place.

Error Intervention

If students are unsure which box to use as they regroup,

then explain that they should always record the regrouped number in the box above the next digit to be multiplied.

ELL Use Vocabulary

To check understanding, ask a student to repeat and complete these sentences: *When you multiply by a two-digit number, first multiply by the _____ and then by the _____ and then add the _____.* [Ones; tens; partial products]

Quick Check Formative Assessment

Find 259 × 36. [9,324]

3 Independent Practice

Use with Exercises 18–22.

Provide extra copies of Multiplication Charts (Teaching Tool 4) as needed. Have students use the "C" charts. Point out that some of the products will have five digits, so they will need to use the ten thousands column when they record their work.

Remind students to record a zero as a place holder when they find the second partial product.

Exercise 22
Is there any extra information not needed to solve the problem? [Each student gets 2 apples.]

Step **1-3**

Divisibility

Objective Students will learn and apply divisibility rules for the numbers 2, 3, 4, 5, 6, 9, and 10.

Vocabulary Divisible, multiple, remainder

Materials Counters

Professional Development

Math Background

- If a number can be evenly divided by another number, then the first number is a multiple of the second number.
- A remainder occurs when a divisor does not evenly divide a dividend. A remainder must be less than the divisor.
- A number is evenly divisible by another number when the quotient is a whole number with remainder zero.

Name ______________________

Step **1-3**

Divisibility

A number such as 1,875 is divisible by a number like 5 if 1,875 ÷ 5 has no remainder. If 1,875 is a multiple of 5, then 1,875 is divisible by 5.

Use the divisibility rules to determine if 1,875 is divisible by 2, 3, 4, 5, 6, 9, or 10, by answering 1 to 15.

Divisibility Rules	
Number	**Rule**
2	The last digit is even: 0, 2, 4, 6, 8.
3	The sum of the digits is divisible by 3.
4	The last two digits of the number make a number that is divisible by 4.
5	The ones digit is 0 or 5.
6	The number is divisible by 2 and 3.
9	The sum of the digits is divisible by 9.
10	The ones digit is a 0.

1. Is the last digit in 1,875 an even number? no

2. Is 1,875 divisible by 2? no

3. Is the ones digit in 1,875 a 0 or 5? yes

4. Is 1,875 divisible by 5? yes

5. Is 1,875 divisible by 10? no

6. What is the sum of the digits of 1,875?
1 + 8 + 7 + 5 = 21

7. Is the sum of the digits divisible by 3? yes

8. Is 1,875 divisible by 3? yes

9. Is the sum of the digits divisible by 9? no

10. Is 1,875 divisible by 9? no

11. Is 1,875 divisible by both 2 and 3? no

Interactive Learning

1 Concept Development

Use with Exercises 1-15.

Purpose

There are rules that tell you if a number can be evenly divided by another number before doing the actual division. Today you will learn about these divisibility rules for certain numbers.

Pose the Problem

Suppose you want to share 46 items with some friends. How can you decide how many items each friend should get? Ask students to share their ideas.

Model

Distribute 46 counters to each pair of students. *Use your counters to see if 46 is divisible by 2. Into how many groups will you divide 46?* [2] Allow time for pairs to divide the counters. *Is 46 divisible by 2?* [Yes] *If 46 is divisible by 2, then 46 is also a multiple of 2. How many counters are in each group?* [23]

Name ______________________ Step 1-3

Divisibility (continued)

12. Is 1,875 divisible by 6? no

13. What number makes up the last two digits of 1,875? 75

14. Is 75 divisible by 4? no

15. Is 1,875 divisible by 4? no

Test each number to see if it is divisible by 2, 3, 4, 5, 6, 9, or 10. List the numbers each is divisible by.

16. 45 — 3, 5, 9
17. 57 — 3
18. 72 — 2, 3, 4, 6, 9
19. 98 — 2

20. 214 — 2
21. 313 — none
22. 425 — 5
23. 670 — 2, 5, 10

24. 845 — 5
25. 400 — 2, 4 , 5, 10
26. 900 — 2, 3, 4, 5, 6, 9, 10
27. 1,002 — 2, 3, 6

28. 430 — 2, 5, 10
29. 635 — 5
30. 3,470 — 2, 5, 10
31. 9,630 — 2, 3, 5, 6, 9, 10

32. 2,345 — 5
33. 5,672 — 2, 4
34. 1,236 — 2, 3, 4, 6
35. 7,305 — 3, 5

36. Camp Many Lakes has 198 campers registered this year. They are planning many activities and games which must be completed in groups of equal number of campers. What different sizes of groups can Camp Many Lakes divide the campers into? 2, 3, 6, or 9

37. Reasoning Are all numbers that are divisible by 2 also divisible by 10? Explain your reasoning.
Not all numbers that are divisible by 2 are also divisible by 10. For example, 24 is divisible by 2 but not by 10.

38. Reasoning Are all numbers that are divisible by 10 also divisible by 2? Explain your reasoning.
All numbers that are divisible by 10 are divisible by 2. If a number ends in a zero, and thus is divisible by 10, it ends in an even number and thus is divisible by 2.

Use your counters to see if 46 is divisible by 3. Have students divide the counters into 3 groups. Discuss how the counters were divided. *Are there any counters left over? How many?* [Yes; 1 left over] *1 is a remainder. So, 46 is not divisible by 3.*

You may continue to have students divide the counters into equal groups if needed.

Using counters may not be the easiest way to decide divisibility of greater numbers. Instead, you can use divisibility rules to determine if a number can be divided evenly by certain numbers. Refer students to the chart on page 6. Read and discuss the chart together. Then have students complete Exercises 1-15.

Students may notice that there are no divisibility rules for 7 and 8. Explain that the rules listed in the chart are the most used divisibility rules.

2 Guided Practice

Use with Exercises 16–19.

Review the divisibility rules and remind students to refer to the chart as needed. Some students may continue using counters.

Exercise 16

Error Intervention

If students have trouble deciding if 45 is evenly divisible by 4,

then ask: *Is 45 evenly divisible by 2?* [No] *How do you know?* [The last digit is odd, not even.] Point out that all multiples of 4 are also multiples of 2, so all multiples of 4 are even numbers. *45 is an odd number so it is not evenly divisible by 4.*

ELL Use Vocabulary

To check understanding, ask a student to repeat and complete this sentence: *If the divisor goes into the dividend evenly, then the quotient has no _____.* [Remainder]

Quick Check Formative Assessment

By which numbers (2, 3, 4, 5, 6, 9, or 10) is 36 divisible? [2, 3, 4, 6, and 9]

3 Independent Practice

Use with Exercises 20–38.

Exercises 19, 25, 26, 27
Encourage students to look for patterns and use reasoning with the divisibility rules. Remind them that any multidigit number that ends in "00" is divisible by 4. Numbers that are two more (or two less) than a multidigit number that ends in 00 are not divisible by 4.

Step 1-4

Dividing by Multiples of 10

Objective Students will use basic facts to find quotients of division problems whose dividends and divisors are multiples of ten.

Vocabulary Multiple of 10, divisor, dividend, quotient

Professional Development

Math Background

- Patterns can be used to mentally divide multiples of 10.
- Divide the basic fact. Then subtract the number of zeros in the divisor from the number of zeros in the dividend. Write that many zeros after the basic fact quotient. For example, 4,000 ÷ 80 = 50.

Name ______________________ Step 1-4

Dividing by Multiples of 10

Use the multiplication sentences to find each quotient. Look for a pattern.

1. 4 × 20 = 80   80 ÷ 20 = 4

40 × 20 = 800   800 ÷ 20 = 40

400 × 20 = 8,000   8,000 ÷ 20 = 400

2. What basic division fact is used in each quotient above?

8 ÷ 2 = 4

Use basic facts and a pattern to find 2,400 ÷ 80. Answer 3 to 5.

3. What basic division fact can be used to find 2,400 ÷ 80?

24 ÷ 8 = 3

In 24 ÷ 8 = 3, 24 is the dividend, 8 is the divisor, and 3 is the quotient.

4. Look for a pattern.

Number Sentence	Zeros in the Dividend	Zeros in the Divisor	Zeros in the Quotient
240 ÷ 80 = 3	1	1	0
240 ÷ 8 = 30	1	0	1
2,400 ÷ 8 = 300	2	0	2
2,400 ÷ 80 = 30	2	1	1

Complete. If the basic division fact does not end in zero,

Zeros in the dividend − Zeros in the divisor = zeros in the quotient.

5. Reasoning Use the pattern to explain why 2,400 ÷ 80 has one zero.

2,400 has 2 zeros and 80 has one zero.
2 − 1 = 1, so the quotient has 1 zero.

Interactive Learning

1 Concept Development

Use with Exercises 1 and 2.

Purpose

You have learned how to use divisibility rules to help you divide. Today you will use patterns to help you divide multiples of 10.

Pose the Problem

Barrettes are sold in packages of 20. How many packages are needed for 8,000 barrettes? Ask students to share their ideas and explain why this is a division problem.

Model

Write 8,000 ÷ 20 on the board. *We can solve this problem by remembering how multiplication and division are related and by looking for patterns.* Write the pairs of related sentences given in Exercise 1.

All of these numbers are multiples of 10. How do you know? [They end in a zero.] *Let's start with the products. Find the first product. What is 4 × 20?* [80] *How do you know?* [Sample answer: 4 × 2 tens is 8 tens.]

Name ______________________

Step **1-4**

Dividing by Multiples of 10 (continued)

Divide. Use mental math.

6. 300 ÷ 30 = 10	**7.** 60 ÷ 20 = 3	**8.** 200 ÷ 40 = 5
9. 240 ÷ 60 = 4	**10.** 490 ÷ 70 = 7	**11.** 450 ÷ 90 = 5
12. 100 ÷ 50 = 2	**13.** 2,700 ÷ 90 = 30	**14.** 1,800 ÷ 60 = 30
15. 3,500 ÷ 70 = 50	**16.** 1,500 ÷ 30 = 50	**17.** 800 ÷ 40 = 20
18. 640 ÷ 80 = 8	**19.** 3,600 ÷ 60 = 60	**20.** 140 ÷ 70 = 2
21. 1,200 ÷ 20 = 60	**22.** 8,100 ÷ 90 = 90	**23.** 560 ÷ 80 = 7
24. 600 ÷ 30 = 20	**25.** 400 ÷ 20 = 20	**26.** 2,400 ÷ 60 = 40
27. 1,200 ÷ 40 = 30	**28.** 2,500 ÷ 50 = 50	**29.** 2,100 ÷ 70 = 30
30. 4,500 ÷ 90 = 50	**31.** 480 ÷ 80 = 6	**32.** 450 ÷ 50 = 9

33. Dan has a coin collection. His sister Michaela has just started collecting. Michaela has 20 coins, and Dan has 400 coins. About how many times as large as Michaela's coin collection is Dan's collection?

20 times as large

34. Hector must store computer CDs in cartons that hold 40 CDs each. How many cartons will he need to store 2,000 CDs?

50 cartons

35. **Reasoning** Write another division problem with the same answer as 2,700 ÷ 90.

Sample answer: 270 ÷ 9

The second product, 40 × 20, is 10 times as much as the first product, so how much is 40 × 20? [80 tens, or 800] *The third product, 400 × 20, is 10 times as much as the second product, so how much is 400 × 20?* [8,000]

Now let's complete the related division sentences. If 4 × 20 is 80, then what is 80 ÷ 20? [4] *If 40 × 20 is 800, then what is 800 ÷ 20?* [40] *If 400 × 20 is 8,000, then what is 8,000 ÷ 20?* [400] Have students complete Exercise 1.

So, how many packages are needed for 8,000 barrettes? [400 packages]

What basic fact do you recognize in each division sentence in the list? [8 ÷ 4 = 2] Have students complete Exercise 2. *Look for a pattern in the division sentences. If the divisor and dividend are both multiples of 10, how can you easily find the quotient?* [Divide the basic fact: 8 ÷ 2 = 4. Then find the difference in the number of zeros in the dividend and divisor and write that number of zeros after the 4.]

2 Guided Practice

Use with Exercises 3–5.

Have students think about the method for easily determining the quotient and see if it works with these exercises as well.

Exercise 3

Error Intervention

If students have difficulty with the basic division fact 24 ÷ 8 = 3,

then have students review the multiplication facts for 8. *How should you complete this multiplication sentence: 8 × _____ = 24?* [3] *The related division sentence uses all of the same numbers, so how should you complete this sentence: 24 ÷ 8 = _____?* [3]

ELL Use Vocabulary

To check understanding, ask a student to repeat and complete these sentences: *To divide multiples of 10, divide the basic fact. Then find the difference between the number of zeros in the _____ and _____ and write that number of zeros after the _____ of the basic fact.* [Dividend; divisor; quotient]

Quick Check Formative Assessment

Use mental math to find 3,600 ÷ 90. [40]

3 Independent Practice

Use with Exercises 6–35.

Exercises 6–11

Encourage students to use multiplication to check their answers to these exercises. Remind them that the pattern for multiplying by multiples of 10 is to multiply the nonzero digits. Then add the number of zeros in the two factors and write that number of zeros after the product.

In Exercises 8 and 34, remind students that the basic fact is 20 ÷ 4, so there are no zeros in the quotient for Exercise 8. In Exercise 34, they will be adding only 2 zeros, not 3 zeros, to the basic fact quotient.

Step **1-5**

Dividing by Two-Digit Divisors

Objective Students will divide a three-digit number by a two-digit divisor.

Vocabulary Estimate, remainder

Materials Division Templates (Teaching Tool 11)

Professional Development

Math Background

- Dividing by two-digit divisors involves the same algorithm as dividing by one-digit divisors.
- Any remainder must be less than the divisor.

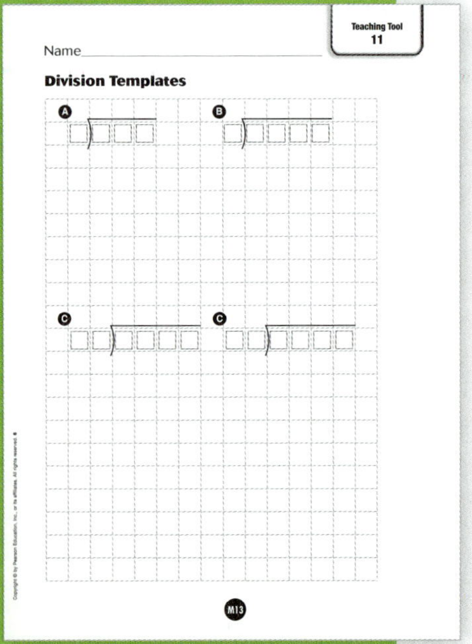

Name ______________________ Step **1-5**

Dividing by Two-Digit Divisors

A carpenter cut a board that is 144 inches long. He cut pieces 32 inches long. How many pieces did he get and how much of the board was left?

Find 144 ÷ 32 by answering 1 to 11.

1. First, estimate to find the approximate number of pieces.

150 ÷ 30 = <u>5</u>

2. Write the estimate in the ones place of the quotient, on the right.

$32\overline{)1\ 4\ 4}$ quotient 5; 1 6 0

3. Multiply. 32 × 5 = <u>160</u>

4. Compare the product to the dividend. Write > or <.

160 (>) 144

Since 160 is too large, 5 was too large. Try 4.

5. Multiply. 32 × 4 = <u>128</u>

6. Compare the product to the dividend. Write > or <.

128 < 144

Since 128 is less than 144, 4 is not too large. Write 4 in the ones place of the quotient on the right. Write 128 below 144.

$32\overline{)1\ 4\ 4}$ quotient 4; 1 2 8; 1 6

7. Subtract. 144 − 128 = <u>16</u>

8. Compare the remainder to the divisor. Write > or <.

16 (<) 32

Since the remainder is less than the divisor, the division is finished.

9. What is 144 ÷ 32? <u>4</u> R <u>16</u>

10. How many 32-inch pieces did the carpenter cut? <u>4</u> pieces

11. How much of the board was left? <u>16</u> inches

10 Dividing by Two-Digit Divisors

Interactive Learning

1 Concept Development

Use with Teaching Tool 11.

Purpose

You have learned how to divide by two-digit multiples of ten. Today you will learn how to divide by any two-digit number.

Pose the Problem

Mrs. Ortega spent 237 hours on a special project at work. She works 44 hours per week. How many weeks did it take her to complete the project? Ask students to discuss their ideas and estimate the answer.

Model

Distribute copies of Division Templates (Teaching Tool 11). Write $44\overline{)237}$ on the board. *Write this division problem in the "C" chart. How did you estimate the answer?* [Sample answer: Use compatible numbers; 240 ÷ 40 = 6 weeks] *Write the estimate in the ones place of the quotient.* At the board, write the 6 above the 7.

Name ______________________

Step 1-5

Dividing by Two-Digit Divisors (continued)

Divide.

12. $32\overline{)202}$ 6 R10	13. $94\overline{)260}$ 2 R72	14. $45\overline{)345}$ 7 R30
15. $62\overline{)137}$ 2 R13	16. $28\overline{)212}$ 7 R16	17. $58\overline{)552}$ 9 R30
18. $82\overline{)657}$ 8 R1	19. $32\overline{)131}$ 4 R3	20. $93\overline{)824}$ 8 R80
21. $89\overline{)465}$ 5 R20	22. $74\overline{)204}$ 2 R56	23. $78\overline{)637}$ 8 R13
24. $77\overline{)561}$ 7 R22	25. $61\overline{)181}$ 2 R59	26. $73\overline{)419}$ 5 R54
27. $63\overline{)564}$ 8 R60	28. $82\overline{)718}$ 8 R62	29. $57\overline{)318}$ 5 R33

30. **Reasoning** To start dividing 126 by 23, Miranda used the estimate $120 \div 20 = 6$. How could she tell 6 is too many?
$6 \times 23 = 138$ and $138 > 120$.

Multiply 44 × 6. How does the product compare to the dividend? [The product, 264, is greater than the dividend, 237.] *That means 6 is too large. You cannot make 6 groups of 44 out of 237. Erase 6 and try 5.* At the board, replace the 6 with a 5.

Multiply 44 × 5 and compare the product to the dividend. How does it compare? [The product, 220, is less than the dividend, 237.] *That means we can make 5 groups of 44.* Show students how to write the product under the dividend and subtract.

What is the remainder? [17] *Is the remainder less than the divisor?* [Yes] *The division is finished. 237 ÷ 44 = 5R17. How many weeks did it take Mrs. Ortega to complete the project?* [Between 5 and 6 weeks] *Why isn't the answer just 5 weeks?* [It took 5 full weeks. Then she used part of another week for the remaining 17 hours.

2 Guided Practice

Use with Exercises 1–11.

Remind students to start the division process with an estimate. *An estimate is used to help you decide where to place the first digit of the quotient, and it gives you a number to try first in the calculations.*

Exercise 4
Point out that the estimate is too large and needs to be adjusted. Other times, however, the estimate might be correct, and other times it may be too small.

Exercise 11
Error Intervention

If students have trouble interpreting the remainder,

then have students reread the problem. *How long was the board before the carpenter cut it?* [144 inches] *How long was each piece?* [32 inches] *How can you tell how many inches the 4 pieces used?* [Multiply 32 × 4 = 128 inches] *How can you tell how much was left?* [Subtract144 − 128 = 16 inches] Point out that the remainder in the division calculation is 16.

ELL Use Vocabulary

To check understanding, ask a student to repeat and complete this sentence: *When you divide by a two-digit number, first make an_____ to help you decide where to place the first digit of the quotient.* [Estimate]

Quick Check Formative Assessment

Find 286 ÷ 38. [7R20]

3 Independent Practice

Use with Exercises 12–30.

Provide extra copies of Division Templates (Teaching Tool 11) as needed. Alternatively, students may do their work on grid paper to help them keep the digits correctly aligned.

Remind students to check that the remainder is less than the divisor.

Step **1-6**

One- and Two-Digit Quotients

Objective Students will divide a three-digit number by a two-digit divisor to find a one- or two-digit quotient.

Vocabulary Tens, ones

Materials Division Templates (Teaching Tool 11)

Professional Development

Math Background

- Dividing to find two-digit quotients involves the same algorithm as dividing to find one-digit divisors.
- After completing the calculations involving the tens digit in the quotient, the ones digit is brought down and the entire process repeats.

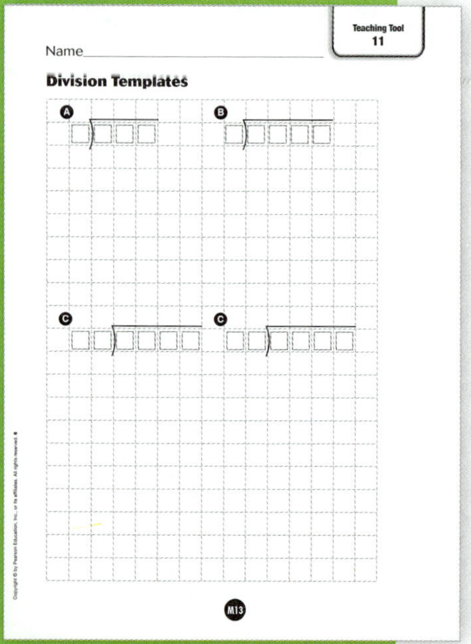

Name ______ Step 1-6

One- and Two-Digit Quotients

Maya wants to buy a guitar that costs \$675. She saves \$40 a week. In how many weeks will she have enough money to buy the guitar?

Find 675 ÷ 40 by answering 1 to 11.

1. Begin by estimating the quotient.
   640 ÷ 40 = **16**

Since the estimate has two digits, begin by dividing the tens.

2. Write the first digit of the estimate in the tens place of the quotient.
3. What is 40 × 1 ten? **40** tens
   Write the product below the 67.
4. What is 67 tens − 40 tens? **27** tens
   Write the difference below the 40 and the line.
5. Bring down the ones. Regroup to show how many ones in all:
   27 tens and 5 ones = **275** ones
6. How many groups of 40 are there in 275? **6**
   Write this number in the ones place of the quotient.
7. What is 40 × 6? **240** Write the product below the 275.
8. What is 275 − 240? **35**
   Write the difference below the 240 and the line.
9. Compare the remainder to the divisor. Write > or <.
   35 (<) 40

Since the remainder is less than the divisor, the division is finished.

10. 675 ÷ 40 = **16** R **35**
11. **Reasoning** How many weeks does Maya need to save to have enough money to buy the guitar? Explain.
    Maya needs to save 16 weeks and part of another week. So, after 17 weeks she will have enough

12 One- and Two-Digit Quotients

1 Concept Development

Interactive Learning

Use with Teaching Tool 11.

Purpose

You have learned how to divide by two-digit numbers to find a one-digit quotient. Today you will learn how to divide by a two-digit number to find a two-digit quotient.

Pose the Problem

The snack stand at a football game sold 567 water bottles. The water bottles come in cases of 24. How many cases of water were sold? Ask students to share their ideas and estimate the answer.

Model

Distribute copies of Division Templates (Teaching Tool 11). Write 24)567 on the board. *Write this division problem in the "C" chart.* How did you estimate the answer? [Sample answer: Use compatible numbers; 600 ÷ 20 = 30 cases] *So, it looks like the quotient will have 2 digits. Write the first digit of the estimate in the tens place of the quotient.* At the board, write the 3 above the 6 in the dividend.

Name ____________________

Step **1-6**

One- and Two-Digit Quotients (continued)

Find 495 ÷ 65 by answering 12 to 17.

12. Begin by estimating the quotient: 490 ÷ 70 = **7**

Since the estimate has one digit, begin by dividing the ones.

13. Write the estimate in the ones place of the quotient.

14. What is 65 × 7? **455**
Write the product below the 495.

15. What is 495 − 455? **40**
Write the difference below the 455 and the line.

$$\begin{array}{r} 7 \\ 65\overline{)495} \\ \underline{455} \\ 40 \end{array}$$

16. Compare the remainder to the divisor. Write > or <.

40 (<) 65

Since the remainder is less than the divisor, the division is finished.

17. 495 ÷ 65 = **7** R **40**

Divide.

18. 23)512 **22 R6** **19.** 82)920 **11 R18** **20.** 35)735 **21**

21. 28)689 **24 R17** **22.** 19)377 **19 R16** **23.** 31)515 **16 R19**

24. 42)883 **21 R1** **25.** 51)987 **19 R18** **26.** 13)525 **40 R5**

27. In July, 912 students toured the nature preserve. There were 24 guided tours and each tour had the same number of students. How many students were on each tour? **38**

28. **Reasoning** Is 45 R49 a reasonable answer for the problem 634 ÷ 13? Why or why not?
No, the remainder is larger than the divisor.

Multiply 24 × 3 tens and compare the product to dividend. How does it compare? [The product, 72 tens, is greater than the dividend, 567.] *That means the estimate was too large. Erase the 3 and try 2.* Do the same at the board.

Multiply 24 × 2 tens and compare the product to the dividend. How does it compare? [The product, 48 tens, is less than the dividend, 567.] Show students how to write 48 under the 56, subtract, and bring down the 7 ones.

Now you need to divide the ones: 87 ÷ 24. Guide students as they repeat the division process to find the second digit of the quotient.

What is the remainder? [15] *Is the remainder less than the divisor?* [Yes] *The division is finished. 567 ÷ 24 = 23 R15. How many cases of water were sold?* [Between 23 and 24 cases] *Explain.* [The snack stand sold 23 full cases and another 15 bottles from part of the 24th case.]

2 Guided Practice

Use with Exercises 1–17.

Remind students to use an estimate to decide how many digits will be in the quotient.

Exercise 1
Error Intervention

If students have difficulty estimating the quotient,

then remind students that they should first round the divisor to the nearest ten, and then use compatible numbers.

Exercise 6
Stress how the steps of the division process repeat as the ones are divided.

Exercises 12–17
This problem yields a one-digit quotient.

ELL Use Vocabulary

To check understanding, ask a student to repeat and complete this sentence: *When you divide by a two-digit number, begin by making an estimate to decide whether to place the first digit of the quotient in the ____ place or the _____ place.* [Tens; ones]

Quick Check — Formative Assessment

Find 887 ÷ 52. [17 R3]

3 Independent Practice

Use with Exercises 18–28.

Provide extra copies of Division Templates (Teaching Tool 11) as needed. Alternatively, students may do their work on grid paper to help them keep the digits correctly aligned.

Exercise 20
This problem has no remainder. Remind students that they need not write "R0" after the quotient.

Step 2-1

Parts of a Region

Objective Students will use models to identify and name fractional parts of a whole.

Vocabulary Equal parts, fraction, denominator, numerator

Materials Fractions Models: Circles (Teaching Tool 6), crayons or markers

Math Background

- A fraction is used to represent equal parts of a whole.
- The denominator of a fraction is the total number of equal parts in the whole.
- The numerator is the number of equal parts being considered.

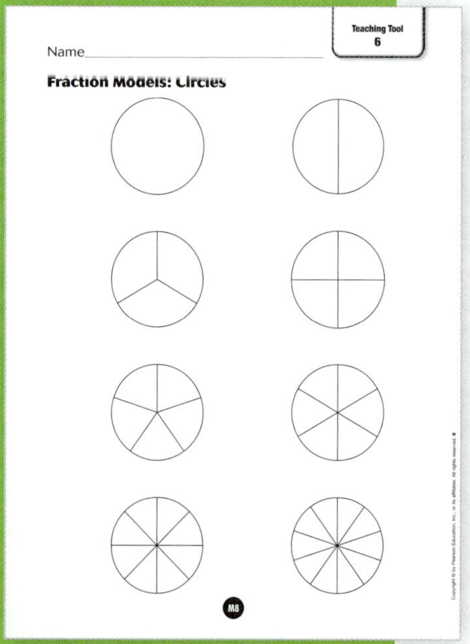
Name

Fraction Models: Circles

Teaching Tool 6

Name ______________________ Step 2-1

Parts of a Region

1. In the circle at the right, color 2 of the equal parts blue and 4 of the equal parts red.

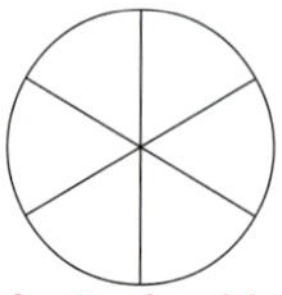

Students should color 2 parts blue and 4 parts red.

Write fractions to name the parts by answering 2 to 6.

2. How many total equal parts does the circle have? 6

3. How many of the equal parts of the circle are blue? 2

4. What fraction of the circle is blue?

$\frac{2}{6} = \frac{\text{number of equal parts that are blue}}{\text{total number of equal parts}} = \frac{\text{(numerator)}}{\text{(denominator)}}$

Two sixths of the circle is blue.

5. How many of the equal parts of the circle are red? 4

6. What fraction of the circle is red?

$\frac{4}{6} = \frac{\text{number of equal parts that are red}}{\text{total number of equal parts}} = \frac{\text{(numerator)}}{\text{(denominator)}}$

Four sixths of the circle is red.

Show the fraction $\frac{3}{8}$ by answering 7 to 9.

7. Color $\frac{3}{8}$ of the rectangle at the right.

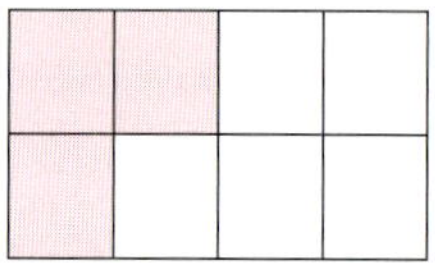

8. How many equal parts does the rectangle have? 8

9. How many parts did you color? 3

14 Parts of a Region

1 Concept Development

Use with Teaching Tool 6.

Purpose

Today you will learn how to use fractions to represent equal parts of a whole.

Pose the Problem

Andy cut a whole pizza into 4 equal parts. He gave 3 of the parts to his friends. What fraction of the pizza did Andy give away? Have students share their ideas.

Model

Distribute copies of Fraction Models: Circles (Teaching Tool 6) and direct the students' attention to the circle that shows 4 equal parts. *Since the parts are equal, each part can be represented by a fraction. How many equal parts are there in all?* [4] *What are the equal parts called?* [Fourths] *Color 3 parts. What fraction*

Name ______________________________

Parts of a Region (continued)

Write the fraction for the shaded part of each region.

10.  $\frac{2}{3}$

11. 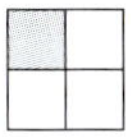 $\frac{1}{4}$

12.  $\frac{4}{5}$

13. 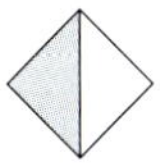 $\frac{1}{2}$

14. 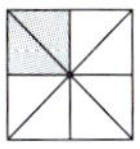 $\frac{2}{8}$

15. 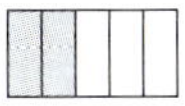 $\frac{2}{5}$

16.  $\frac{1}{3}$

17.  $\frac{3}{5}$

18.  $\frac{5}{8}$

Color to show each fraction.

19. $\frac{3}{4}$ 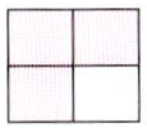

20. $\frac{5}{6}$ 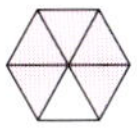

21. $\frac{7}{10}$ 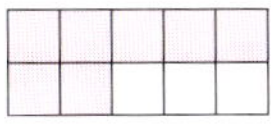

22. Math Reasoning Draw a picture to show $\frac{1}{3}$. Then divide each of the parts in half. What fraction of the whole does the $\frac{1}{3}$ represent now? Check students' drawings. $\frac{2}{6}$

23. Ben divided a pie into 8 equal pieces and ate 3 of them. How much of the pie remains? $\frac{5}{8}$

represents the part of the circle you colored? [$\frac{3}{4}$] Write $\frac{3}{4}$ on the board and have students say "three fourths" aloud. *The denominator of the fraction is 4 because there are 4 equal parts in all. The numerator is 3 because 3 of the parts are colored. So, what fraction of the pizza did Andy give away to his friends?* [$\frac{3}{4}$ of the pizza]

Find the circle that shows 10 equal parts. Color $\frac{7}{10}$ of that circle. How many equal parts did you color? [7] *How many equal parts are there in all?* [10] *What fraction represents the part that you colored?* [$\frac{7}{10}$] *What fraction of the circle is not colored?* [$\frac{3}{10}$]

Give pairs of students time to work together, using the remainder of the circles on Teaching Tool 6. After one student colors a chosen number of parts of a circle, his or her partner will write the fraction represented by the colored part. Then partners exchange roles and use another circle.

2 Guided Practice

Use with Exercises 1–9.

Remind students that the denominator of a fraction represents equal parts of a whole. For example, three equal parts can be named as thirds. If there are three unequal parts, those parts are not thirds.

Exercises 4, 6

Look at the numerator in each fraction. Is the numerator above or below the line? [Above] *Where is the denominator in each fraction?* [Below the line]

Exercise 7

Error Intervention

If students have difficulty knowing how many parts to color,

then ask: *How many equal parts are there?* [8] *How many eighths should be colored?* [3]

ELL Use Vocabulary

To check understanding, ask a student to repeat and complete these sentences: *When a whole is divided into equal parts, each part can be represented by a ____.* [Fraction] *The total number of equal parts is the ____.* [Denominator] *The number of equal parts being considered is the ____.* [Numerator]

Quick Check Formative Assessment

How could you show $\frac{7}{8}$ of a circle colored red? [Divide the circle into 8 equal parts. Color 7 of the parts red.]

3 Independent Practice

Use with Exercises 10–23.

For Exercises 10–18, some students may have difficulty knowing which number to write above the line and which to write below the line. Remind them that the total number of equal parts is the denominator and is written below the fraction bar. For these exercises, the numerator is the number of shaded parts. That number is written above the fraction bar.

Step **2-2**

Equivalent Fractions

Objective Students will use models and then multiplication and division to write equivalent fractions.

Vocabulary Equivalent fractions

Materials Fraction Models: Strips (Teaching Tool 5), crayons or markers

Professional Development Math Background

- You can multiply or divide any number by 1 and not change the value of that number.
- The whole number 1 can be written as a fraction such as $\frac{3}{3}$ or $\frac{5}{5}$.
- When you multiply the numerator and denominator of a fraction by the same number, it is the same as multiplying by 1.

Name ____________________ Step **2-2**

Equivalent Fractions

1. Show $\frac{2}{3}$ by coloring 2 of the $\frac{1}{3}$ strips.

2. Color as many $\frac{1}{6}$ strips as it takes to cover the same region as the $\frac{2}{3}$.

1					
$\frac{1}{3}$		$\frac{1}{3}$		$\frac{1}{3}$	
$\frac{1}{6}$	$\frac{1}{6}$	$\frac{1}{6}$	$\frac{1}{6}$	$\frac{1}{6}$	$\frac{1}{6}$

How many $\frac{1}{6}$ strips did you color? 4

3. So, $\frac{2}{3}$ is equivalent to four $\frac{1}{6}$ strips. $\frac{2}{3} = \frac{4}{6}$

You can use multiplication to find a fraction equivalent to $\frac{2}{3}$. To do this, multiply the numerator and the denominator by the same number.

4. What number is the denominator of $\frac{2}{3}$ multiplied by to get 6? 2

$\frac{2}{3} = \frac{4}{6}$ (× 2, × 2)

5. Since the denominator was multiplied by 2, the numerator must also be multiplied by 2. Put the product of 2 × 2 in the numerator of the second fraction above.

6. Show $\frac{9}{12}$ by coloring 9 of the $\frac{1}{12}$ strips.

7. Color as many $\frac{1}{4}$ strips as it takes to cover the same region as $\frac{9}{12}$.

1											
$\frac{1}{4}$			$\frac{1}{4}$			$\frac{1}{4}$			$\frac{1}{4}$		
$\frac{1}{12}$	$\frac{1}{12}$	$\frac{1}{12}$	$\frac{1}{12}$	$\frac{1}{12}$	$\frac{1}{12}$	$\frac{1}{12}$	$\frac{1}{12}$	$\frac{1}{12}$	$\frac{1}{12}$	$\frac{1}{12}$	$\frac{1}{12}$

How many $\frac{1}{4}$ strips did you color? 3

8. So, $\frac{9}{12}$ is equivalent to three $\frac{1}{4}$ strips. $\frac{9}{12} = \frac{3}{4}$

16 Equivalent Fractions

Name ____________________ Teaching Tool 5

Fraction Models: Strips

1
$\frac{1}{2}$ (2 parts)
$\frac{1}{3}$ (3 parts)
$\frac{1}{4}$ (4 parts)
$\frac{1}{5}$ (5 parts)
$\frac{1}{6}$ (6 parts)
$\frac{1}{8}$ (8 parts)
$\frac{1}{10}$ (10 parts)
$\frac{1}{12}$ (12 parts)

M7

Interactive Learning 1 Concept Development

Use with Teaching Tool 5.

Purpose

You know how to use fractions to represent equal parts of a whole. Today you will learn to find two different fractions that represent the same part of a whole.

Pose the Problem

Distribute copies of Fraction Models: Strips (Teaching Tool 5). Instruct students to cut out whole strips. *Use your fraction strips to find as many fractions as you can that name the same part of a whole as $\frac{1}{2}$.* Give students time to work in pairs. Then ask them to share their results with the class.

Model

Fractions that name the same part of a whole but have different numerators and denominators are equivalent fractions. What are some fractions that are equivalent to $\frac{1}{2}$? [Sample answers: $\frac{2}{4}$, $\frac{3}{6}$, $\frac{4}{8}$, $\frac{6}{12}$] *Write a number sentence showing that $\frac{1}{2}$ and $\frac{2}{4}$ are equivalent.* [$\frac{1}{2} = \frac{2}{4}$] Write $\frac{1}{2} = \frac{2}{4}$ on the board.

Name ______________________ Step 2-2

Equivalent Fractions (continued)

You can use division to find a fraction equivalent to $\frac{9}{12}$. To do this, divide the numerator and the denominator by the same number.

9. What number is the denominator of $\frac{9}{12}$ divided by to get 4? **3** $\qquad \frac{9}{12} \overset{\div 3}{=} \frac{\boxed{3}}{4}$

10. Since the denominator was divided by 3, the numerator must also be divided by 3. Put the quotient of 9 ÷ 3 in the numerator of the second fraction above.

Multiply the numerator and denominator of each fraction by the same number to find a fraction equivalent to each.

11. $\frac{2}{3} \overset{\times 3}{=} \frac{\boxed{6}}{9}$ **12.** $\frac{1}{2} \overset{\times 4}{=} \frac{\boxed{4}}{8}$

Divide the numerator and denominator of each fraction by the same number to find a fraction equivalent to each.

13. $\frac{8}{10} \overset{\div 2}{=} \frac{\boxed{4}}{5}$ **14.** $\frac{10}{15} \overset{\div 5}{=} \frac{\boxed{2}}{3}$

Find each equivalent fraction.

15. $\frac{1}{5} = \frac{\boxed{3}}{15}$ **16.** $\frac{8}{10} = \frac{\boxed{4}}{5}$ **17.** $\frac{2}{8} = \frac{\boxed{1}}{4}$

18. $\frac{7}{10} = \frac{\boxed{14}}{20}$ **19.** $\frac{6}{14} = \frac{\boxed{3}}{7}$ **20.** $\frac{8}{11} = \frac{\boxed{16}}{22}$

Write a fraction equivalent to each fraction given. Sample answers are given.

21. $\frac{6}{8}$ $\frac{3}{4}$ **22.** $\frac{8}{12}$ $\frac{2}{3}$ **23.** $\frac{7}{35}$ $\frac{1}{5}$ **24.** $\frac{16}{24}$ $\frac{2}{3}$

25. Reasoning Explain why $\frac{1}{2}$ and $\frac{2}{4}$ are equivalent fractions.
Sample answer: The numerator and denominator of $\frac{1}{2}$ can both be multiplied by 2 to get $\frac{2}{4}$.

Now use your fraction strips to find as many fractions as you can that are equivalent to $\frac{1}{4}$. [Sample answers: $\frac{2}{8}$, $\frac{3}{12}$] *Write a number sentence showing that $\frac{1}{4}$ and $\frac{2}{8}$ are equivalent.* [$\frac{1}{4} = \frac{2}{8}$] Write $\frac{1}{4} = \frac{2}{8}$ on the board.

Look at the two number sentences. What do you notice about each pair of numerators and each pair of denominators? [For $\frac{1}{2} = \frac{2}{4}$, $1 \times 2 = 2$, and $2 \times 2 = 4$; For $\frac{1}{4} = \frac{2}{8}$, $1 \times 2 = 2$ and $4 \times 2 = 8$] *To find a fraction equivalent to a given fraction, you can multiply the numerator and denominator by the same number.* Write $\frac{1}{2} \times \frac{2}{2} = \frac{2}{4}$ and $\frac{1}{4} \times \frac{2}{2} = \frac{2}{8}$ below each respective equation on the board.

You can also divide the numerator and denominator by the same number to find an equivalent fraction. If you start with $\frac{2}{4}$, you can find $\frac{1}{2}$ by dividing both the numerator and denominator by 2. Write $\frac{3}{12} \div \frac{3}{3} = \frac{1}{4}$ on the board. *For $\frac{3}{12}$, you can find $\frac{1}{4}$ by dividing 3 and 12 by 3. You can use division whenever both the numerator and denominator are divisible by the same number.*

2 Guided Practice

Use with Exercises 1–10.

Be sure students understand that they can always multiply the numerator and denominator by the same number to find a fraction equivalent to the given fraction. To use division, they need to find a number greater than 1 by which both the numerator and denominator are divisible.

Exercises 1–3
The fraction strips show that $\frac{2}{3} = \frac{4}{6}$. Notice that they also show that $\frac{1}{3} = \frac{2}{6}$ and that $\frac{3}{3} = \frac{6}{6}$, or 1.

Exercises 9–10
Error Intervention

If students have trouble finding an equivalent fraction for $\frac{9}{12}$,

then have them line up the $\frac{1}{12}$ fraction strips with the $\frac{1}{4}$ fraction strips to show that $\frac{9}{12}$ covers the same region as $\frac{3}{4}$.

ELL Use Vocabulary

To check understanding, ask a student to repeat and complete this sentence: *Fractions that name the same part of a whole are _____.* [Equivalent]

Quick Check Formative Assessment

How could you show that $\frac{6}{8}$ and $\frac{3}{4}$ are equivalent? [Sample answer: Use fraction strips. Line up the $\frac{1}{8}$ strips and the $\frac{1}{4}$ strips. Color 6 of the eighths. Color 3 of the fourths and show that they match.]

3 Independent Practice

Use with Exercises 11–25.

For Exercises 15–20, some students may have difficulty deciding whether to multiply or divide. Remind them to look at the given denominators in each pair. *In Exercise 15, what would you do to 5 to get 15?* [Multiply by 3.] *So what will you do to the numerator 1 to get the numerator for the second fraction?* [Multiply by 3.] *In Exercise 16, what will you do to 10 to get 5?* [Divide by 2.] *So what will you do to the numerator 8 to get the numerator for the second fraction?* [Divide by 2.]

Step 2-3

Mixed Numbers

Objective Students will use improper fractions and mixed numbers to name fractions greater than 1.

Vocabulary Improper fraction, mixed number

Materials Fraction Models: Strips (Teaching Tool 5)

Math Background

- An amount greater than 1 can be named using an improper fraction. The same amount can be named using a mixed number.

Name ______________________ Teaching Tool 5

Fraction Models: Strips

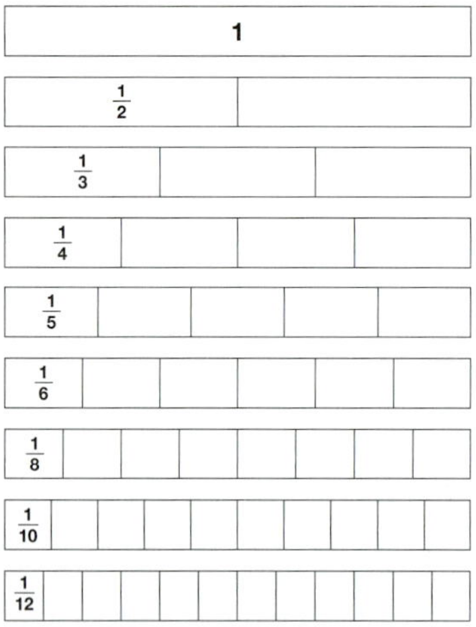

M7

Name ______________________ Step 2-3

Mixed Numbers

A mixed number is a number written with a whole number and a fraction. An improper fraction is a fraction in which the numerator is greater than or equal to the denominator.

1. Circle the number that is a mixed number. 3 $4\frac{1}{3}$ $\frac{8}{5}$ ($4\frac{1}{3}$ circled)

2. Circle the number that is an improper fraction. $\frac{3}{4}$ $2\frac{3}{5}$ $\frac{9}{4}$ ($\frac{9}{4}$ circled)

Write the improper fraction $\frac{7}{3}$ as a mixed number by answering 3 to 6.

3. Show seven $\frac{1}{3}$ fraction strips.

4. Use fraction strips. How many 1 strips can you make with seven $\frac{1}{3}$ strips? 2

5. How many $\frac{1}{3}$ strips do you have left over? 1

6. Write $\frac{7}{3}$ as a mixed number. $2\frac{1}{3}$

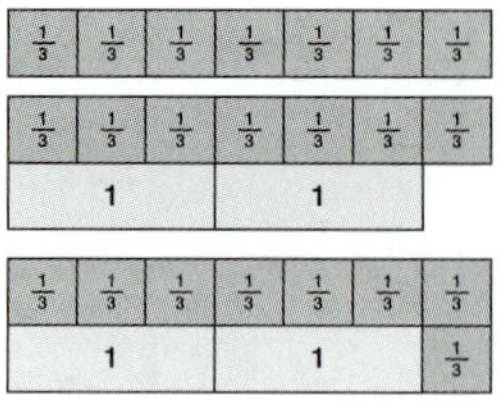

Write $\frac{7}{3}$ as a mixed number without fraction strips by answering 7 to 9.

7. Divide 7 by 3 at the right.

8. Fill in the missing numbers below.

Quotient → [2] $\frac{[1]}{3}$ ← Remainder ← Divisor

$$\begin{array}{r} \boxed{2\ R1} \\ 3\overline{)7} \\ -\boxed{6} \\ \boxed{1} \end{array}$$

Notice, the quotient 2 tells how many one strips you can make. The remainder 1 tells how many $\frac{1}{3}$ strips are left over.

9. Write $\frac{7}{3}$ as a mixed number. $2\frac{1}{3}$

18 Mixed Numbers

1 Concept Development

Interactive Learning

Use with Teaching Tool 5.

Purpose

Today you will be learning how to write an amount that is more than one whole as an improper fraction and as a mixed number.

Pose the Problem

Four friends divide 5 snack bars equally. How much does each friend get? Allow students to work in pairs to solve the problem using any method.

Model

What operation will you use? [Division] *What division sentence represents this problem?* [5 ÷ 4 = ?] *What fraction represents the division?* [$\frac{5}{4}$] *This is called an improper fraction.*

Name ________________

Mixed Numbers (continued)

10. Since $14 \div 5 = 2$ R4, what is $\frac{14}{5}$ as a mixed number? $2\frac{4}{5}$

Write $2\frac{1}{5}$ as an improper fraction by answering 11 to 13.

11. Show $2\frac{1}{5}$ with fractions strips.

12. Use fraction strips. How many $\frac{1}{5}$ strips does it take to equal $2\frac{1}{5}$? 11

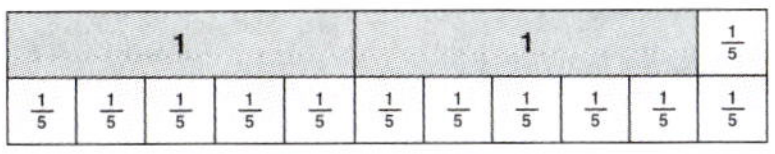

13. What improper fraction equals $2\frac{1}{5}$? $\frac{11}{5}$

Write $2\frac{1}{5}$ as an improper fraction without using fraction strips by answering 14 to 16.

14. Fill in the missing numbers.

Whole Number × Denominator + Numerator

2 × 5 + 1 = 10 + 1 = 11

15. Write the 11 you found in Exercise 14 over the denominator, 5. $\frac{11}{5}$

16. What improper fraction equals $2\frac{1}{5}$? $\frac{11}{5}$

Notice, 2×5 tells how many $\frac{1}{5}$ strips equal 2 wholes. The 1 tells there is one additional $\frac{1}{5}$ strip.

17. Since $6 \times 4 + 3 = 27$, what is $6\frac{3}{4}$ as an improper fraction? $\frac{27}{4}$

Change each improper fraction to a mixed number or a whole number and change each mixed number to an improper fraction.

18. $3\frac{2}{7}$ $\frac{23}{7}$ **19.** $\frac{7}{3}$ $2\frac{1}{3}$ **20.** $\frac{7}{2}$ $3\frac{1}{2}$ **21.** $1\frac{1}{10}$ $\frac{11}{10}$

How can we find a mixed number that is equivalent to the improper fraction $\frac{5}{4}$? On the board, draw 5 rectangles, each the same size and shape. *Each rectangle will represent 1 snack bar. How many whole snack bars will each friend get?* [1] On the board, cross out 4 rectangles. *How many are left?* [1] *How could the friends divide the remaining snack bar?* [Divide it into 4 equal parts.] *What fraction represents the part each friend will get from the remaining snack bar?* [$\frac{1}{4}$] Draw 1 whole rectangle with another rectangle below to represent $\frac{1}{4}$. *What is the total amount each friend will get?* [1 whole bar plus $\frac{1}{4}$ bar] On the board write $1\frac{1}{4}$ next to the drawing.

2 Guided Practice

Use with Exercises 1–9.

Exercise 2
Why is $\frac{3}{4}$ not an improper fraction?
[The numerator is not greater than the denominator.]

Error Intervention

If students have difficulty dividing when converting from an improper fraction to a mixed number,

then have them make a drawing to model the division.

ELL Use Vocabulary

To check understanding, have a student repeat and complete this sentence: *A number written with a whole number and fraction is called a ______.*
[Mixed number]

Quick Check Formative Assessment

What improper fraction is equivalent to $4\frac{2}{3}$? [$\frac{14}{3}$] *What mixed number is equivalent to $\frac{19}{8}$?* [$2\frac{3}{8}$]

3 Independent Practice

Use with Exercises 10–21.

Suggest that students write the word DoWN on their paper to remind them how to change a mixed number to an improper fraction (multiply the **d**enominator and the **w**hole number and then add the **n**umerator.)

For Exercises 19 and 20, if students have trouble finding the fraction, have them continue to use fraction strips to model the problem. Students can also use the fraction strips to check their work for reasonableness.

Step 2-5

Simplest Form

Objective Students will identify fractions that are in simplest form and find the simplest form of a fraction.

Vocabulary Simplest form

Materials Fraction Models: Strips (Teaching Tool 5)

Professional Development

Math Background

- You can find a fraction equivalent to a given fraction by multiplying the numerator and denominator by the same number or by dividing both by a common factor.
- If the numerator and denominator of a fraction have no common factors other than 1, the fraction is in simplest form.

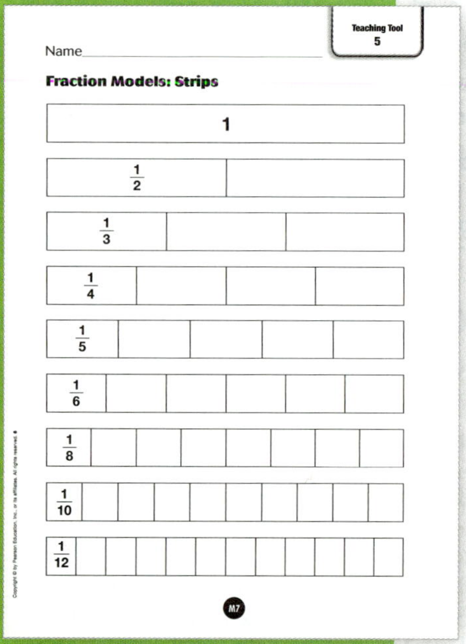

Name ______________________ Step 2-5

Simplest Form

Anita saw that $\frac{12}{30}$ of the students in her class wore t-shirts one day.

Write $\frac{12}{30}$ in simplest form by answering 1 to 5.

To write a fraction in simplest form, you need to use the greatest common factor (GCF) of the numerator and the denominator.

1. What is the GCF of 12 and 30? 6
2. Divide both the numerator and the denominator by the GCF to find an equivalent fraction. $\frac{12 \div 6}{30 \div 6} = \frac{2}{5}$
3. What is the fraction that you found that is equivalent to $\frac{12}{30}$? $\frac{2}{5}$

A fraction is in simplest form when the GCF of the numerator and the denominator is 1.

4. Is the GCF of the numerator and the denominator of the fraction you found 1? yes
5. What is $\frac{12}{30}$ in simplest form? $\frac{2}{5}$

Nine out of 24 girls on the cross county team went to the state finals.

6. What fraction of the girls went to the state finals? $\frac{9}{24}$

Write $\frac{9}{24}$ in simplest form by answering 7 to 11.

7. What is the GCF of 9 and 24? 3
8. Divide both the numerator and the denominator by the GCF to find an equivalent fraction. $\frac{9 \div 3}{24 \div 3} = \frac{3}{8}$
9. What is the GCF of the numerator and the denominator of the fraction you found? 1
10. Is this fraction written in simplest form? yes
11. What fraction in simplest form represents the part of girls on the cross country team that went to the state finals? $\frac{3}{8}$

22 Simplest Form

Interactive Learning 1 Concept Development

Use with Teaching Tool 5.

Purpose

You know how to find equivalent fractions. Today you will learn how to write a fraction in simplest form.

Pose the Problem

How do you write a fraction such as $\frac{9}{12}$ in simplest form? Allow time for students to share their ideas.

Model

Distribute copies of Fraction Models: Strips (Teaching Tool 5). Instruct students to cut out whole strips. *Use your fraction strips to find fractions equivalent to $\frac{9}{12}$.* Give students time to work in pairs. Then ask them to share their results with the class. Write $\frac{9}{12}$, $\frac{6}{8}$, and $\frac{3}{4}$ on the board.

Which of these three fractions ($\frac{9}{12}$, $\frac{6}{8}$, or $\frac{3}{4}$) do you think is the simplest? Why? Students might answer that $\frac{3}{4}$ is the simplest because it uses numbers that are easy to work with.

Name ______________________________

Simplest Form (continued)

Write each fraction in simplest form. If it is in simplest form, write simplest form.

12. $\frac{5}{10}$	**13.** $\frac{14}{16}$	**14.** $\frac{27}{45}$	**15.** $\frac{10}{15}$
$\frac{1}{2}$	$\frac{7}{8}$	$\frac{3}{5}$	$\frac{2}{3}$
16. $\frac{5}{20}$	**17.** $\frac{14}{18}$	**18.** $\frac{5}{11}$	**19.** $\frac{1}{15}$
$\frac{1}{4}$	$\frac{7}{9}$	simplest form	simplest form
20. $\frac{6}{20}$	**21.** $\frac{36}{45}$	**22.** $\frac{11}{33}$	**23.** $\frac{24}{60}$
$\frac{3}{10}$	$\frac{4}{5}$	$\frac{1}{3}$	$\frac{2}{5}$
24. $\frac{18}{24}$	**25.** $\frac{12}{160}$	**26.** $\frac{6}{12}$	**27.** $\frac{9}{81}$
$\frac{3}{4}$	$\frac{3}{40}$	$\frac{1}{2}$	$\frac{1}{9}$
28. $\frac{16}{48}$	**29.** $\frac{7}{13}$	**30.** $\frac{21}{25}$	**31.** $\frac{14}{35}$
$\frac{1}{3}$	simplest form	simplest form	$\frac{2}{5}$

32. Reasoning Explain how to tell $\frac{100}{105}$ is not in simplest form without finding all the factors.

Since each number ends in 0 or 5, each is divisible by 5. Simplify $\frac{100}{105}$ by dividing the numerator and denominator by 5.

A fraction is in simplest form when the greatest common factor of its numerator and denominator is 1. Look at the fractions $\frac{9}{12}$, $\frac{6}{8}$, and $\frac{3}{4}$. What is the greatest common factor of 9 and 12? [3] *What is the greatest common factor of 6 and 8?* [2] *What is the greatest common factor of 3 and 4?* [1] *So, $\frac{3}{4}$ is the simplest form of $\frac{9}{12}$ and of $\frac{6}{8}$.*

You can find the simplest form of a fraction by dividing the numerator and denominator by their greatest common factor. How could you use the greatest common factor of 9 and 12 to find the simplest form of $\frac{9}{12}$? [Divide both the numerator and denominator by 3.] Write $\frac{9 \div 3}{12 \div 3} = \frac{3}{4}$ on the board. *How could you use the greatest common factor of 6 and 8 to find the simplest form of $\frac{6}{8}$?* [Divide both the numerator and denominator by 2.] Write $\frac{6 \div 2}{8 \div 2} = \frac{3}{4}$ on the board.

If the greatest common factor is 1, the fraction is already in simplest form. Write the fraction $\frac{3}{4}$ on the board. *Since 3 and 4 can not be divided by any other factor than 1, it is already in simplest form.*

2 Guided Practice

Use with Exercises 1–11.

Be sure students understand that they can divide the numerator and denominator by any common factor to find a fraction equivalent to the given fraction. Then they might have to divide by another common factor to get the simplest form of the fraction. However, dividing by the greatest common factor will give the simplest form with just one division.

Exercises 1–5
Why are 12 and 30 divided by 6 instead of by 2 or 3? [Dividing by 2 would give $\frac{6}{15}$ and dividing by 3 would give $\frac{4}{10}$. Neither of these is in simplest form.]

Error Intervention

If students have difficulty finding the GCF of the numerator and denominator,

then remind them that they can list all the factors of each number, choose the common factors, and then identify the greatest common factor.

ELL Use Vocabulary

To check understanding, ask a student to repeat and complete this sentence: *A fraction is in _____ when the greatest common factor of the numerator and denominator is 1.* [Simplest form]

Quick Check Formative Assessment

How could you show that $\frac{6}{8}$ in simplest form is $\frac{3}{4}$? [Sample answer: Use fraction strips. Line up the $\frac{1}{8}$ strip and the $\frac{1}{4}$ strip. Color 6 of the eighths. Color 3 of the fourths and show that they match.]

2 Independent Practice

Use with Exercises 12–32.

Exercises 22 and 28
Some students might notice that the answers for these two exercises are the same, $\frac{1}{3}$. Point out that one way to find out if two fractions are equivalent is to find the simplest form of each of them. If the simplest form is the same, the fractions are equivalent.

Step 3-1

Multiplying Two Fractions

Objective Students will multiply a fraction by a fraction.

Vocabulary Numerator, denominator

Materials Rectangular paper for folding, markers or colored pencils

Math Background

- The algorithm for multiplying fractions is simple: multiply the numerators and multiply the denominators. $\frac{a}{b} \times \frac{c}{d} = \frac{a \times c}{b \times d}$
- The multiplication of two fractions can be modeled as taking "a part of a part."

Name ______________________ Step 3-1

Multiplying Two Fractions

Pablo's yard is $\frac{3}{4}$ of an acre. One-half of the yard is woods. What part of an acre is the wooded part of Pablo's yard?

Find $\frac{1}{2}$ of $\frac{3}{4}$ or $\frac{1}{2} \times \frac{3}{4}$ by answering 1 to 5.

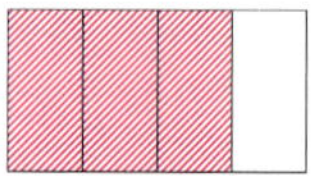

1. Fold a sheet of paper into 4 equal parts, as shown at the right. Color 3 parts with slanted lines to show $\frac{3}{4}$. Color the rectangle at the right to show what you did.

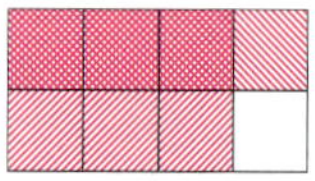

2. Now fold the paper in half the other way. Shade one half with lines slanted the opposite direction of the first set. Color the rectangle at the right to show what you did.

3. What fraction of the paper is shaded with crisscrossed lines? $\frac{3}{8}$

4. The part shaded with crisscrossed lines shows $\frac{1}{2}$ of $\frac{3}{4}$ or $\frac{1}{2} \times \frac{3}{4}$. So, what is $\frac{1}{2} \times \frac{3}{4}$? $\frac{3}{8}$

5. In Pablo's yard, what part of an acre is wooded? $\frac{3}{8}$ acre

6. To find $\frac{1}{2} \times \frac{3}{4}$, how many sections did you divide the paper into? 8

7. What is the product of the denominators in $\frac{1}{2} \times \frac{3}{4}$? $2 \times 4 =$ 8

8. To find $\frac{1}{2} \times \frac{3}{4}$, how many sections did you crisscross? 3

9. What is the product of the numerators in $\frac{1}{2} \times \frac{3}{4}$? $1 \times 3 =$ 3

10. Write the product of the numerators over the product of the denominators. $\frac{1 \times 3}{2 \times 4} = \frac{3}{8}$

11. Is your answer to item 10 the same as item 4? yes

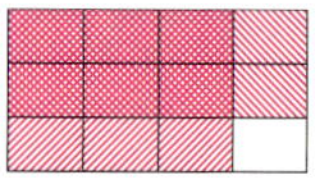

12. Use paper folding to find $\frac{2}{3} \times \frac{3}{4}$. Color the rectangle at the right to show what you did. So, $\frac{2}{3} \times \frac{3}{4} = \frac{6}{12}$.

13. To find $\frac{2}{3} \times \frac{3}{4}$, how many sections did you divide the paper into? 12

1 Concept Development

Use with Exercises 1–11.

Purpose

You have learned how to multiply whole numbers. Today you will learn how to multiply fractions.

Pose the Problem

Pablo's yard is $\frac{3}{4}$ of an acre. One-half of the yard is woods. What part of an acre is the wooded part of Pablo's yard? Ask students to share their ideas about how to solve this problem. Explain that solving this problem requires finding the product of two fractions, $\frac{1}{2} \times \frac{3}{4}$.

Model

Distribute pieces of rectangular paper to students. *Let's say that your piece of paper represents an acre. What part of an acre is Pablo's yard?* [$\frac{3}{4}$] *How many equal parts do you have to divide the paper into to show $\frac{3}{4}$?* [4 equal parts] Ask students to complete Exercise 1 to show the part of an acre that is Pablo's yard.

Name ______________________

Multiplying Two Fractions (continued)

14. What is the product of the denominators in $\frac{2}{3} \times \frac{3}{4}$? $3 \times 4 =$ 12

15. To find $\frac{2}{3} \times \frac{3}{4}$ how many sections did you crisscross? 6

16. What is the product of the numerators in $\frac{2}{3} \times \frac{3}{4}$? $2 \times 3 =$ 6

17. Complete: $\frac{2}{3} \times \frac{3}{4} = \frac{2 \times 3}{3 \times 4} = \frac{6}{12}$

To multiply two fractions, you can multiply the numerators and then the denominators. Then simplify, if possible.

$\frac{2}{3} \times \frac{3}{4} = \frac{2 \times 3}{3 \times 4} = \frac{6}{12} = \frac{1}{2}$

18. Reasoning Shari found $\frac{3}{10} \times \frac{5}{9}$ as shown at the right. Why does Shari's method work?

She simplified before multiplying, instead of after.

$\frac{3}{10} \times \frac{5}{9} = \frac{\overset{1}{\cancel{3}} \times \overset{1}{\cancel{5}}}{\underset{2}{\cancel{10}} \times \underset{3}{\cancel{9}}} = \frac{1}{6}$

Multiply. Simplify, if possible.

19. $\frac{1}{8} \times \frac{2}{3} = \frac{1}{12}$ **20.** $\frac{5}{6} \times \frac{1}{2} = \frac{5}{12}$ **21.** $\frac{1}{4} \times \frac{3}{5} = \frac{3}{20}$

22. $\frac{6}{7} \times \frac{1}{3} = \frac{2}{7}$ **23.** $\frac{3}{4} \times \frac{3}{8} = \frac{9}{32}$ **24.** $\frac{1}{5} \times \frac{4}{5} = \frac{4}{25}$

25. $\frac{2}{3} \times \frac{4}{7} = \frac{8}{21}$ **26.** $\frac{3}{7} \times \frac{3}{10} = \frac{9}{70}$ **27.** $\frac{4}{9} \times \frac{3}{4} = \frac{1}{3}$

28. $\frac{5}{8} \times \frac{4}{5} = \frac{1}{2}$ **29.** $\frac{7}{9} \times \frac{3}{5} = \frac{7}{15}$ **30.** $\frac{1}{10} \times \frac{5}{7} = \frac{1}{14}$

31. $\frac{7}{8} \times \frac{5}{14} = \frac{5}{16}$ **32.** $\frac{3}{11} \times \frac{1}{9} = \frac{1}{33}$ **33.** $\frac{1}{12} \times \frac{4}{5} = \frac{1}{15}$

34. There are 45 tents at the summer camp. Girls will use $\frac{2}{3}$ of the tents. How many tents will the girls use? 30 tents

The three sections with slanted lines represent Pablo's yard. What part of Pablo's yard is woods? [$\frac{1}{2}$] *How can you use the paper to show the wooded part of Pablo's yard?* [Fold the paper in half so that each of the parts that represent Pablo's yard is folded in half.] Ask students to complete Exercise 2.

How many parts are shaded with crisscrossed lines? [3] *How many parts are there in all?* [8] Have students complete Exercises 3 and 4.

To multiply fractions, multiply the numerators and multiply the denominators. Simplify the fraction that is the product if possible. Have students complete Exercises 5 through 11. *So, what part of an acre is the wooded part of Pablo's yard?* [$\frac{3}{8}$ of an acre]

2 Guided Practice

Use with Exercises 12–18.

Allow students to continue to use paper for folding and coloring.

Exercise 18
Some students may prefer to simplify the problem before multiplying. Remind them to use the greatest common factor of one of the numerators and one of the denominators.

Error Intervention

If students have difficulty understanding why the product of two fractions that are less than 1 is less than either factor,

then say: *The paper model shows that the product of two fractions is "part of a part," so the product will be less than either factor.*

ELL Use Vocabulary

To check understanding, ask a student to repeat and complete this sentence: *The ____ is the bottom number of the fraction, and it tells the number of equal parts in the whole.* [Denominator]

Quick Check Formative Assessment

How do you find the product of two fractions? [Multiply the numerators, multiply the denominators, and simplify if possible.]

2 Independent Practice

Use with Exercises 19–34.

Point out to students that if 1 is the only common factor of the numerator and denominator in the product, that fraction is already in simplest form.

Exercise 34
Remind students that the whole number 45 can be written as the fraction $\frac{45}{1}$. *To find $\frac{2}{3}$ of 45, you multiply $\frac{2}{3} \times \frac{45}{1}$.*

Multiplying Fractions by Whole Numbers

Objective Students will multiply a fraction by a whole number.

Vocabulary Numerator, denominator, common factor

Materials Counters, 18-inch pieces of yarn

Professional Development

Math Background

- The multiplication of a fraction by a whole number, such as $\frac{1}{3} \times 6$, can be interpreted as *one third of a group of six.*
- Any whole number n can be written as a fraction in the form $\frac{n}{1}$. For example, 6 can be written as the fraction $\frac{6}{1}$.
- The algorithm for multiplying fractions is simple: multiply the numerators and multiply the denominators.
  $\frac{a}{b} \times \frac{c}{d} = \frac{a \times c}{b \times d}$

Name ______________________ Step **3-2**

Multiplying Fractions by Whole Numbers

Brianna has 15 model cars in her collection. Of the 15, $\frac{2}{3}$ are vintage cars. How many of her cars are vintage?

Find $\frac{2}{3}$ of 15 or $\frac{2}{3} \times 15$ by answering 1 to 5.

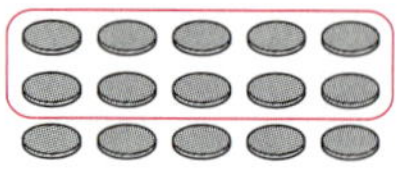

1. Show 15 counters in 3 equal rows.
2. Each row has $\frac{1}{3}$ of the counters. Put the loop of yarn around 2 rows to find $\frac{2}{3}$. Circle 2 rows of counters at the right.
3. How many counters did you circle? **10**
4. What is $\frac{2}{3}$ of 15 or $\frac{2}{3} \times 15$? **10**
5. How many of Brianna's cars are vintage? **10**

When you put the 15 counters into 3 rows, you found $15 \div 3$. This can also be shown as: $\frac{2}{\cancel{3}_1} \times \frac{\cancel{15}^5}{1}$

6. What is left is 2×5. What is the product? **10**

Find $\frac{5}{6} \times 24$ by answering 7 to 10.

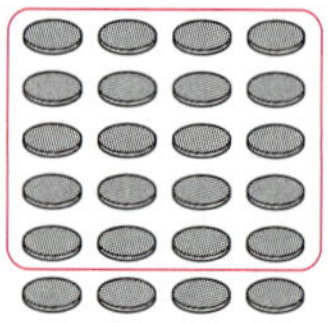

7. Show the product with counters and yarn. Circle the counters at the right.
8. What is $24 \div 6$? **4**
   Show this by crossing out and changing numbers below.
   $\frac{5}{\cancel{6}_{1}} \times \frac{\cancel{24}^{4}}{1}$
9. What product is left? **5** × **4** = **20**
10. What is $\frac{5}{6} \times 24$? **20**

26 Multiplying Fractions by Whole Numbers

Interactive Learning

1 Concept Development

Use with Exercises 1–6.

Purpose

You have learned how to multiply fractions. Today you will multiply a fraction and a whole number.

Pose the Problem

Brianna has 15 model cars in her collection, and $\frac{2}{3}$ of the cars are vintage. How many of Brianna's cars are vintage? Ask students to share their ideas about this problem.

Model

Distribute 24 counters and the pieces of yarn to each student. *Let's say that each counter represents a car. Arrange your counters in an array to model the rows of cars as shown in Exercise 1. What does your array look like?* [3 rows of counters with 5 counters in each row]

Now loop your piece of yarn around two rows of counters. Ask students to read and complete Exercises 2 and 3.

Name ______________________________ Step 3-2

Multiplying Fractions by Whole Numbers (continued)

Find each product.

11. $\frac{8}{9} \times 45$ **40**
12. $42 \times \frac{3}{7}$ **18**
13. $\frac{7}{12}$ of 96 **56**
14. $\frac{2}{11} \times 77$ **14**

15. $\frac{3}{8} \times 64$ **24**
16. $\frac{1}{6}$ of 102 **17**
17. $\frac{2}{9} \times 72$ **16**
18. $\frac{3}{4} \times 168$ **126**

19. $\frac{2}{5}$ of 25 **10**
20. $\frac{7}{9} \times 81$ **63**
21. $\frac{1}{2} \times 52$ **26**
22. $\frac{2}{3}$ of 66 **44**

Use the information in the table for Exercises 23 and 24.

Zoo Animals	Population	Zoo Animals	Population
Wild Dogs	10	Elephants	3
Monkeys	21	Tigers	8
Bears	18	Giraffes	5

23. If $\frac{2}{7}$ of the monkey population are spider monkeys, how many spider monkeys are at the zoo? **6**

24. If $\frac{3}{5}$ of the animals listed are female, how many females are in the list? **39**

25. You earned $141 babysitting last month. You told your parents that you saved $\frac{2}{3}$ of your earnings. How much did you save last month? **$94**

26. Emperor penguins are approximately 45 inches tall, while rockhopper penguins are about $\frac{5}{9}$ of that height. How tall is a typical rockhopper penguin? **25 inches**

27. **Reasoning** If you know that $\frac{3}{4}$ of a number is 18, what is $\frac{1}{4}$ of the same number? **6**

When you placed the yarn around two of the three rows, you were finding $\frac{2}{3}$ of the whole group of 15. What is another way of writing $\frac{2}{3}$ of 15? [$\frac{2}{3} \times 15$] Have students complete Exercises 4 and 5.

You can write any whole number as a fraction. The whole number becomes the numerator and the denominator is always 1. How can you write 15 as a fraction? [$\frac{15}{1}$] *What is another way of writing $\frac{2}{3} \times 15$?* [$\frac{2}{3} \times \frac{15}{1}$] Write $\frac{2}{3} \times \frac{15}{1}$ on the board.

You can simplify first by finding a common factor of one of the numerators and one of the denominators. What is a common factor of 15 and 3? [3] *What is 15 ÷ 3?* [5] Cross out the numerator 15 and write 5. *What is 3 ÷ 3?* [1] Cross out the denominator 3 and write 1.

The simplified problem is $\frac{2}{1} \times \frac{5}{1}$. What is another way of writing $\frac{2}{1} \times \frac{5}{1}$? [$2 \times 5$] Have students complete Exercise 6. *So, how many of Brianna's model cars are vintage?* [10]

2 Guided Practice

Use with Exercises 7–10.

Allow students to continue to use counters and yarn as needed.

Exercise 7
Why does it make sense to model the problem with an array of 6 rows? [Sample answer: To find $\frac{5}{6}$ of 24, I need to break 24 into 6 equal parts.]

Error Intervention

If students have difficulty understanding why the product is less than the whole number being multiplied,

then tell them that they are trying to find just a part of the whole number, so the answer will be less than the whole number.

ELL Use Vocabulary

To check understanding, ask a student to repeat and complete this sentence: *A whole number can be written as a fraction by placing the whole number in the _____ and the number 1 in the _____.* [Numerator; denominator]

Quick Check — Formative Assessment

Find $\frac{2}{3} \times 18$. [12]

3 Independent Practice

Use with Exercises 11–27.

Exercises 23 and 24
Students should recognize that the table provides important information. *What information does the table provide?* [The number of each type of animal in the zoo]

Exercise 26
Remind students that the word "of" used in this way means that they should multiply. *How can you find $\frac{5}{9}$ of 45?* [Multiply $\frac{5}{9} \times 45$ or $\frac{5}{9} \times \frac{45}{1}$.]

Step **3-3**

Multiplying Mixed Numbers

Objective Students multiply a mixed number by a mixed number, fraction, or whole number.

Vocabulary Mixed number, improper fraction

Materials Markers or colored pencils

Math Background

- Any whole number n can be written as a fraction in the form $\frac{n}{1}$. For example, 5 can be written as a fraction as $\frac{5}{1}$.
- A mixed number can be thought of as an improper fraction. For example, $3\frac{1}{2}$ can be thought of as $\frac{6}{2} + \frac{1}{2}$ and written as $\frac{7}{2}$.
- The simple algorithm for multiplying fractions is the same for improper fractions: multiply numerators and multiply denominators, then simplify. $\frac{a}{b} \times \frac{c}{d} = \frac{a \times c}{b \times d}$

Name ____________________ Step 3-3

Multiplying Mixed Numbers

George made a rectangular quilt that is $2\frac{1}{2}$ yards long and $1\frac{2}{3}$ yards wide. Answer 1 to 6 to find the area of the quilt.

Find $1\frac{2}{3} \times 2\frac{1}{2}$.

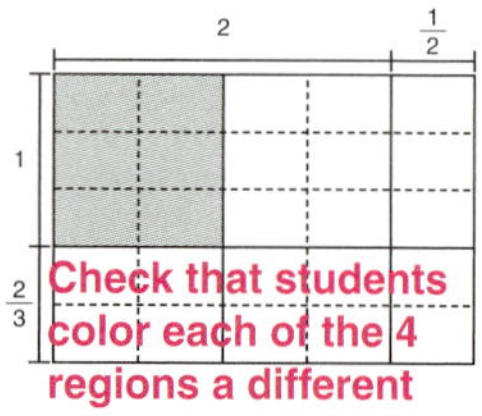

1. The rectangular quilt at the right is $2\frac{1}{2}$ units by $1\frac{2}{3}$ units. The shaded area represents one whole square yard. Shade another region that is equal to one whole square yard.

Check that students color each of the 4 regions a different color.

2. The quilt is divided into equal parts. Six equal parts equal one whole square yard. Each part is what fraction of one whole square yard? $\frac{1}{6}$

3. Color another whole square yard with a different color. Then another, as many times as you can. How many total whole square yards are there in the quilt? 4

4. What part of a whole square yard is left over? $\frac{1}{6}$

5. So, what is $1\frac{2}{3} \times 2\frac{1}{2}$? $4\frac{1}{6}$

6. What is the area of George's quilt? $4\frac{1}{6}$ square yards

Find $1\frac{2}{3} \times 2\frac{1}{2}$ another way by answering 7 to 9.

7. Write $1\frac{2}{3}$ as an improper fraction. $\frac{5}{3}$

8. Write $2\frac{1}{2}$ as an improper fraction. $\frac{5}{2}$

9. Now find $\frac{5}{3} \times \frac{5}{2}$. $\frac{25}{6}$ = $4\frac{1}{6}$

Notice that the product of the numerators, $5 \times 5 = 25$, is the number of equal parts in the rectangle. Also, the products of the denominators, $3 \times 2 = 6$, is the number of equal parts in each whole.

28 Multiplying Mixed Numbers

Interactive Learning 1 Concept Development

Use with Exercises 1–9.

Purpose

You have learned how to multiply fractions. Today you will learn how to multiply a mixed number by a mixed number, fraction, or whole number.

Pose the Problem

George made a rectangular quilt that is $2\frac{1}{2}$ yards long and $1\frac{2}{3}$ yards wide. To find the area of the quilt, we need to multiply the length times the width. What is $1\frac{2}{3} \times 2\frac{1}{2}$? Ask students to share their ideas about this problem.

Model

Each student should have several markers or colored pencils for shading the model of the quilt. *Look at the model of the quilt. Which part shows the length of the quilt?* [The top, labeled 2 and $\frac{1}{2}$] *Which part shows the width of the quilt?* [The side, labeled 1 and $\frac{2}{3}$] *How do we find the area of the quilt?* [Multiply $1\frac{2}{3} \times 2\frac{1}{2}$.]

Name ______________________ Step 3-3

Multiplying Mixed Numbers (continued)

Fill in the blanks to find each product. Change mixed numbers to improper fractions. Write whole numbers over 1. Remove common factors before multiplying to make the computations easier.

10. $\frac{2}{3} \times 1\frac{3}{8} = \frac{2}{3} \times \frac{11}{8} = \frac{\overset{1}{\cancel{2}} \times 11}{3 \times \underset{4}{\cancel{8}}} = \frac{11}{12}$

11. $5 \times 1\frac{3}{10} = \frac{5}{1} \times \frac{13}{10} = \frac{\overset{1}{\cancel{5}} \times 13}{1 \times \underset{2}{\cancel{10}}} = \frac{13}{2} = 6\frac{1}{2}$

Multiply. Simplify, if possible.

12. $2\frac{6}{7} \times 1\frac{3}{4} =$ 5

13. $\frac{3}{4} \times 3\frac{1}{5} =$ $2\frac{2}{5}$

14. $3\frac{2}{5} \times \frac{5}{7} =$ $2\frac{3}{7}$

15. $5\frac{5}{8} \times 3\frac{4}{5} =$ $21\frac{3}{8}$

16. $2\frac{2}{7} \times 5\frac{3}{5} =$ $12\frac{4}{5}$

17. $2\frac{1}{10} \times 2\frac{1}{7} =$ $4\frac{1}{2}$

18. $4\frac{1}{12} \times \frac{4}{5} =$ $3\frac{4}{15}$

19. $2\frac{1}{10} \times 6\frac{5}{7} =$ $14\frac{1}{10}$

20. $3\frac{4}{5} \times 5 =$ 19

21. Pam is making a cake. The recipe calls for $2\frac{1}{8}$ cups of flour. How much flour is needed for 4 cakes? $8\frac{1}{2}$ cups

22. Reasoning Find each product and compare it to $2\frac{1}{2}$. What is true when multiplying by numbers less than 1 and when multiplying by numbers greater than 1?

$\frac{1}{3} \times 2\frac{1}{2} = \frac{5}{6}$ $1\frac{1}{3} \times 2\frac{1}{2} = 3\frac{1}{3}$ $\frac{2}{3} \times 2\frac{1}{2} = 1\frac{2}{3}$ $1\frac{2}{3} \times 2\frac{1}{2} = 4\frac{1}{6}$

Sample answer: When $2\frac{1}{2}$ is multiplied by a number less than 1, the product is less than $2\frac{1}{2}$. When $2\frac{1}{2}$ is multiplied by a number greater than 1, the product is greater than $2\frac{1}{2}$.

Multiplying Mixed Numbers **29**

Have students complete Exercise 1. *Into how many parts is each whole square yard divided?* [6] It may help some students to change the label along the top of the quilt so that the length of each part is labeled $\frac{1}{2}$. They can also change the labels on the side so that the width of each part is labeled $\frac{1}{3}$. *What is $\frac{1}{2} \times \frac{1}{3}$?* [$\frac{1}{6}$] Have students complete Exercise 2.

So, each whole square yard is divided into 6 parts. We need to find how many whole square yards are in the quilt, and how many parts are left over. Have students complete Exercises 3–6. As they color the groups of 6 parts, point out to students that any group of six equal parts can make up a whole square yard.

Remind students of the algorithm they have learned for multiplying fractions, $\frac{a}{b} \times \frac{c}{d} = \frac{a \times c}{b \times d}$. *You know how to multiply a fraction by a fraction. Improper fractions can be multiplied in the same way. How do you write $2\frac{1}{2}$ as an improper fraction?* [$\frac{5}{2}$] *How do you write $1\frac{2}{3}$ as an improper fraction?* [$\frac{5}{3}$] Have students complete Exercises 7–9.

2 Guided Practice

Use with Exercises 10–11.

Students continue to solve multiplication problems with mixed numbers by writing them as improper fractions and using the fraction multiplication algorithm.

Exercise 10
Why can you simplify the 2 in the numerator to a 1 and the 8 in the denominator to a 4? [Sample answer: Because this is the same as dividing both the numerator and the denominator by 2.]

Error Intervention

If students have difficulty understanding why the fractions are being simplified before being multiplied,

then remind them of how they simplified when multiplying fractions.

ELL Use Vocabulary

To check understanding, ask a student to repeat and complete this sentence: *A ______ is a number that combines a whole number and a fraction.* [Mixed number]

Quick Check Formative Assessment

What is $\frac{1}{3}$ of $4\frac{1}{8}$? [$1\frac{3}{8}$]

3 Independent Practice

Use with Exercises 12–22.

Exercises 12–22
Students may have difficulty remembering to multiply the numerators and the denominators. After they have changed the mixed numbers to improper fractions, have them rewrite the problem as the product of the numerators over the product of the denominators.

Step **3-4**

Understanding Division with Fractions

Objective Students divide a whole number or a fraction by a fraction.

Vocabulary Reciprocal

Materials Markers or colored pencils, fraction models or Teaching Tool 6

Professional Development

Math Background

- When dividing with fractions it is important to understand what the quotient means. For $3 \div \frac{1}{2} = 6$, the quotient means that there are "six halves in three."
- The reciprocal method for division of fractions requires multiplying by the reciprocal of the divisor.

Name ________________ Step **3-4**

Understanding Division with Fractions

Donna has 3 pounds of clay. She uses $\frac{1}{2}$ pound for each vase. Answer 1 to 3 to find the number of vases she can make.

Find $3 \div \frac{1}{2}$ using a model.

1. Color each half of a rectangle at the right a different color. How many $\frac{1}{2}$s are in 3? 6
2. What is $3 \div \frac{1}{2}$? 6
3. How many vases can Donna make? 6 vases

Check that students color each half differently.

You could also find $3 \div \frac{1}{2}$ by multiplying $3 \times \frac{2}{1}$.

The numbers $\frac{1}{2}$ and $\frac{2}{1}$ or 2 have a special relationship because $\frac{1}{2} \times 2 = 1$. The numbers $\frac{1}{2}$ and 2 are reciprocals. Similarly, $\frac{3}{4}$ and $\frac{4}{3}$ are reciprocals. Note that $\frac{3}{4} \times \frac{4}{3} = 1$.

4. What is the reciprocal of $\frac{1}{3}$? 3 or $\frac{3}{1}$
5. What is the reciprocal of $\frac{5}{7}$? $\frac{7}{5}$

So, $3 \div \frac{1}{2}$ can be written as 3×2, because 2 is the reciprocal of $\frac{1}{2}$.

The model shows the $\frac{9}{10}$ pound of clay that Thomas has. He uses $\frac{3}{10}$ pound for each small bowl. Answer 6 to 8 to find how many small bowls Thomas can make.

Find $\frac{9}{10} \div \frac{3}{10}$ using a model.

6. Color each $\frac{3}{10}$ of the rectangle at the right a different color. How many $\frac{3}{10}$s are in $\frac{9}{10}$? 3
7. What is $\frac{9}{10} \div \frac{3}{10}$? 3
8. How many small bowls can Thomas make? 3 small bowls

Check that students use 3 different colors to color 3 sections each time.

Find $\frac{9}{10} \div \frac{3}{10}$ by using the reciprocal.

9. What is the reciprocal of $\frac{3}{10}$? $\frac{10}{3}$

Interactive Learning

1 Concept Development

Use with Exercises 1–5.

Purpose

You have learned how to model multiplying fractions. Today you will use similar skills and new ideas to divide with fractions.

Pose the Problem

Donna has 3 pounds of clay to use to make vases. She uses $\frac{1}{2}$ pound for each vase. How many vases can she make? Ask students to share their ideas about this problem.

Model

Each student should have several markers or colored pencils for shading the division model. *Look at the model on page 30. Each big box represents 1 whole, and each of the three boxes is divided in half. Does this model show how much clay Donna has?* [Sample answer: Yes, the 3 boxes represent the 3 pounds of clay.] Have students complete Exercise 1.

Name ______________________

Step 3-4

Understanding Division with Fractions (continued)

10. To find $\frac{9}{10} \div \frac{3}{10}$, can you multiply $\frac{9}{10}$ by the reciprocal of $\frac{3}{10}$? yes

11. Complete: $\frac{9}{10} \times \frac{10}{3} = \frac{9 \times 10}{10 \times \boxed{3}} = \frac{90}{\boxed{30}} = \boxed{3}$

12. Is the answer to item 11 the same as item 8? yes

Find the reciprocal of each number.

13. $\frac{3}{4}$ $\frac{4}{3}$ **14.** $\frac{1}{15}$ $\frac{15}{1}$ **15.** $\frac{7}{9}$ $\frac{9}{7}$ **16.** $1\frac{3}{7}$ $\frac{7}{10}$

Find each quotient.

17. How many $\frac{1}{4}$s are in 2? 8

18. How many $\frac{1}{2}$s are in 3? 6

19. How many $\frac{1}{4}$s are in 4? 16

20. How many $\frac{3}{4}$s are in 3? 4

21. How many $\frac{1}{8}$s are in 2? 16

22. How many $\frac{2}{8}$s are in 1? 4

23. How many $\frac{3}{8}$s are in 3? 8

24. How many $\frac{6}{8}$s are in 3? 4

25. $3 \div \frac{1}{6}$ 18 **26.** $9 \div \frac{3}{5}$ 15 **27.** $8 \div \frac{1}{2}$ 16

28. $10 \div \frac{5}{6}$ 12 **29.** $9 \div \frac{3}{4}$ 12 **30.** $6 \div \frac{1}{3}$ 18

31. $2 \div \frac{1}{7}$ 14 **32.** $6 \div \frac{3}{5}$ 10 **33.** $10 \div \frac{1}{10}$ 100

34. Bonnie is cutting 7 apples. Each apple is cut into eighths. How many slices of apple will she have? 56

35. **Reasoning** Explain how to find $\frac{3}{4} \div \frac{3}{8}$ by using the reciprocal of $\frac{3}{8}$.

$\frac{3}{4} \div \frac{3}{8} = \frac{3}{4} \times \frac{8}{3} = 2$

Into how many parts is each whole pound divided? [2] *Does the model show the amount of clay Donna needs to make a vase?* [Sample answer: Yes, each equal part that the pounds are divided into are $\frac{1}{2}$ pounds.] Have students complete Exercises 2 and 3.

A simple method for dividing with fractions is to multiply by the reciprocal. Reciprocals are two numbers whose product is one. The reciprocal of $\frac{3}{4}$ is $\frac{4}{3}$. The reciprocal of 8 is $\frac{1}{8}$. What is the reciprocal of $\frac{1}{2}$? [2] *What is the reciprocal of $\frac{2}{3}$?* [$\frac{3}{2}$] Have students read and complete Exercises 4 and 5.

Make sure students understand that, when using the reciprocal method for dividing fractions, they use the reciprocal of only the divisor when they switch to multiplication. *Using the reciprocal method, what problem would you use to find $\frac{5}{6} \div \frac{3}{8}$?* [$\frac{5}{6} \times \frac{8}{3}$] *Can you find $6 \div \frac{2}{5}$ by multiplying $\frac{1}{6} \times \frac{5}{2}$?* [No; Sample answer: you use the reciprocal of only the divisor. It is the second factor when you multiply; the correct operation is $6 \times \frac{5}{2}$ or $\frac{6}{1} \times \frac{5}{2}$.]

2 Guided Practice

Use with Exercises 6–20.

Students continue to solve division problems with fractions and by using the reciprocal method.

Exercises 17–20
Students should recognize that these questions represent division problems. For Exercise 17, ask *How can you write this as a division problem?* [$2 \div \frac{1}{4}$]

Exercise 20
Error Intervention

If students have difficulty solving the problem,

then ask: *How can you use a diagram to help you?* [Sample answer: Draw 3 boxes and divide each box into 4 equal parts; find how many groups of 3 equal parts are in the boxes in all. There are 4 groups of 3 parts in all the boxes, so the answer is 4.] *How can you use a reciprocal to help you?* [$3 \div \frac{3}{4} = 3 \times \frac{4}{3} = 4$]

ELL Use Vocabulary

To check understanding, ask a student to repeat and complete this sentence: *The ______ of 6 is $\frac{1}{6}$.* [Reciprocal]

Quick Check Formative Assessment

How many $\frac{2}{3}$s are in 8? [12]

3 Independent Practice

Use with Exercises 21–35.

Students may wish to make paper models, like those in Exercises 1–9, to help them visualize the problem. Provide them with paper, fraction models, or Teaching Tool 6 to model the divisions.

Remind students to use reciprocals to multiply. Use Exercise 30 as an example. *What multiplication problem should you solve to find the quotient $6 \div \frac{1}{3}$?* [6×3]

Step **3-5**

Dividing Fractions

Objective Students will divide a fraction by a fraction.

Vocabulary Reciprocal, greatest common factor

Materials Index cards (4 blank cards, 1 card with a division symbol on one side and a multiplication symbol on the other side)

Professional Development

Math Background

- Division of fractions requires multiplying by the reciprocal of the divisor.
- When a greater fraction is divided by a lesser fraction, the quotient will be greater than 1.
- When a lesser fraction is divided by a greater fraction, the quotient will be less than 1.

Name ____________________ Step **3-5**

Dividing Fractions

A serving of juice is $\frac{1}{16}$ of a gallon. Answer 1 to 6 to find how many servings are in $\frac{7}{8}$ of a gallon.

Find $\frac{7}{8} \div \frac{1}{16}$.

1. What is the reciprocal of $\frac{1}{16}$? **16**
2. Write $\frac{7}{8} \div \frac{1}{16}$ as $\frac{7}{8}$ times the reciprocal of $\frac{1}{16}$. $\frac{7}{8} \div \frac{1}{16} = \frac{7}{8} \times$ **16**
3. Does $16 = \frac{16}{1}$? **yes**
4. Multiply. Simplify for any common factors first. $\frac{7}{8} \times \frac{16}{1} = \frac{7 \times \cancel{16}^{2}}{\cancel{8}_{1} \times 1} = \frac{\boxed{14}}{1}$
5. What is $\frac{7}{8} \div \frac{1}{16}$? $\frac{7}{8} \div \frac{1}{16} = \frac{7}{8} \times 16 =$ **14**
6. How many $\frac{1}{16}$-gallon servings are in $\frac{7}{8}$ gallon of juice? **14 servings**

Answer 7 to 11 to find how many $\frac{3}{8}$-gallon servings are in $\frac{1}{2}$ gallon of water.

Find $\frac{1}{2} \div \frac{3}{8}$.

7. What is the reciprocal of $\frac{3}{8}$? $\mathbf{\frac{8}{3}}$
8. Write $\frac{1}{2} \div \frac{3}{8}$ as $\frac{1}{2}$ times the reciprocal of $\frac{3}{8}$. $\frac{1}{2} \div \frac{3}{8} = \frac{1}{2} \times$ $\mathbf{\frac{8}{3}}$
9. Multiply. Simplify for any common factors first. $\frac{1}{2} \times \frac{8}{3} = \frac{1 \times \cancel{8}^{4}}{\cancel{2}_{1} \times 3} = \frac{\boxed{4}}{\boxed{3}}$
10. Write the answer in simplest form. So, $\frac{1}{2} \div \frac{3}{8} = \frac{1}{2} \times \frac{8}{3} =$ $\mathbf{\frac{4}{3}}$ $=$ $\mathbf{1\frac{1}{3}}$
11. How many $\frac{3}{8}$-gallon servings are in $\frac{1}{2}$ gallon of water? $\mathbf{1\frac{1}{3}}$ **servings**
12. Fill in the missing numbers to divide. Simplify for any common factors before multiplying.

$\frac{2}{3} \div \frac{5}{12} = \frac{2}{3} \times$ $\mathbf{\frac{12}{5}}$ $= \frac{8}{5} =$ $\mathbf{1\frac{3}{5}}$

32 Dividing Fractions

Interactive Learning 1

Concept Development

Use with Exercises 1–6.

Purpose

You have learned how to multiply fractions. Today you will learn how to divide a fraction by a fraction.

Pose the Problem

Read the problem from Exercises 1–5 aloud. Have students complete the exercises as you model the problem.

Model

Distribute the index cards to each student. Write $\frac{7}{8} \div \frac{1}{16}$ on the board. Direct students to write the numerator and the denominator of each fraction on an index card and set up the expression shown on the board at their desks.

Dividing by a fraction is the same as multiplying by its reciprocal. What is the reciprocal of $\frac{1}{16}$? [$\frac{16}{1}$] Change the fraction $\frac{1}{16}$ on the board to show $\frac{16}{1}$. Have students model this by switching the numerator and denominator

Name ______________________

Step 3-5

Dividing Fractions (continued)

Divide. Simplify, if possible.

13. $\frac{1}{8} \div \frac{2}{3} =$ $\frac{3}{16}$

14. $\frac{5}{6} \div \frac{1}{2} =$ $1\frac{2}{3}$

15. $\frac{1}{4} \div \frac{3}{5} =$ $\frac{5}{12}$

16. $\frac{6}{7} \div \frac{3}{4} =$ $1\frac{1}{7}$

17. $\frac{3}{4} \div \frac{3}{8} =$ 2

18. $\frac{1}{5} \div \frac{4}{5} =$ $\frac{1}{4}$

19. $\frac{2}{3} \div \frac{4}{7} =$ $1\frac{1}{6}$

20. $\frac{3}{7} \div \frac{3}{10} =$ $1\frac{3}{7}$

21. $\frac{4}{9} \div \frac{3}{4} =$ $\frac{16}{27}$

22. $\frac{5}{8} \div \frac{4}{5} =$ $\frac{25}{32}$

23. $\frac{7}{9} \div \frac{3}{5} =$ $1\frac{8}{27}$

24. $\frac{1}{10} \div \frac{5}{7} =$ $\frac{7}{50}$

25. $\frac{7}{8} \div \frac{5}{14} =$ $2\frac{9}{20}$

26. $\frac{3}{11} \div \frac{1}{9} =$ $2\frac{5}{11}$

27. $\frac{1}{12} \div \frac{4}{5} =$ $\frac{5}{48}$

28. $\frac{2}{5} \div \frac{5}{7} =$ $\frac{14}{25}$

29. $\frac{1}{3} \div \frac{3}{8} =$ $\frac{8}{9}$

30. $\frac{1}{4} \div \frac{1}{4} =$ 1

31. $\frac{5}{12} \div \frac{3}{5} =$ $\frac{25}{36}$

32. $\frac{9}{10} \div \frac{5}{7} =$ $1\frac{13}{50}$

33. $\frac{4}{5} \div \frac{5}{9} =$ $1\frac{11}{25}$

34. **Reasoning** For the school cafeteria, 15 pounds of vegetables were ordered by the chef. If each student usually gets $\frac{3}{8}$ of a pound of vegetables each day for lunch, how many students could be fed with the vegetables in one day? **40 students**

35. Draw a picture to show $\frac{7}{8} \div \frac{1}{16} = 14$.

Answers will vary. Drawings should show $\frac{7}{8}$ divided into sixteenths and that there are 14 sixteenths in $\frac{7}{8}$.

of the fraction $\frac{1}{16}$ to show the reciprocal. *Now, you can multiply the two fractions.* Change the symbol on the board. *What does the new problem become?* [$\frac{7}{8} \times \frac{16}{1}$] Have students flip over the division symbol card to show the multiplication symbol.

You can simplify the fraction multiplication first by finding the greatest common factor for one of the numerators and one of the denominators. What is a common factor of 16 and 8? [8] *What is 16 ÷ 8* [2] Cross out the numerator 16 and write 2. *What is 8 ÷ 8?* [1] Cross out the denominator 8 and write 1.

The simplified problem is $\frac{7}{1} \times \frac{2}{1}$. What is another way of writing $\frac{7}{1} \times \frac{2}{1}$? [7 × 2] *How many $\frac{1}{16}$ gallon servings are in $\frac{7}{8}$ gallon of juice?* [14 servings]

2 Guided Practice

Use with Exercises 7–12.

Exercise 9

Why does it help to remove the common factors first? [Sample answer: The numbers are smaller and easier to work with.]

Exercise 12

Error Intervention

If students have difficulty changing an improper fraction to a mixed number,

then remind them to divide the numerator by the denominator. *What is 8 ÷ 5?* [1] *So, 1 is the whole number part of the mixed number. How many are left?* [3] *The remainder, 3, is written over the divisor, 5.*

ELL Use Vocabulary

To check understanding, ask a student to repeat and complete this sentence: *The largest number that is a factor of two or more numbers is the _____.* [Greatest common factor]

Quick Check Formative Assessment

What is the reciprocal of $\frac{2}{9}$? [$\frac{9}{2}$]

3 Independent Practice

Use with Exercises 13–35.

For more practice, allow students to use index cards to find the reciprocal of the divisors.

For Exercises 13–33, to avoid computation errors, encourage students to simplify the fractions before multiplying the two fractions.

Exercise 34

How can you write 15 as a fraction? [$\frac{15}{1}$]

Step 3-6

Dividing Mixed Numbers

Objective Students divide with mixed numbers.

Vocabulary Mixed number, improper fraction, reciprocal

Materials Index cards, markers or colored pencils

Professional Development

Math Background

- Any whole number n can be written as a fraction in the form $\frac{n}{1}$. For example, 5 can be written as the fraction $\frac{5}{1}$.
- A mixed number can be written as an improper fraction. For example, $3\frac{1}{2}$ can be thought of as $\frac{6}{2} + \frac{1}{2}$ and written as $\frac{7}{2}$.
- Dividing a number by a fraction is the same as multiplying the number by the reciprocal of the fraction.

Name ____________________ Step 3-6

Dividing Mixed Numbers

Sierra used $3\frac{1}{2}$ cups of shredded paper and $1\frac{1}{6}$ cups of paste to make a piñata. Answer 1 to 6 to find how many times as much paper as paste Sierra used.

1. If Sierra used 6 cups of paper and 3 cups of paste, what computation would you do to solve the problem? $6 \div 3$

Find $3\frac{1}{2} \div 1\frac{1}{6}$.

2. Four large rectangles are shown below. Color $3\frac{1}{2}$ rectangles.

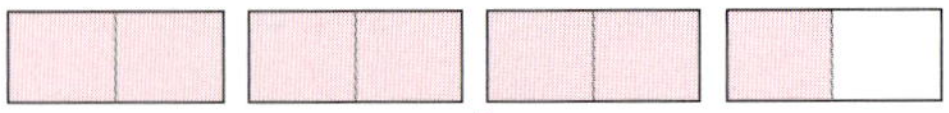

3. Write $1\frac{1}{6}$ as an improper fraction. $\frac{7}{6}$

4. To find how many groups of $1\frac{1}{6}$ are in $3\frac{1}{2}$, each rectangle below is divided into 6 equal parts. Color $1\frac{1}{6}$ or $\frac{7}{6}$ of the rectangles. Now color another $\frac{7}{6}$ with a different color. Repeat as many times as you can.

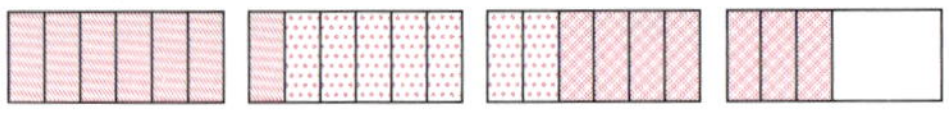

5. What is $3\frac{1}{2} \div 1\frac{1}{6}$? 3

6. How many times as much paper as paste did Sierra use? 3 times

Find $3\frac{1}{2} \div 1\frac{1}{6}$ another way by writing the missing numbers.

7. $3\frac{1}{2} \div 1\frac{1}{6} = \frac{7}{2} \div \frac{7}{6}$ Change to improper fractions.

$= \frac{7}{2} \times \frac{6}{7}$ Multiply by the reciprocal.

$= \frac{\overset{1}{\cancel{7}} \times \overset{3}{\cancel{6}}}{\underset{1}{\cancel{2}} \times \underset{1}{\cancel{7}}}$ Multiply the numerators and denominators and simplify for any common factors.

$= 3$ Find the result.

Interactive Learning

1 Concept Development

Use with Exercises 1–7.

Purpose

You have learned how to multiply mixed numbers. Today you will learn how to divide with mixed numbers.

Pose the Problem

Sierra used $3\frac{1}{2}$ cups of shredded paper and $1\frac{1}{6}$ cups of paste to make a piñata. How many times as much paper as paste did Sierra use? Ask students to share their ideas about this problem.

Model

Each student should have several markers or colored pencils for shading the division model. Have students read and complete Exercises 1 and 2. *What does the section that you colored show?* [The number of cups of shredded paper] Have students complete Exercises 3 and 4.

Name ____________________

Step 3-6

Dividing Mixed Numbers (continued)

Find $4 \div 2\frac{1}{5}$ by writing the missing numbers.

8. $4 \div 2\frac{1}{5} = \frac{4}{1} \div \frac{\boxed{11}}{5}$ — Change to improper fractions.

$= \frac{4}{1} \times \frac{\boxed{5}}{\boxed{11}}$ — Multiply by the reciprocal.

$= \frac{\boxed{4} \times \boxed{5}}{\boxed{1} \times \boxed{11}}$ — Multiply the numerators and denominators and remove common factors.

$= \frac{\boxed{20}}{11} = 1\frac{\boxed{9}}{11}$ — Simplify.

Divide. Simplify if possible.

9. $7 \div 3\frac{4}{10} =$ $2\frac{1}{17}$

10. $3\frac{4}{5} \div 5 =$ $\frac{19}{25}$

11. $3\frac{1}{4} \div 4\frac{1}{4} =$ $\frac{13}{17}$

12. $1\frac{3}{5} \div 4\frac{2}{3} =$ $\frac{12}{35}$

13. $2\frac{6}{7} \div 1\frac{3}{4} =$ $1\frac{31}{49}$

14. $1\frac{4}{9} \div 4 =$ $\frac{13}{36}$

15. $3\frac{7}{9} \div 6\frac{2}{3} =$ $\frac{17}{30}$

16. $2\frac{7}{8} \div 1\frac{11}{12} =$ $1\frac{1}{2}$

17. $1 \div 2\frac{2}{3} =$ $\frac{3}{8}$

18. Horatio is making a necklace. He has large beads that are $1\frac{1}{8}$ inches long. How many beads are needed to make a necklace 18 inches long? **16 beads**

19. Reasoning If $3 \times 2\frac{1}{2} = 7\frac{1}{2}$, what is $7\frac{1}{2} \div 2\frac{1}{2}$? **3**

20. Reasoning Use estimation to explain why 26 is NOT a reasonable solution for $10\frac{1}{4} \div 1\frac{3}{4}$.

Sample answer: $10\frac{1}{4} \div 1\frac{3}{4}$ is about $10 \div 2 = 5$, and 26 is not close to 5.

What do the groups of 7 sixths show? [The number of cups of paste] *Why don't we color in the section on the right that is not divided into sixths?* [Sample answer: Because we are dividing $3\frac{1}{2}$; if we included the undivided section, that would be dividing 4.]

Remind students of how they used the reciprocal method for dividing fractions. *What multiplication problem should you use to find the quotient $\frac{3}{4} \div \frac{2}{5}$?* [$\frac{3}{4} \times \frac{5}{2}$] When dividing with mixed numbers, we first have to change each mixed number in the problem to an improper fraction. *How do you write $4\frac{2}{3}$ as an improper fraction?* [$\frac{14}{3}$] Have students complete Exercise 7.

2 Guided Practice

Use with Exercises 8–11.

Students continue to solve division problems with mixed numbers. Remind students to convert mixed numbers to improper fractions.

Exercise 9
Watch for students who multiply by the reciprocal of the wrong number, or who use the reciprocal for both factors when multiplying. Say, *Circle the divisor and determine its reciprocal.*

Exercise 10
Error Intervention

If students state that they should change only the mixed number to a fraction,

then remind them that every whole number can be written as a fraction with a denominator of 1. *How can you write 5 as a fraction?* [$\frac{5}{1}$]

ELL Use Vocabulary

To check understanding, ask a student to repeat and complete this sentence: *The mixed number $5\frac{1}{2}$ can be converted to the ______ $\frac{11}{2}$.* [Improper fraction]

Quick Check Formative Assessment

What is $4\frac{2}{5} \div 2\frac{3}{4}$? [$1\frac{3}{5}$]

3 Independent Practice

Use with Exercises 12–20.

Remind students to use reciprocals to multiply. Use Exercise 17 as an example. *What multiplication problem can you use to find the quotient $1 \div 2\frac{2}{3}$?* [$1 \times \frac{3}{8}$]

Students may find it easier to simplify before multiplying. They can simplify by finding the greatest common factor of either numerator and one of the denominators, and then dividing both by that factor.

Step 4-1

Place Value Through Thousandths

Objective Students will read and write decimals through thousandths.

Vocabulary Tenths, hundredths, thousandths

Materials Decimal Place-Value Chart (Teaching Tool 7)

Professional Development Math Background

- One digit to the right of the decimal point indicates tenths.
- Two digits to the right of the decimal point indicate hundredths.
- Three digits to the right of the decimal point indicate thousandths.
- 0.387 is read "three hundred eighty-seven thousandths."

Name ____________________ Teaching Tool 7

Decimal Place-Value Chart

ONES				DECIMALS		
hundreds	tens	ones	.	tenths	hundredths	thousandths
			.			

M9

Name ____________________ Step 4-1

Place Value Through Thousandths

1. Write 5.739 in the place-value chart below.

ones		tenths	hundredths	thousandths
5	.	7	3	9

2. What is the value of the 5 in 5.739? 5
3. What is the value of the 7 in 5.739? 0.7
4. What is the value of the 3 in 5.739? 0.03
5. What is the value of the 9 in 5.739? 0.009
6. Write 5.739 in expanded form. 5 + 0.7 + 0.03 + 0.009
7. Write 5.739 in words.
   five and seven hundred thirty-nine thousandths

Write seven and two hundred four thousandths in standard form by answering 8 to 12.

8. How many ones are in seven and two hundred four thousandths? 7
   Write 7 in the ones place of the place-value chart below.

ones		tenths	hundredths	thousandths
7	.	2	0	4

9. How many tenths are in seven and two hundred four thousandths? 2
   Write 2 in the tenths place of the place-value chart above.
10. How many hundredths are in seven and two hundred four thousandths? 0
    Write 0 in the hundredths place of the place-value chart above.
11. How many thousandths are in seven and two hundred four thousandths? 4
    Write 4 in the thousandths place of the place-value chart.
12. Write 7.204 in expanded form. 7 + 0.2 + 0.004

36 Place Value Through Thousandths

Interactive Learning 1 Concept Development

Use with Teaching Tool 7.

Purpose

You have learned about the place value of whole numbers. Today you will learn about the place value of decimals.

Pose the Problem

Write 0.741 on the board. *How can you use place value to read and understand this decimal?* Have students share their ideas.

Model

Distribute copies of Decimal Place-Value Chart (Teaching Tool 7). *What is the first place to the right of the decimal point?* [Tenths] *What digit is in the tenths place?* [7]

Step 4-1

Name ______________________

Place Value Through Thousandths (continued)

Write each number in standard form.

13. 426 thousandths 0.426
14. 631 thousandths 0.631
15. 3 and 3 thousandths 3.003
16. 507 thousandths 0.507
17. 5 and 6 thousandths 5.006
18. 9 and 62 thousandths 9.062

Write the value of the underlined digit.

19. 2.553 0.05
20. 0.381 0.001
21. 6.647 0.6
22. 9.097 0.09

Write each decimal in expanded form.

23. 4.685 4 + 0.6 + 0.08 + 0.005
24. 3.056 3 + 0.05 + 0.006
25. 0.735 0.7 + 0.03 + 0.005
26. 4.004 4 + 0.004

Write each decimal in word form.

27. 2.598 two and five hundred ninety-eight thousandths

28. 0.008 eight thousandths

29. 0.250 two hundred fifty thousandths

Place Value Through Thousandths **37**

What is the value of the 7? [7 tenths] *What is the second place to the right of the decimal point?* [Hundredths] *What digit is in the hundredths place?* [4] *What is the value of the 4?* [4 hundredths] *What is the third place to the right of the decimal point?* [Thousandths] *What digit is in the thousandths place?* [1] *What is the value of the 1?* [1 thousandth]

Use the decimal place-value chart to write 0.741. Write this decimal in expanded form. [0.7 + 0.04 + 0.001] *How do you say this decimal?* [Seven hundred forty-one thousandths]

Have students model other decimals with the place-value chart.

2 Guided Practice

Use with Exercises 1–12.

Remind students that the digits to the left of the decimal point show ones, tens, hundreds, thousands, and so on.

Exercises 2–5
Error Intervention

If students have difficulty finding the value of each digit,

then say: *Look at the place-value chart. What digit is placed in the tenths place?* [7] *So, 7 has a value of 7 tenths or 0.7.*

ELL Use Vocabulary

To check understanding, ask a student to repeat and complete this sentence: *In the decimal 6.095, the 0 is in the _____ place and the 5 is in the _____ place.* [Tenths, thousandths]

Quick Check Formative Assessment

What is the value of the 4 in the decimal 2.704? [4 thousandths or 0.004]

3 Independent Practice

Use with Exercises 13–29.

Remind students that the decimal point separates the whole numbers from the tenths, hundredths, and thousandths.

Exercises 15, 17, and 18
Remind students that the word *and* is used to represent the decimal point when the number is read.

For Exercises 23–26, some students may have difficulty writing the decimal in expanded form. Remind them that an addition symbol is used to separate the value of each digit of the decimal.

Step **4-2**

Relating Fractions and Decimals

Objective Students will write decimals for fractions and fractions for decimals.

Vocabulary Tenths, hundredths

Materials Decimal Models (Teaching Tool 8), crayons or markers

Professional Development

Math Background

- Tenths refer to 10 equal parts of the whole. Hundredths refer to 100 equal parts of the whole.
- A zero is written to the left of the decimal point for positive decimals less than 1.
- $0.7 = \frac{7}{10}$ and $0.07 = \frac{7}{100}$

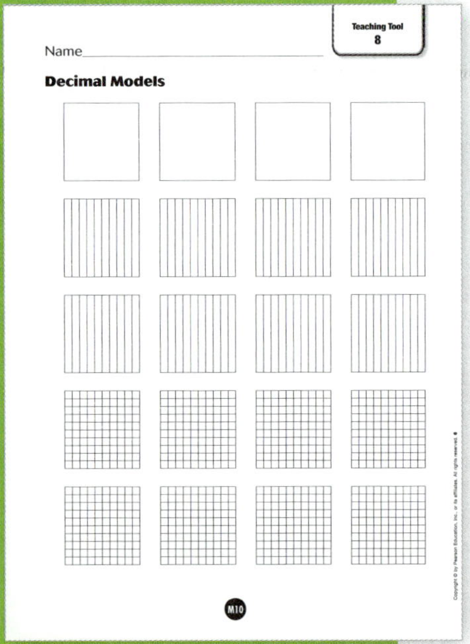

Name ______ Step **4-2**

Relating Fractions and Decimals

1. How many equal parts are in the rectangle on the right? 10
2. Color 3 equal parts of the rectangle.
3. What fractional part of the rectangle did you color? $\frac{3}{10}$
4. The fraction $\frac{3}{10}$ is read "three tenths", what is three tenths written in decimal form? 0.3

So, $\frac{3}{10}$ and 0.3 are both three tenths. They are the same amount.

$\frac{3}{10} = 0.3$

5. How many equal parts are in the grid on the right? 100
6. Color 4 columns and 3 more squares in the grid. How many small squares did you color? 43
7. What decimal represents the part of the grid you colored? 0.43
8. Write 0.43 in words. forty-three hundredths
9. What is 43 hundredths written as a fraction? $\frac{43}{100}$
10. So, 0.43 and $\frac{43}{100}$ are the same amount. $0.43 = \frac{43}{100}$

38 Relating Fractions and Decimals

Interactive Learning

1 Concept Development

Use with Teaching Tool 8.

Purpose

You have learned about the place value of decimals. Today you will learn about the relationship between fractions and decimals.

Pose the Problem

Write $\frac{8}{10}$ and $\frac{27}{100}$ on the chalkboard. *How can you use decimals to represent the same amounts as these fractions?* Have students share their ideas.

Model

Distribute copies of Decimal Models (Teaching Tool 8). *Look at the first large square in the second row. How many equal parts are there?* [10] *Shade 8 parts. What fraction describes what you shaded?* [Eight tenths] *We can also use a decimal to show eight tenths.* Write $\frac{8}{10} = 0.8$ on the board. Have students write the number sentence under the shaded square. *Remember, the first digit to the right of the decimal point tells how many tenths. Both the fraction and the decimal are read as "eight tenths."*

Name ______________________

Step 4-2

Relating Fractions and Decimals (continued)

Write a fraction and a decimal for each shaded part.

11. 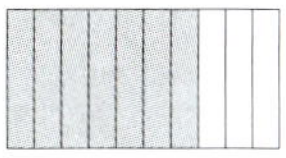

$\frac{7}{10}$; 0.7

12. 

$\frac{39}{100}$; 0.39

13. 

$\frac{53}{100}$; 0.53

Write each fraction as a decimal.

14. $\frac{8}{10}$ 0.8

15. $\frac{56}{100}$ 0.56

16. $\frac{7}{10}$ 0.7

17. $\frac{13}{100}$ 0.13

18. $\frac{85}{100}$ 0.85

19. $\frac{77}{100}$ 0.77

20. $\frac{6}{100}$ 0.06

21. $3\frac{5}{10}$ 3.5

Write each decimal as a fraction or mixed number.

22. 0.3 $\frac{3}{10}$

23. 0.63 $\frac{63}{100}$

24. 6.9 $6\frac{9}{10}$

25. 0.17 $\frac{17}{100}$

26. 4.23 $4\frac{23}{100}$

27. 0.01 $\frac{1}{100}$

28. 0.33 $\frac{33}{100}$

29. 1.1 $1\frac{1}{10}$

Katie bought 100 plants for her garden. She bought 37 tomato plants, 8 cucumber plants, 12 pumpkin plants, and the rest of her plants were onions.

30. Write a fraction and a decimal to express the part of the plants that are tomatoes. $\frac{37}{100}$; 0.37

31. **Reasoning** Write a fraction and a decimal to express the part of the plants that are onions. $\frac{43}{100}$; 0.43

Look at the first grid in the fourth row. How many equal parts are there? [100] *Shade 27 parts. What fraction describes what you shaded?* [Twenty-seven hundredths] Write $\frac{27}{100}$ = 0.27 on the board, and have students write the number sentence under the shaded square. *Both the fraction and the decimal are read "twenty-seven hundredths."*

Have students shade 5 little squares in another hundredths grid. Then discuss that $\frac{5}{100}$ written as a decimal is 0.05, not 0.5.

2 Guided Practice

Use with Exercises 1–10.

Remind students that one place to the right of the decimal point shows tenths and two places to the right of the decimal point show hundredths.

Exercises 3, 9
Error Intervention

If students have difficulty writing the fraction,

then remind them that the numerator tells how many equal parts are shaded, and the denominator tells how many equal parts are in the whole.

ELL Use Vocabulary

To check understanding, ask a student to repeat and complete these sentences: *The fraction $\frac{3}{10}$ is read "three _____ ."* [Tenths] *The fraction $\frac{83}{100}$ is read "eighty-three _____ ".* [Hundredths]

Quick Check Formative Assessment

What is the decimal 0.4 written as a fraction? [$\frac{4}{10}$] *What is $\frac{59}{100}$ written as a decimal?* [0.59]

3 Independent Practice

Use with Exercises 11–31.

Remind students that when they write a decimal, they should write a zero in the ones place if the amount is less than 1.

For Exercise 21, some students may be uncertain about how to work with decimals or fractions greater than 1. Remind them that the fraction part of a mixed number is represented by the digit(s) to the right of the decimal point in a decimal number. The whole-number part of a mixed number is represented by the digit(s) to the left of the decimal point.

Step 4-3

Multiplying with Decimals and Whole Numbers

Objective Students will find the product of a decimal and whole number.

Vocabulary Decimal point, decimal places

Materials Place-value blocks

Professional Development Math Background

- The steps for multiplying whole numbers by decimals are similar to the steps for multiplying two whole numbers.
- Add the number of decimal places in each factor to find the number of decimal places in the product.

Name ______________________ Step 4-3

Multiplying with Decimals and Whole Numbers

A small jar of spice weighs 0.54 ounce. What is the weight of three jars?

Find 3 × 0.54 by answering 1 to 10.

Let the block at the right represent one unit, or 1.0.

1.0

So, [rod] represents one tenth, or 0.1 and [cube] represents one hundredth or 0.01.

1. Show three groups of 0.54 using place-value blocks.

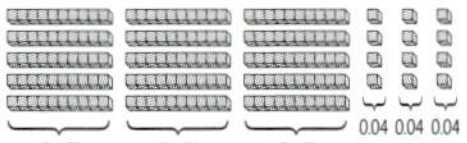
0.5 0.5 0.5 0.04 0.04 0.04

2. Multiply the hundredths.

   3 × 4 hundredths = __12__ hundredths

3. Trade 10 hundredths for one tenth.

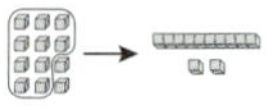

   12 hundredths = __1__ tenth

   and __2__ hundredths

   Record the 2 in the answer and write the 1 above the 5 tenths to show the regrouping.

11	
0.54	← 2 decimal places
× 3	← 0 decimal places
1.62	2 decimal places

4. Multiply the tenths.

   3 × 5 tenths = __15__ tenths

40 Multiplying with Decimals and Whole Numbers

Interactive Learning 1 Concept Development

Purpose

You have learned how to multiply whole numbers. Today you will learn how to multiply a decimal and a whole number.

Pose the Problem

Yogurt is on sale for $0.33 each. Karen bought 4 packages of yogurt. How much did the yogurt cost in all? Have students share their ideas before modeling the solution.

Model

Distribute 1 one, 13 tenths, and 12 hundredths blocks per pair. Write 4 × 0.33 vertically on the board and show 4 groups of 0.33 with the place-value blocks. Have students record the problem and complete the calculation as you model each step.

Multiplying with a decimal is similar to multiplying whole numbers. What do you do first? [Multiply each digit in 0.33 by 4 from right to left.]

Name ____________________

Step 4-3

Multiplying with Decimals and Whole Numbers (continued)

5. Add the regrouped tenth. 15 tenths + 1 tenth = 16 tenths

6. Trade 10 tenths for 1 one. 16 tenths = 1 one and 6 tenths

Record the 6 in the answer and write the 1 above the 0 to show the regrouping.

7. Multiply the ones. 3 × 0 ones = 0 ones

8. Add the regrouped one. 0 ones + 1 one = 1 one

Record the 1 in the answer.

9. What is 3 × 0.54? 1.62

10. What is the weight of three jars? 1.62 ounces

11. How many decimal places are there in 0.54? 2

12. How many decimal places are there in 3? 0

13. How many decimal places are there in both factors combined? 2

14. How many decimal places are in the product of 0.54 × 3 = 1.62? 2

The total number of decimal places in the factors always equals the number of decimal places in the product.

15. Reasoning If 5 × 83 = 415, what is 5 × 0.83? Explain.

4.15; 5 × 0.83 has two decimal places.

Find each product.

16. 8.6 × 4	**17.** 42.5 × 6	**18.** 40 × 1.3	**19.** $9.12 × 3
34.4	255.0	52.0	$27.36

20. Louis bought 5 pens that cost $0.79 each. How much did he pay for them? $3.95

21. A small bottle of perfume holds 0.25 ounce. How many ounces would 5 of these bottles hold? 1.25 ounces

Look at the hundredths blocks. How many hundredths are in 4 × 0.03? [12 hundredths] *Trade 10 hundredths for 1 tenth. So, 12 hundredths is equal to 1 tenth and 2 hundredths.* Record the 2 in the product at the far right and the regrouped 1 above the 3 in the tenths column. *Look at the tenths blocks.* Continue to model how to multiply the tenths and the ones.

What do you get after you multiply each digit? [132] *You must place the decimal point in the product to get the correct answer. Add the number of decimal places in each factor to find the number of decimal places in the product. How many decimal places are in the first factor?* [2] *How many decimal places are in the second factor?* [0] *How many decimal places are there in all?* [2] Have students demonstrate how to place the decimal point in the product. *How much did the yogurt cost in all?* [$1.32]

2 Guided Practice

Use with Exercises 1–14.

Remind students that they need to find the total number of decimal places in both factors in order to place the decimal point correctly.

Exercise 9

Error Intervention

If students have difficulty placing the decimal in the product,

then have them draw arrows from the last digit of the product to help place the decimal. *Starting at the right of the 2, draw arrows and move the decimal point 2 places to the left.*

ELL Use Vocabulary

To check understanding, ask a student to repeat and complete this sentence: *The _____ is used to separate the ones from the tenths and hundredths.* [Decimal point]

Quick Check Formative Assessment

How many decimal places are in the product 6 × 1.7? Find the product. [1; 10.2]

3 Independent Practice

Use with Exercises 15–21.

For Exercises 16–19, some students may forget to add the regrouped numbers. Encourage them to cross out the regrouped numbers when they are added. Have students look back at their work to see that all of the regrouped numbers have been crossed out.

Step 4-4

Multiplying Decimals by Decimals

Objective Students will find the product of two decimals.

Vocabulary Decimal places

Materials Multiplication Charts (Teaching Tool 4)

Professional Development Math Background

- The steps for multiplying decimals are similar to the steps for multiplying whole numbers.
- Place value determines the location of the decimal point in the product.

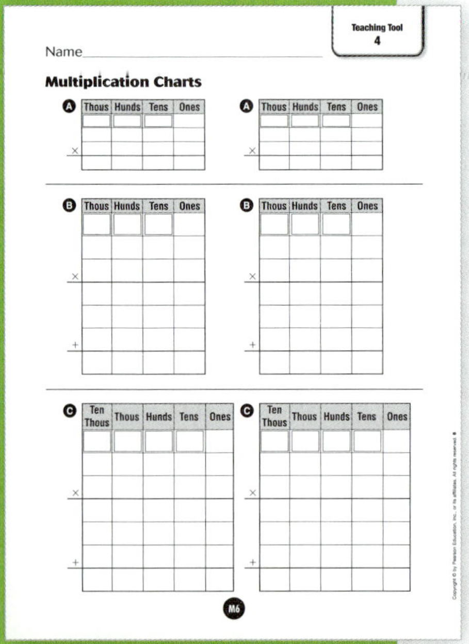

Name ____________ **Step 4-4**

Multiplying Decimals by Decimals

Hans lives 2.35 miles from school. Jamal lives 1.2 times as far. How far from school does Jamal live?

Find 1.2 × 2.35 by answering 1 to 7.

235
× 12
2,820

1. Multiply 1.2 × 2.35 as you would with whole numbers. What is 12 × 235? **2,820**
2. How many decimal places are in 1.2? **1**
3. How many decimal places are in 2.35? **2**
4. How many decimal places are in both factors together? **3**

The number of decimal places in the product equals the total number of decimal places in the factors.

5. How many decimal places should be in the product 1.2 × 2.35? **3**
6. So, what is 1.2 × 2.35? **2.820**
7. How far from the school does Jamal live? **2.82** miles
8. **Reasoning** Why are there only 2 decimal places in the correct answer of 2.82 when 1.2 and 2.35 have 3 decimal places in all?
   Because the last decimal place was a zero and zeros on the end of decimals don't have to be written in the answer.

Rico lives 0.03 times as far from the school as Hans. How far from the school does Rico live?

Find 0.03 × 2.35 by answering 9 to 13.

9. What is 3 × 235? **705**
10. How many decimal places are in both factors, 0.03 and 2.35, together? **4**
11. How many decimal places should be in the product? **4**

Interactive Learning 1 Concept Development

Use with Teaching Tool 4.

Purpose

You have learned how to multiply with decimals and whole numbers. Today you will learn how to multiply a decimal by a decimal.

Pose the Problem

Sheri bought 1.5 pounds of chicken salad. Each pound cost $5.40. How much did it cost Sheri to buy the chicken salad? Have students share their ideas.

Model

Distribute copies of Multiplication Charts (Teaching Tool 4). *What information are you given?* [Sheri bought 1.5 pounds of chicken salad and each pound cost $5.40.] *What are you asked to find?* [The total cost of the chicken salad]

To find how much the chicken salad cost, you can multiply the decimals as if they were whole numbers. Write 15 × 540 vertically on the board. Have students copy the problem using the chart to help them align

Name ______________________ Step 4-4

Multiplying Decimals by Decimals (continued)

If necessary, zeros may need to be added at the beginning of the number to place the decimal point correctly.

12. So, what is 0.03 × 2.35? **0.0705**

13. How far from the school does Rico live? **0.0705** miles

Find each product.

14. 0.8 × 0.01	**15.** 1.5 × 0.02	**16.** 6.7 × 0.005	**17.** 0.2 × 0.03
0.008	0.03	0.0335	0.006
18. 0.5 × 0.05	**19.** 1.2 × 0.03	**20.** 0.9 × 0.08	**21.** 0.3 × 0.3
0.025	0.036	0.072	0.09
22. 0.06 × 0.3	**23.** 1.2 × 0.07	**24.** 0.04 × 0.09	**25.** 0.7 × 0.09
0.018	0.084	0.0036	0.063

26. 9.8 × 1.2	**27.** 5.6 × 3.7	**28.** 0.4 × 0.6	**29.** 0.85 × 0.2	**30.** 1.95 × 0.4
11.76	20.72	0.24	0.17	0.78
31. 17.6 × 0.23	**32.** 4.05 × 8.1	**33.** 6.10 × 5.2	**34.** 2.09 × 0.7	**35.** 0.49 × 0.3
4.048	32.805	31.720	1.463	0.147

36. An inch is 2.54 centimeters. How many centimeters are in 6.5 inches? **16.51 centimeters**

37. A cell phone company offers telephone calls for $0.05 for one minute. How much should it cost to make a cell phone call for 0.5 minute? **$0.025**

38. Reasoning Is the product 1.01 × 1.01 less than or greater than 1? Explain.

Greater than 1, since 1.01 is greater than 1.

each digit. *What do you do first?* [Multiply each digit in 540 by 5 from right to left.] Have students find the first partial product as you record the calculations on the board. *What is the partial product?* [2,700] *How do you find the next partial product?* [Multiply each digit in 540 by 10.] Have students find the second partial product as you record the calculations on the board. *What is the second partial product?* [5,400] *What is the product?* [2,700 + 5,400 = 8,100] Place the decimal points in the original problem written on the board. *How many decimal places are in 5.40?* [2] *How many decimal places are in 1.5?* [1] *How many decimal places are there in both factors?* [3] *The number of decimal places in the product equals the total number of decimal places in the factors. So, how many decimal places should be in the product of 1.5 × 5.40?* [3] *How much did the chicken salad cost?* [8.100 or $8.10]

2 Guided Practice

Use with Exercises 1–13.

Remind students that multiplying decimals is like multiplication of whole numbers. Students need to remember to write the decimal point in the product.

Exercises 12 and 13
Error Intervention

If students forget to write a zero in the ones place of the product,

then remind them that zero is used as a placeholder to show the whole number value in the decimal.

Exercises 9 and 13
If 3 × 235 = 705, how do you know 0.03 × 2.35 = 0.0705? [There are 4 decimal places in the factors so there should be 4 decimal places in the product.]

ELL Use Vocabulary

To check understanding, ask a student to repeat and complete this sentence: *The number of ______ in the product is equal to the sum of the number of decimal places in the factors.* [Decimal places]

Quick Check — Formative Assessment

What is the relationship between the number of decimal places in the factors and the number of decimal places in the product? [The number of decimal places is the same.]

3 Independent Practice

Use with Exercises 14–38.

Remind students to start at the far right of the product when counting decimal places.

Exercise 16
Point out that a decimal written to the thousandths place does not change the way to find the product of decimals. *How many decimal places are in 6.7? 0.005?* [1; 3] *How many decimal places are in the product 6.7 × 0.005?* [4]

Step **4-5**

Dividing a Decimal by a Whole Number

Objective Students will divide a decimal by a whole number.

Vocabulary Decimal point

Materials Centimeter Grid Paper (Teaching Tool 10)

Professional Development

Math Background

- The process of dividing a decimal by a whole number is similar to the process of dividing whole numbers.
- The placement of the decimal point in the quotient is directly related to the placement of the decimal point in the dividend.

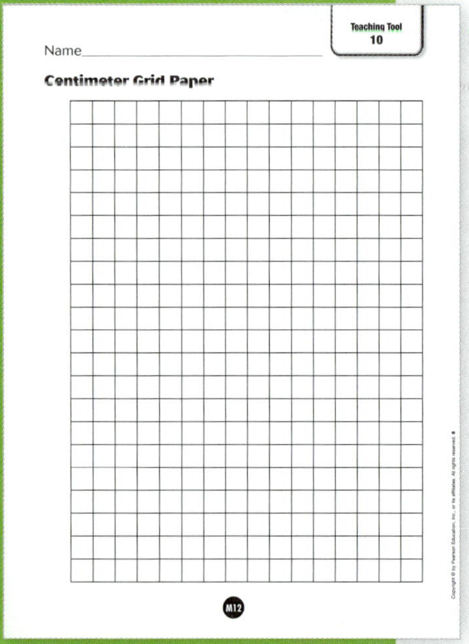
Name

Teaching Tool 10

Centimeter Grid Paper

M12

Name ______ Step **4-5**

Dividing a Decimal by a Whole Number

A plot of land that is 29.4 acres is divided into 12 equal parts. How many acres is each part?

Find 29.4 ÷ 12 by answering 1 to 11 and completing the long division problem at the right.

```
     2.45
12)29.40
   24
    54
    48
     60
     60
      0
```

1. How many groups of 12 are there in 29? **2**

Record the 2 above the 9 in 29.4 at the right.

2. Multiply and subtract.
How many ones are leftover? 29 − 24 = **5** ones

Record this value below the 24 and the line.

3. How many tenths are 5 ones and 4 tenths? **54** tenths
Bring down the 4 next to the 5, to show the 54 tenths.

4. How many groups of 12 are there in 54? **4**

Record the 4 above the 4 in 29.4.

5. Multiply and subtract.
How many tenths are leftover? 54 tenths − 48 tenths = **6** tenths

Record this value below the 48 and the line.

6. Does 29.4 = 29.40? **yes** Since there is a remainder, add a zero to the dividend to change 29.4 to 29.40.

7. How many hundredths are in 6 tenths and 0 hundredths? **60** hundredths

Bring down the 0 next to the 6, to show the 60 hundredths.

8. How many groups of 12 are there in 60? **5**

Record the 5 above the 0 in 29.40.

9. Multiply and subtract.
How many hundredths are leftover? 60 − 60 = **0** hundredths

Since there are no hundredths left, the division is finished. Notice that the decimal point in the quotient is directly above the decimal point in the dividend.

10. So, what is 29.4 ÷ 12? **2.45**

11. How many acres is each piece of land? **2.45 acres**

Interactive Learning **1**

Concept Development

Use with Teaching Tool 10.

Purpose

You have learned how to multiply a decimal by a whole number. Today you will learn how to divide a decimal by a whole number.

Pose the Problem

A movie theater is selling ticket booklets for $36.25. Each booklet has 5 tickets. What is the value of each movie ticket? Allow time for students to share their ideas.

Model

Distribute copies of Centimeter Grid Paper (Teaching Tool 10). *What are you asked to find?* [The value of each movie ticket] *To find the value of each movie ticket, you can divide.*

Name ____________________ Step 4-5

Dividing a Decimal by a Whole Number (continued)

Find each quotient.

12. 4)12.8 — 3.2	**13.** 37)55.5 — 1.5	**14.** 35)2.1 — 0.06	**15.** 2)37.4 — 18.7
16. 11)97.9 — 8.9	**17.** 41)129.15 — 3.15	**18.** 30)13.5 — 0.45	**19.** 9)45.54 — 5.06
20. 6)72.24 — 12.04	**21.** 5)43.75 — 8.75	**22.** 3)7.41 — 2.47	**23.** 30)188.4 — 6.28
24. 9)67.86 — 7.54	**25.** 3)39.09 — 13.03	**26.** 52)72.8 — 1.4	**27.** 81)32.4 — 0.4
28. 2)621.5 — 310.75	**29.** 16)75.2 — 4.7	**30.** 24)151.2 — 6.3	**31.** 9)132.3 — 14.7

32. A 12-pack of canned juice costs $3.24. What is the cost of each juice can? $0.27

33. Reasoning How many zeros can be placed after the last digit in a decimal without changing the value of the number?
There is no limit to the number of zeros that may be added.

Write 5)$36.25 on the board. Have students write the problem on grid paper to help them keep each place value aligned correctly. Have them record the calculations as you model the problem. *Place a decimal point in the quotient directly above the decimal point in the dividend. Why is it helpful to write the decimal point before you start dividing?* [Sample answer: So you remember to include the decimal point in the quotient.] *Divide the same way you would with whole numbers. How many groups of 5 are in 36?* [7] Record the 7 in the ones place of the quotient. *Are there any ones left over?* [Yes] *How many?* [1 one is left over.] *What is the next step?* [Divide the tenths.] Continue to model how to divide the tenths and the hundredths. *What is the quotient?* [7.25] *So, what is the value of each movie ticket?* [$7.25]

2 Guided Practice

Use with Exercises 1–11.

Remind students that dividing a decimal by a whole number is like dividing a whole number by a whole number.

Exercise 6
Why do you need to place a zero to the right of the tenths place in the dividend? [Sample answer: So you can continue dividing the 6 tenths that are left.]

Exercises 10
Error Intervention

If students forget to place the decimal in the quotient,

then encourage them to write the decimal point before dividing to find the quotient.

ELL Use Vocabulary

To check understanding, ask a student to repeat and complete this sentence: *A decimal point is used to separate the ______ from the tenths and hundredths in a number.* [Whole numbers]

Quick Check Formative Assessment

How is dividing a decimal by a whole number similar to dividing whole numbers? [Sample answer: The process is the same, but when you divide a decimal by a whole number you need to place the decimal point in the quotient.]

3 Independent Practice

Use with Exercises 12–33.

Remind students to annex zeros to the dividend to continue dividing any left over values.

Exercises 14, 18, and 32
Have students write a zero in the ones place of the quotient as a placeholder for the ones.

Step 4-6

Dividing a Decimal by a Decimal

Objective Students will divide a decimal by a decimal.

Vocabulary Powers of ten

Materials Decimal Models (Teaching Tool 8)

Professional Development

Math Background

- Division of decimals is similar to division of whole numbers.
- To divide a decimal by a decimal, multiply the divisor and the dividend by the least power of ten that eliminates decimals in the divisor.

Name ______________________ Step 4-6

Dividing a Decimal by a Decimal

Simon has 2.25 gallons of filtered water. How many 0.75 gallon servings of water does Simon have?

Find 2.25 ÷ 0.75 by answering 1 to 4.

1. Show 2.25 with place-value blocks.

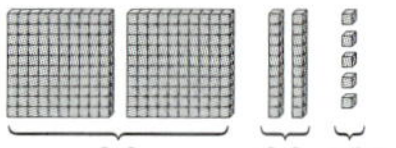

2. Divide 2.25 into groups with 0.75 in each. Trade ones for tenths and tenths for hundredths, as needed. How many groups of 0.75 are in 2.25? 3

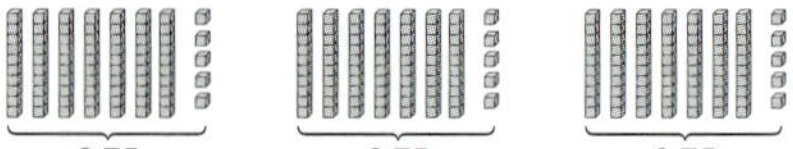

3. So, what is 2.25 ÷ 0.75? 3

4. How many 0.75 gallon servings of water does Simon have? 3 servings

Find 2.25 ÷ 0.75 another way by answering 5 to 8.

5. What number makes the number sentence true? $0.75 \times \underline{100} = 75$

6. You can change 2.25 ÷ 0.75 to make it easier to divide. Fill in the missing number below to see how.

$$2.25 \div 0.75 = \frac{2.25}{0.75} = \frac{2.25 \times 100}{0.75 \times 100} = \frac{\boxed{225}}{75} = \underline{225} \div 75$$

7. What is 225 ÷ 75? 3

8. Since 225 ÷ 75 = 2.25 ÷ 0.75, what is 2.25 ÷ 0.75? 3

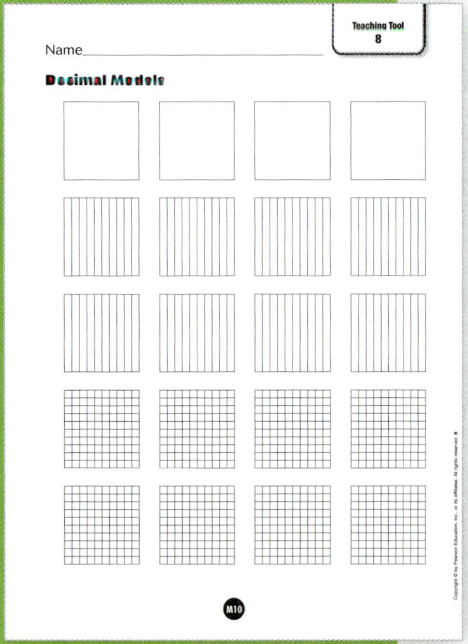
Name
Teaching Tool 8
Decimal Models
M10

1 Concept Development

Interactive Learning

Use with Teaching Tool 8.

Purpose

You have learned how to multiply two decimals. Today you will learn how to divide a decimal by a decimal.

Pose the Problem

Jenna bought 0.5 yard of fabric. She paid $3.50. What is the price per yard of the fabric? Allow time for students to share their ideas before modeling the solution.

Model

Distribute copies of Decimal Models (Teaching Tool 8). *How much did Jenna pay for the fabric?* [$3.50] *How much fabric did Jenna buy?* [0.5 yard] *What division must you complete to find the price per yard of the fabric?* [$3.50 ÷ 0.5]

Name ______________________

Step 4-6

Dividing a Decimal by a Decimal (continued)

To divide decimals, multiply the divisor by 10 or 100 to make it a whole number. Multiply the dividend by the same amount. The quotient of the resulting amounts equals the quotient of the original numbers.

Find 2.96 ÷ 0.4 by answering 9 to 12.

9. What number makes the number sentence true? 0.4 × 10 = 4

10. Multiply 2.96 by the same number. 2.96 × 10 = 29.6

11. What is 29.6 ÷ 4? 7.4

12. What is 2.96 ÷ 0.4? 7.4

Divide.

13. 12.2 ÷ 6.1	**14.** 35.7 ÷ 5.1	**15.** 0.18 ÷ 0.2	**16.** 53.4 ÷ 8.9
2	7	0.9	6
17. 1.25 ÷ 0.25	**18.** 0.48 ÷ 0.16	**19.** 26.8 ÷ 6.7	**20.** 1.008 ÷ 5.6
5	3	4	0.18

21. Baseball card packages cost $3.50 each. How many packages can be purchased for $17.50? 5 packages

22. Reasoning When dividing a number which is greater than 1 by a number less than 1, will the quotient be greater than or less than the dividend? Explain.

The quotient will be greater than the dividend. For example, 5 ÷ 0.2 = 25.

Look at the second row of grids. Shade 3 whole grids and 5 columns in the fourth grid to represent the amount Jenna paid. How many equal groups of 0.5 can you make? Model division into equal groups of 5 tenths by circling the first group of 5 columns. Have students continue to circle groups of 5 columns, or 5 tenths. *There are 7 groups of 5 tenths, so each yard of fabric cost $7.*

Remind students that numbers such as 10, 100, and 1,000 are powers of ten written in standard form. *You can use powers of ten to divide a decimal by a decimal.* Write 0.5)3.50 on the board. *What number can you multiply the divisor by to make it a whole number?* [10] Write 0.5 × 10 = 5 on the board. *Now the dividend must be multiplied by the same number. What is 3.50 × 10?* [35.0] Write 0.5 × 3.50 = 35.0 on the board. *What does the division problem become?* [5)35.0] Write 5)35.0 on the board. *Multiplying the divisor and dividend by the same power of ten makes the division of decimals easier. So, how much does each yard of fabric cost?* [$7]

2 Guided Practice

Use with Exercises 1–8.

Remind students to multiply the divisor by the least power of ten that makes it a whole number. Then multiply the dividend by the same power of ten.

Exercise 6

Why do you multiply 2.25 and 0.75 by 100? [Multiplying the divisor by 100 will make the decimal a whole number. The dividend must be multiplied by the same number.]

Exercise 8

Error Intervention

If students do not understand the relationship between the two problems,

then point out to students that the quotient does not change when the divisor and the dividend are multiplied by the same number.

ELL Use Vocabulary

To check understanding, ask a student to repeat and complete this sentence: *Numbers such as 10, 100, and 1,000 that are the products of 10 multiplied by itself are called* ______ [Powers of ten].

Quick Check Formative Assessment

What number would you multiply the divisor and dividend by to find 44.2 ÷ 1.3? [10]

3 Independent Practice

Use with Exercises 9–22.

Exercises 11 and 12

Why is the quotient for 29.6 ÷ 4 the same as the quotient of 2.96 ÷ 0.4? [2.96 and 0.4 were multiplied by the same power of ten to make the division easier to calculate. 2.96 ÷ 0.4 = 29.6 ÷ 4]

Multiple-Step Problems

Objective Students will solve multiple-step word problems.

Vocabulary Hidden question

Materials Problem-Solving Recording Sheet (Teaching Tool 14)

Professional Development Math Background

- A four-step problem-solving process is used to solve multiple-step problems: Understand, Plan, Solve, and Look Back.
- The result of one computation is used in a subsequent computation.

Name ____________ Step 4-7

Multiple-Step Problems

Melanie mixed 64 ounces of pineapple juice and 32 ounces of cherry juice to make a punch. She then poured all the punch into cups, with 8 ounces in each cup. How many cups of punch did Melanie pour?

Solve by answering 1 to 8.

Answer 1 and 2 to **understand** the problem.

1. What do you know from reading the problem?

Melanie used __64 ounces__ of pineapple juice.

Melanie used __32 ounces__ of cherry juice.

Melanie poured __8 ounces__ of punch into each cup.

2. What do you need to find?

How many cups of punch did Melanie pour?

Answer 3 to 7 to **plan and solve** the problem.

3. How can you find how many cups of punch Melanie poured?

Divide the total ounces of punch by 8.

4. Does the problem tell you how many ounces of punch Melanie made? __no__

5. Do you have enough information to find out how many ounces of punch Melanie made? __yes__

"How many ounces of punch did Melanie make?" is the **hidden question** in the problem. You need to answer the hidden question before you can solve the problem.

48 Multiple-Step Problems

Name ____________ Teaching Tool 14

Problem Solving Recording Sheet

Problem:

Find?

Know?

Strategies?

Show the Problem
- ☐ Draw a Picture
- ☐ Make an Organized List
- ☐ Make a Table
- ☐ Make a Graph
- ☐ Act It Out/Use Objects

- ☐ Look for a Pattern
- ☐ Try, Check, Revise
- ☐ Write an Equation
- ☐ Use Reasoning
- ☐ Work Backwards
- ☐ Solve a Simpler Problem

Show the Problem?

Solution?

Answer?

Check? Reasonable?

M16

Interactive Learning 1 Concept Development

Use with Teaching Tool 14.

Purpose

Sometimes you need to find additional information before you can solve a problem. Today you will learn how to find the additional information needed to solve multiple-step problems.

Pose the Problem

T-Shirts Plus is selling shirts for $8.99 each. Sheryl wants to buy 2 shirts. If she pays with a $20-bill, how much change should she get? Allow time for students to decide if they have all the information needed to solve the problem.

Model

Distribute copies of Problem-Solving Recording Sheet (Teaching Tool 14) and have students complete the sheet as you discuss the problem. *What information are you given?* [Price of each shirt, the amount Sheryl pays] *What are you asked to find?* [How much change she gets]

Name ________________________

Step 4-7

Multiple-Step Problems (continued)

6. How many ounces of punch did Melanie make? 96 ounces

7. How many cups of punch did Melanie pour? 12 cups

Answer 8 to **look back** at your solution to the problem.

8. Reasoning Describe another way to find how many cups of punch Melanie poured.

Find how many 8-ounce cups of pineapple juice were in the punch and how many 8-ounce cups of cherry juice were in the punch. Then add the numbers of cups. $64 \div 8 = 8$ cups of pineapple juice; $32 \div 8 = 4$ cups of cherry juice.
$8 + 4 = 12$ cups of punch.

Write and answer the hidden question. Then solve the problem.

9. Lacy bought 2 yards of blue material, 6 yards of red material, and 6 yards of white material, each for \$2 a yard. How much change did she receive if she paid with a \$50 bill?

How many yards of material did Lacy buy in all? 14 yards; How much did the material cost in all? \$28; \$22 change

10. Trevor spent \$34 on a video game at one store. Then at another store he spent a total of \$38 on two model cars. How much more did the video game cost than one model car if each model car cost the same?

How much did each model car cost? \$19; \$15 more

11. Elise ordered 5 pounds of hamburger packaged in freezer paper and the rest packaged for immediate use. Her total bill was \$36. If each pound cost \$4, how many pounds of hamburger were packaged for immediate use?

How many pounds of hamburger did Elise buy in all? 9 pounds; 4 pounds

Explain that all the necessary information is provided in the problem, but an extra step is hidden within the words. *What hidden question do you need to answer before you solve the problem?* [What is the cost of 2 shirts?] *We can use the multiple-step problem-solving strategy to solve the problem. How much does each shirt cost?* [\$8.99] *How many shirts does Sheryl want to buy?* [2] Write $2 \times \$8.99$ vertically on the board and have students solve the hidden question. *How much does it cost to buy 2 shirts?* [\$17.98]

Now we can use this answer to solve the original problem. How does Sheryl pay for the 2 shirts? [She pays with a \$20-bill.] *Using the answer you found from the hidden question, write a number sentence to find how much change Sheryl should receive. How much change does she get back?* [\$20.00 − \$17.98 = \$2.02]

2 Guided Practice

Use with Exercises 1–8.

Remind students that multiple-step problems require more than one step to find the solution.

Exercise 6
What operation do you use to find how many ounces of punch Melanie made? Write a number sentence. [Addition; 64 + 32 = 96 ounces]

Exercise 8
Error Intervention

If students have difficulty finding another way to solve the problem,

then ask: *How many cups of pineapple juice can Melanie pour?* [8 cups] *How many cups of cherry juice can she pour?* [4 cups]

ELL Use Vocabulary

To check understanding, ask a student to repeat and complete this sentence: *The answer to a ______ can be used to solve the original problem.* [Hidden question]

Quick Check Formative Assessment

Identify the hidden question: Mark bought 2 notebooks that cost \$2.39 each and a highlighter for \$1.78. How much did he spend in all? [How much did the 2 notebooks cost?]

3 Independent Practice

Use with Exercises 9–11.

Remind students to identify and solve the hidden question in each exercise before solving the original problem.

For Exercise 9, point out to students that some multiple-step problems have two hidden questions that must be answered. *What is the first hidden question?* [How many yards did Lacy buy in all?] *What is the second hidden question?* [How much did all the material cost?]

Grade 6 NCTM Focal Point

Number and Operations 2: Connecting ratio and rate to multiplication and division

BOOK B

Number and Operations 2

Step 1-1

Multiplying Two-Digit Numbers

Objective Students will multiply two-digit numbers by one-digit numbers.

Vocabulary Tens, ones

Materials Multiplication Charts (Teaching Tool 4), place-value blocks

Math Background

- Place-value blocks can be used to model the standard multiplication algorithm.
- The ones are multiplied first, and then the tens.
- Each group of 10 ones can be regrouped as 1 ten.

Teaching Tool 4

Name________________________

Multiplication Charts

A

Thous	Hunds	Tens	Ones
×			

B

Thous	Hunds	Tens	Ones
×			
+			

C

Ten Thous	Thous	Hunds	Tens	Ones
×				
+				

M6

Step 1-1

Name ________________________________

Multiplying Two-Digit Numbers

Jenny's Market has 4 boxes. Each box holds 16 cans of soup. Answer 1 to 7 to find the number of cans of soup Jenny's Market has in all.

Find 4 × 16.

1. Show 4 groups of 16 using place-value blocks.

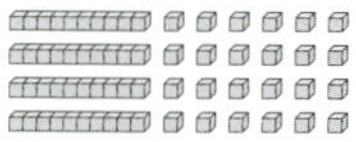

2. Multiply the ones. 4 × 6 ones = __24__ ones

3. Regroup the ones. Trade groups of ten ones for tens.

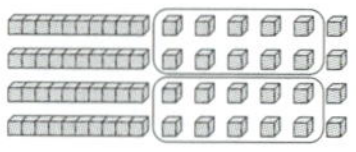

4. 24 = 2 tens and __4__ ones. Record the ones in the ones column of the Tens and Ones chart. Record the tens at the top of the tens column of the chart.

	Tens	Ones
	2	
	1	6
×		4
	6	4

5. Multiply the tens. 4 × 1 ten = __4__ tens

6. Add the regrouped tens to the 4 tens and record this value in the tens column of the chart.

4 tens + 2 tens = __6__ tens

7. So, 4 × 16 = __64__. How many cans of soup does Jenny's Market have in all? __64__

Interactive Learning

1 Concept Development

Use with Teaching Tool 4.

Purpose

There are different ways to record multiplication. Today you will learn how to multiply a two-digit number by a one-digit number using the standard algorithm for multiplication.

Pose the Problem

Mr. Gates wants to order new chairs for the 3 sixth-grade classrooms. How many chairs will he order if each room gets 14 chairs? Have students share their ideas. They should recognize that this is a multiplication problem.

Model

Distribute 4 tens and 12 ones blocks per student and copies of Multiplication Charts (Teaching Tool 4). Explain that students will use the place-value blocks to model multiplication and use the charts to record their work. Write 3 × 14 in vertical form on the board. *Write this multiplication problem in the "A" chart.*

Name ______________________________

Step **1-1**

Multiplying Two-Digit Numbers (continued)

Multiply.

8. 17×2 = 34	**9.** 25×3 = 75	**10.** 21×7 = 147	**11.** 34×4 = 136
12. 22×6 = 132	**13.** 48×3 = 144	**14.** 37×5 = 185	**15.** 47×4 = 188
16. 14×6 = 84	**17.** 18×3 = 54	**18.** 23×4 = 92	**19.** 31×5 = 155
20. 27×7 = 189	**21.** 43×4 = 172	**22.** 52×2 = 104	**23.** 65×3 = 195
24. 57×5 = 285	**25.** 62×3 = 186	**26.** 75×3 = 225	**27.** 37×8 = 296

28. Ron is 26 years old. His grandmother is 3 times his age. How old is his grandmother? 78 years

29. A basketball player usually scores 17 points in each game. How many points would she be expected to score in 5 games? 85 points

30. Reasoning Write a two-digit number multiplied by a one-digit number that does not require regrouping.

Answers will vary. Sample answer: 4 × 21

Place each digit in the correct place-value column. How many tens and ones do I need to show 14? [1 ten 4 ones] Have students use place-value blocks to show 14 at their desks. *How many groups of 14 do I need to show for the 3 classes?* [3] Have students show the three groups at their desks with the tens on the left and the ones on the right.

What is the first step? [Multiply the ones; 3 × 4] *Combine the 3 groups of ones. How many ones in all did you get?* [12] *There are more than 10 ones, so you need to regroup. How many tens and how many ones is that?* [1 ten 2 ones] Show students how to record the 2 ones at the bottom of the ones column and the 1 ten in the box at the top of the tens column.

What is the next step? [Multiply the tens; 3 × 10] *Combine the 3 groups of ten. Then add the 1 ten from regrouping the ones. How many tens in all did you get?* [4] Have students record 4 tens at the bottom of the tens column. *What is the product?* [42] *So, how many chairs will Mr. Gates order?* [42 chairs]

2 Guided Practice

Use with Exercises 1–7.

Remind students that when they are regrouping, they are trading groups of ten ones for tens.

Exercise 1
Point out to students that there are 4 rows with 1 ten and 4 ones in each row.

Exercise 3
Error Intervention

If students have difficulty regrouping the ones,

then say: *How many groups of 10 can be made with 24 ones?* [2] *How many ones are left over?* [4]

ELL Use Vocabulary

To check understanding, ask a student to repeat and complete this sentence: *When you multiply two-digit numbers, first multiply the _____, and then the _____.* [Ones, tens]

Quick Check — Formative Assessment

How many groups of ten do you get when you regroup the ones to find 7 × 42? Find the product. [1; 294]

3 Independent Practice

Use with Exercises 8–30.

Provide extra copies of Multiplication Charts (Teaching Tool 4) as needed. Some of the products will have three digits, so students will need to use the hundreds column when they record the product.

For Exercises 11–15, 20–21, and 23–27, point out to students that these problems require more than one regrouping. Each time they regroup, remind students that these values need to be added.

One- and Two-Digit Quotients

Objective Students will a divide a three-digit number by a two-digit divisor to find a one- or two-digit quotient.

Vocabulary Tens, ones

Materials Division Templates (Teaching Tool 11)

Math Background

- Dividing to find two-digit quotients involves the same algorithm as dividing to find one-digit quotients.
- After completing the calculations involving the tens digit in the quotient, the ones digit is brought down and the entire process repeats.

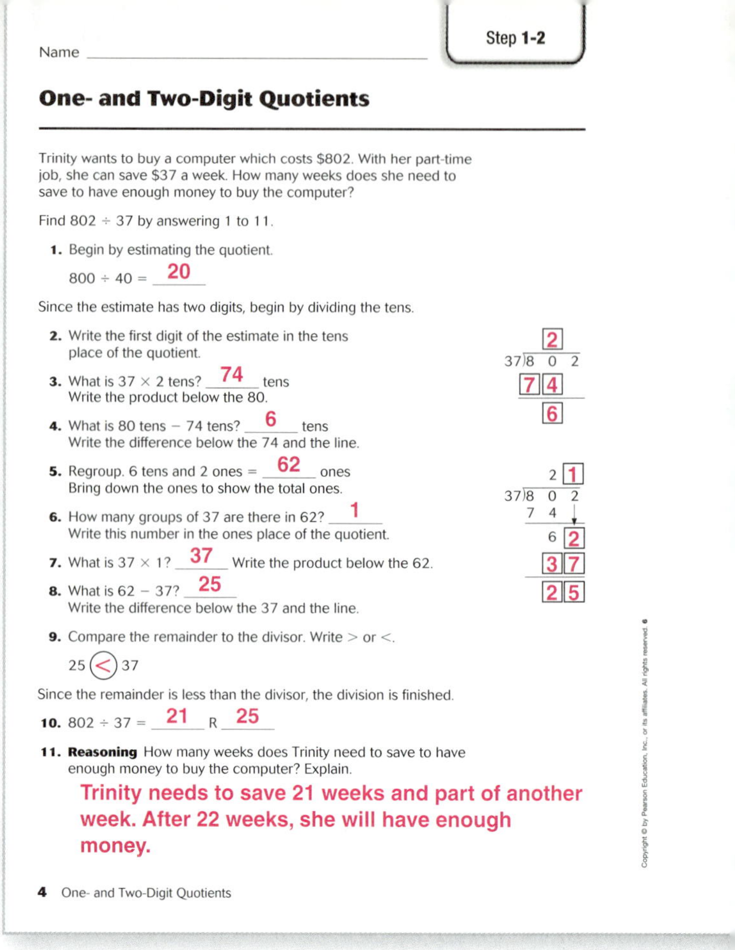
Name ______ Step 1-2

One- and Two-Digit Quotients

Trinity wants to buy a computer which costs $802. With her part-time job, she can save $37 a week. How many weeks does she need to save to have enough money to buy the computer?

Find 802 ÷ 37 by answering 1 to 11.

1. Begin by estimating the quotient.
800 ÷ 40 = 20

Since the estimate has two digits, begin by dividing the tens.

2. Write the first digit of the estimate in the tens place of the quotient.
3. What is 37 × 2 tens? 74 tens
Write the product below the 80.
4. What is 80 tens − 74 tens? 6 tens
Write the difference below the 74 and the line.
5. Regroup. 6 tens and 2 ones = 62 ones
Bring down the ones to show the total ones.
6. How many groups of 37 are there in 62? 1
Write this number in the ones place of the quotient.
7. What is 37 × 1? 37 Write the product below the 62.
8. What is 62 − 37? 25
Write the difference below the 37 and the line.
9. Compare the remainder to the divisor. Write > or <.
25 < 37

Since the remainder is less than the divisor, the division is finished.

10. 802 ÷ 37 = 21 R 25
11. **Reasoning** How many weeks does Trinity need to save to have enough money to buy the computer? Explain.
Trinity needs to save 21 weeks and part of another week. After 22 weeks, she will have enough money.

4 One- and Two-Digit Quotients

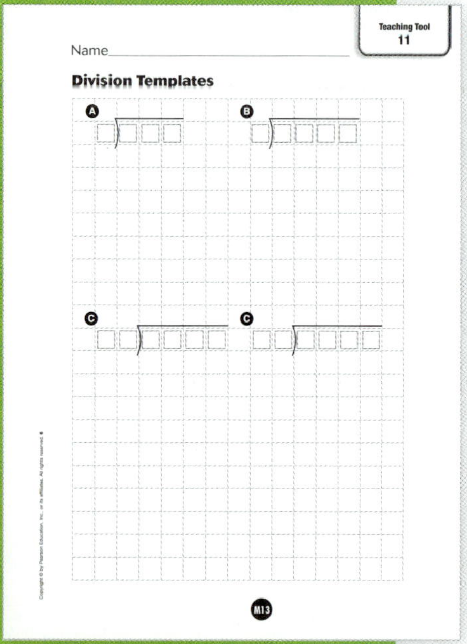

1 Concept Development

Use with Teaching Tool 11.

Purpose

You have learned how to divide by two-digit numbers to find a one-digit quotient. Today you will learn how to divide by a two-digit number to find a one or two-digit quotient.

Pose the Problem

The school secretary wants to mail the school newsletter to 917 homes. Mailing labels come on sheets of 33. How many sheets will be needed? Ask students to share their ideas and estimate the answer.

Model

Distribute copies of Division Templates (Teaching Tool 11). Write 33)917 on the board. *Write this division problem in the "C" chart.* How can you estimate the answer? [Sample answer: Use compatible numbers; 900 ÷ 30 = 30 sheets] *Based on the estimate, the quotient will have two digits. Write the first digit of the estimate in the tens place of the quotient.* At the board, write the 3 in the quotient above the 1 in the dividend.

Name ______________________

One- and Two-Digit Quotients (continued)

Find 516 ÷ 63 by answering 12 to 17.

12. Begin by estimating the quotient: 480 ÷ 60 = 8

Since the estimate has one digit, begin by dividing the ones.

13. Write the estimate in the ones place of the quotient.

14. What is 63 × 8? 504
Write the product below the 516.

15. What is 516 − 504? 12
Write the difference below the 504 and the line.

				8
63)	5	1	6	
	5	0	4	
		1	2	

16. Compare the remainder to the divisor. Write > or <.

12 (<) 63

Since the remainder is less than the divisor, the division is finished.

17. 516 ÷ 63 = 8 R 12

Divide.

18. 32)602 18 R26   **19.** 94)960 10 R20   **20.** 25)545 21 R20

21. 43)285 6 R27   **22.** 28)147 5 R7   **23.** 61)485 7 R58

24. 35)993 28 R13   **25.** 19)213 11 R4   **26.** 31)558 18

27. The local museum's records indicate that 874 people participated in the guided tours in June. There were 38 guided tours in the month of June and each tour had the same number of people. How many people were on each tour? 23

28. Reasoning Is 25 R32 a reasonable answer for the problem 607 ÷ 23? Why or why not?
No, the remainder is larger than the divisor.

Multiply 33 × 3 tens and compare the product to the dividend. How does it compare? [The product, 99 tens, is greater than the dividend, 917.] *That means the estimate was too large. Erase the 3 and try 2.* Do the same at the board.

Multiply 33 × 2 tens and compare the product to the dividend. How does it compare? [The product, 66 tens, is less than the dividend, 917.] Show students how to write 66 under the 91, subtract, and write the difference, 25, below the 66.

Bring down the 7 ones. Now you need to divide the ones: 257 ÷ 33. Guide students as they repeat the division process to find the second digit of the quotient.

What is the remainder? [26] *Is the remainder less than the divisor?* [Yes] *The division is finished. 917 ÷ 33 = 27 R26. How many sheets of labels will be needed?* [28] *Explain.* [The secretary needs 27 full sheets and a 28th sheet for the remaining 26 labels.]

2 Guided Practice

Use with Exercises 1–17.

Remind students to use an estimate to decide how many digits will be in the quotient.

Exercise 1

Error Intervention

If students have difficulty estimating the quotient,

then suggest that they round the divisor and the dividend to the nearest ten, and then use place-value patterns and mental math.

Exercises 3, 7, and 14

Remember to compare the product to the dividend. If it is too great to subtract from the dividend, the digit you wrote in the quotient is also too great.

Exercise 6

Stress how the steps of the division process repeat as the ones are divided.

ELL Use Vocabulary

To check understanding, ask a student to repeat and complete this sentence: *Estimating a quotient can help you decide whether to place the first digit of the quotient in the ____ place or the _____ place* [Tens, ones].

Quick Check Formative Assessment

Find 956 ÷ 63. [15 R11]

3 Independent Practice

Use with Exercises 18–28.

Provide extra copies of Division Templates (Teaching Tool 11) as needed. Alternatively, students may do their work on grid paper (Teaching Tool 10) or lined paper turned sideways to help them keep the digits correctly aligned.

Exercise 26

This problem has no remainder. Remind students that they do not need to write "R0" after the quotient.

Step **1-3**

Dividing with Decimals and Whole Numbers

Objective Students will divide a decimal by a whole number.

Vocabulary Decimal point, tenths, hundredths

Materials Division Templates (Teaching Tool 11), place-value blocks

Math Background

- The process of dividing a decimal by a whole number is similar to the process of dividing whole numbers.
- The decimal point in the quotient is placed directly above the decimal point in the dividend.

Name ______________________ Step **1-3**

Dividing with Decimals and Whole Numbers

Danica has 5.32 yards of ribbon to use on a craft project. If she divides the ribbon into 4 equal parts, how long is each part?

Find 5.32 ÷ 4 by answering 1 to 20 and completing the division problem below.

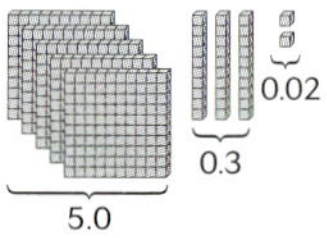

1. Use place-value blocks to show 5.32.
2. Divide the 5 ones evenly into 4 equal groups.
3. How many ones can go into each group? __1__
4. Record the 1 above the 5 in 5.32, at the right.
5. How many ones were used?
   4 × 1 one = __4__ ones
6. Record the ones used below the 5 in 5.32, at the right.
7. How many ones are leftover? 5 − 4 = __1__ one
8. Record the ones left below the 4 and the line.
9. Regroup the one into tenths and add the other 3 tenths.
   __1__ one + 3 tenths =
   __13__ tenths
10. Bring down the 3 next to the 1, to show the 13 regrouped tenths.
11. Divide the 13 tenths evenly into the 4 groups. How many tenths can go in each group? __3__
12. Record the 3 above the 3 in 5.32.

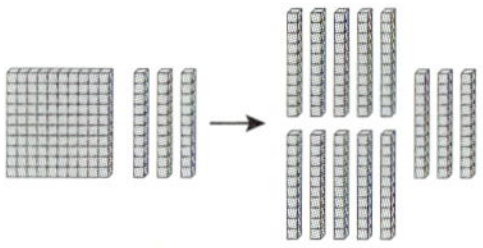

```
   1.33
 4)5.32
   4      ← 4 × 1
   13
   12     ← 4 × 3
    12
    12    ← 4 × 3
     0
```

6 Dividing with Decimals and Whole Numbers

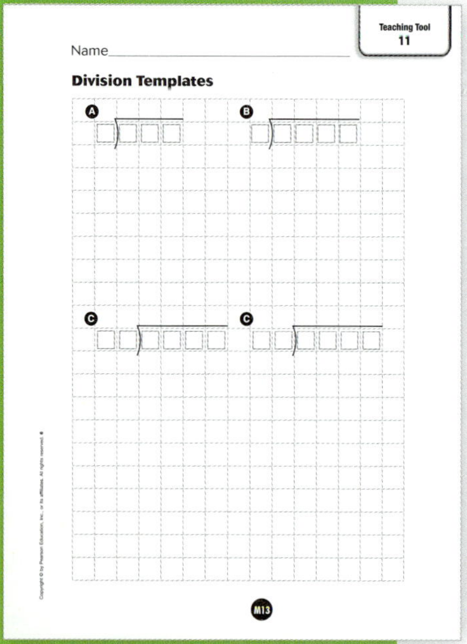
Name ______________________ Teaching Tool 11

Division Templates

A B C C

M13

---

1 Concept Development

Interactive Learning

Use with Teaching Tool 11.

Purpose

You have learned how to divide whole numbers. Today you will learn how to divide a decimal by a whole number.

Pose the Problem

Joy bought 3 pens at the school store. She spent $4.35. How much did each pen cost? Allow time for students to solve and share their ideas.

Model

Distribute 4 ones, 13 tenths, and 12 hundredths blocks per pair and copies of Division Templates (Teaching Tool 11). Explain to students that the grid lines will help keep each place value aligned correctly. *How much did Joy spend?* [$4.35] Have students show 4 ones, 3 tenths, and 5 hundredths with the place-value blocks. *To find the cost of each pen, you can divide.* Write 3)$4.35 on the board. Have students write the problem in the "B" chart and record the calculations as you complete the division.

Name ____________________

Step 1-3

Dividing with Decimals and Whole Numbers (continued)

13. How many tenths were used? 4×3 tenths = **12** tenths

14. Record the tenths used below the 3 in 5.32, and subtract to find the tenths left over.

15. Regroup the tenths into hundredths and add the other 2 hundredths.

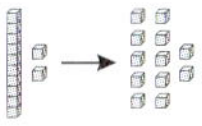

1 tenth + 2 hundredths = **12** hundredths

16. Bring down the 2 next to the 1, to show the 12 regrouped hundredths.

17. Divide the 12 hundredths evenly into the 4 groups. How many hundredths can go in each group? **3**

18. Record the 3 above the 2 in 5.32.

19. How many hundredths were used? 4×3 hundredths = **12** hundredths

20. How long is each part of the ribbon? **1.33 yards**

21. Reasoning Where is the decimal point placed in the quotient when a decimal is divided by a whole number?

The decimal point is placed above the decimal point in the dividend.

Find each quotient.

22. $8\overline{)36.08}$ **4.51**	**23.** $5\overline{)6.15}$ **1.23**	**24.** $6\overline{)36.12}$ **6.02**	**25.** $7\overline{)49.21}$ **7.03**
26. $7\overline{)56.98}$ **8.14**	**27.** $3\overline{)56.88}$ **18.96**	**28.** $6\overline{)18.84}$ **3.14**	**29.** $7\overline{)63.84}$ **9.12**

30. Three friends are equally sharing a 19.5 ounce drink. How many ounces does each friend get? **6.5 ounces**

Dividing a decimal is similar to dividing a whole number. First, place a decimal point in the quotient directly above the decimal point in the dividend. Why is it helpful to write the decimal point before you start dividing? [Sample answer: So you remember to include the decimal point in the quotient.] *Divide 4 ones into 3 groups. Using the blocks, show how many ones are in each group.* [1] Record the 1 in the ones place of the quotient. *Are there any ones left over?* [Yes] *How many?* [1 one is left over.]

What is the next step? [Divide the tenths.] *How many tenths are in each group?* [4] Continue to model how to divide the tenths and the hundredths with the blocks. *What is the quotient?* [1.45] *So, how much did each pen cost?* [$1.45]

2 Guided Practice

Use with Exercises 1–21.

Remind students that flats are used to represent the number of ones, rods are used to represent the number of tenths, and cubes are used to represent the number of hundredths.

Exercises 9 and 15

Error Intervention

If students forget how to regroup the ones and tenths,

then say: *How many tenths are in 1 one?* [10] *How many hundredths are in 1 tenth?* [10]

ELL Use Vocabulary

To check understanding, ask a student to repeat and complete this sentence: *In the number 2.97, the 9 is in the _____ place, and the 7 is in the _____ place.* [Tenths; hundredths]

Quick Check Formative Assessment

How is dividing a decimal dividend different from dividing a whole number dividend? [Sample answer: The first step is to place the decimal point in the quotient.]

3 Independent Practice

Use with Exercises 22–30.

Provide extra copies of Division Templates (Teaching Tool 11) as needed. Remind students to write the decimal point in the quotient before dividing the dividend. Assist them in recording each digit in the appropriate column to find each quotient.

For Exercises 24 and 25, remind students to write a 0 in the quotient as a place-holder when there are not enough tenths to divide into equal groups.

Step 1-4

Dividing a Decimal by a Decimal

Objective Students will divide a decimal by a decimal.

Vocabulary Powers of ten

Materials Decimal Models (Teaching Tool 8)

Professional Development

Math Background

- Division of decimals is similar to division of whole numbers.
- Multiply the divisor and the dividend by the least power of ten that eliminates decimals in the divisor.

Name ______________________ Step 1-4

Dividing a Decimal by a Decimal

Colin has 3.75 cups of sugar to make muffins. How many batches can he make if each batch uses 0.75 cup of sugar?

Find 3.75 ÷ 0.75 by answering 1 to 4.

1. Show 3.75 with place-value blocks.

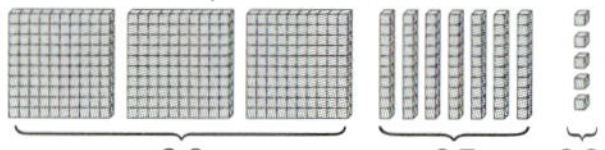

2. Divide 3.75 into groups with 0.75 in each. Trade ones for tenths and tenths for hundredths, as needed. How many groups of 0.75 are in 3.75? 5

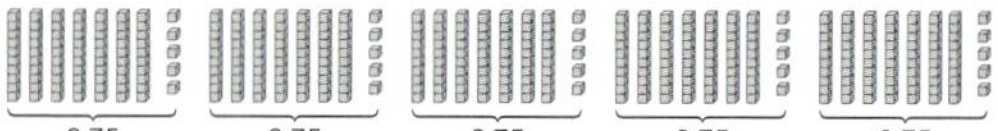

3. So, what is 3.75 ÷ 0.75? 5

4. How many batches can Colin make? 5 batches

Find 3.75 ÷ 0.75 another way by answering 5 to 8.

5. What number makes the number sentence true? $0.75 \times \underline{100} = 75$

6. You can change 3.75 ÷ 0.75 to make it easier to divide. Fill in the missing number below to see how.

$3.75 \div 0.75 = \frac{3.75}{0.75} = \frac{3.75 \times 100}{0.75 \times 100} = \frac{\boxed{375}}{75} = \underline{375} \div 75$

7. What is 375 ÷ 75? 5

Interactive Learning 1 Concept Development

Use with Teaching Tool 8.

Purpose

You have learned how to divide a decimal by a whole number. Today you will learn how to divide a decimal by a decimal.

Pose the Problem

Leah bought 1.5 pounds of trail mix from the store. She divided the trail mix into equal snack-size bags. If each bag contained 0.25 pound of trail mix, how many bags did she make? Allow time for students to share their ideas before modeling the solution.

Model

Distribute copies of Decimal Models (Teaching Tool 8). *How much trail mix did Leah buy?* [1.5 pounds] *How much did Leah put in each bag?* [0.25 pound] *What division must you complete to find how many bags Leah made?* [1.5 ÷ 0.25]

Name ______________________ Teaching Tool 8

Decimal Models

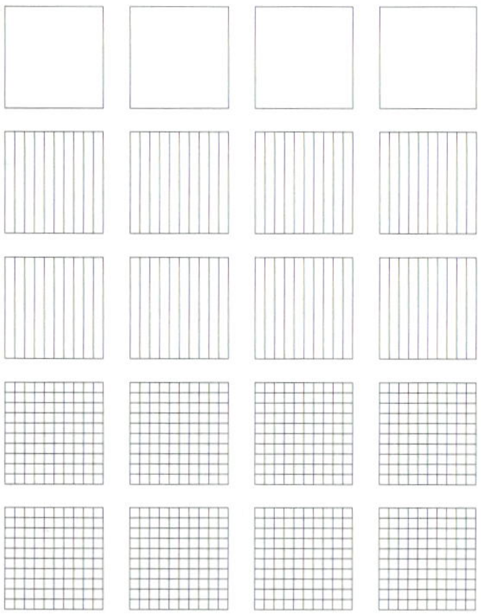

M10

Name ____________________

Step 1-4

Dividing a Decimal by a Decimal (continued)

8. Since 375 ÷ 75 = 3.75 ÷ 0.75, what is 3.75 ÷ 0.75? **5**

To divide decimals, multiply the divisor by 10 or 100 to make it a whole number. Multiply the dividend by the same amount. The quotient of the resulting amounts equals the quotient of the original numbers.

Find 6.24 ÷ 0.8 by answering 9 to 12.

9. What number makes the number sentence true? 0.8 × **10** = 8

10. Multiply 6.24 by the same number. 6.24 × 10 = **62.4**

11. What is 62.4 ÷ 8? **7.8**

12. What is 6.24 ÷ 0.8? **7.8**

Divide.

13. 27.2 ÷ 3.4 **8**

14. 9.2 ÷ 2.3 **4**

15. 1.6 ÷ 0.8 **2**

16. 0.36 ÷ 0.9 **0.4**

17. 31.8 ÷ 5.3 **6**

18. 0.72 ÷ 0.2 **3.6**

19. 44.1 ÷ 6.3 **7**

20. 2.4 ÷ 1.2 **2**

21. Packages of invitation cards cost $6.25 each. How many packages can be purchased for $25.00? **4 packages**

22. Reasoning When dividing a number which is less than 1 by a number greater than 1, will the quotient be greater than or less than the dividend? Explain.

The quotient will be less than the dividend. For example, 0.56 ÷ 7 = 0.08.

Look at the second row of grids. Shade 1 whole grid and 5 columns in the second grid to show what Leah bought. How many equal groups of 0.25 can you make? Model division into equal groups of 2 tenths and 5 hundredths, or 25 hundredths, by circling the first group of 25 squares. Have students continue to identify and circle equal groups of 25 squares. *There are 6 groups of 0.25 hundredths, so Leah made 6 bags of trail mix.*

You can also use ***powers of ten*** *to divide a decimal by a decimal. Some powers of 10 written in standard form are 10, 100, and 1,000.* Write 0.25)1.5 on the board. *What number can you multiply the divisor by to make it a whole number?* [100] Write 0.25 × 100 = 25 on the board. *Now multiply the dividend by the same number. What is 1.5 × 100?* [150] Write 1.5 × 100 = 150 on the board. *What is the new division problem?* [25)150] Write 25)150 on the board. *Multiplying the divisor and dividend by the same number makes the division of decimals easier. So, how many bags of trail mix did Leah make?* [6 bags]

2 Guided Practice

Use with Exercises 1–8.

Remind students to multiply the divisor and the dividend by the least power of ten that will make the divisor a whole number.

Exercise 5
Why do you multiply 0.75 by 100 instead of 10? [Multiplying the divisor by 10 will not make the decimal a whole number. The least number that is a power of 10 that will make the decimal a whole number is 100.]

Exercises 1 and 2
Error Intervention

If students do not understand how to show decimal division using place-value blocks,

then remind them that the flats represent the number of ones, rods represent the number of tenths, and cubes represent the number of hundredths.

ELL Use Vocabulary

To check understanding, ask a student to repeat and complete this sentence: *To change a decimal divisor into a whole number, multiply the divisor and the dividend by the same* _____ [Power of ten].

Quick Check Formative Assessment

Find 20.1 ÷ 6.7. [3]

3 Independent Practice

Use with Exercises 9–22.

Some students may have difficulty organizing their work. You may provide copies of Centimeter Grid Paper (Teaching Tool 10) to help them keep the digits correctly aligned.

Exercises 13–20
Remind students that the dividend is multiplied by the same power of ten that was used to multiply the divisor.

Step 1-5

Solving Multiplication and Division Equations

Objective Students will multiply and divide to solve an equation.

Vocabulary Variable, inverse operations

Materials Equation Tables (Teaching Tool 12), counters, index cards

Professional Development

Math Background

- If you multiply or divide the quantity on one side of an equation, you must also multiply or divide the quantity on the other side by the same nonzero number.
- To undo multiplying, divide. To undo dividing, multiply.

Name ____________________ Teaching Tool 12

Equation Tables

Example: $12p = 48$

	Expression on Left	Inverse Operation	Equal Sign	Expression on Right	Inverse Operation
Equation	$12p$		=	48	
Inverse	$12p$	÷ 12	=	48	÷ 12
Answer	p		=	4	

	Expression on Left	Inverse Operation	Equal Sign	Expression on Right	Inverse Operation
Equation			=		
Inverse			=		
Answer			=		

	Expression on Left	Inverse Operation	Equal Sign	Expression on Right	Inverse Operation
Equation			=		
Inverse			=		
Answer			=		

	Expression on Left	Inverse Operation	Equal Sign	Expression on Right	Inverse Operation
Equation			=		
Inverse			=		
Answer			=		

	Expression on Left	Inverse Operation	Equal Sign	Expression on Right	Inverse Operation
Equation			=		
Inverse			=		
Answer			=		

M14

Name ____________________ Step 1-5

Solving Multiplication and Division Equations

1. Show $2x = 6$ with counters and paper as shown below. Use a blank sheet of paper for each x.

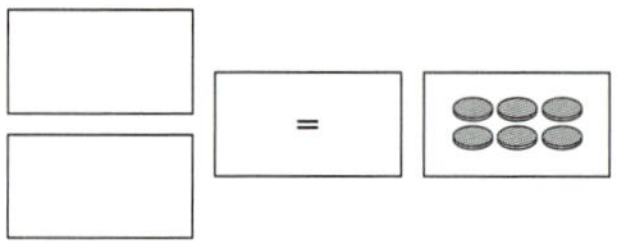

2. Equals divided by equals are equal. Divide each side of the equals sign into 2 equal parts.

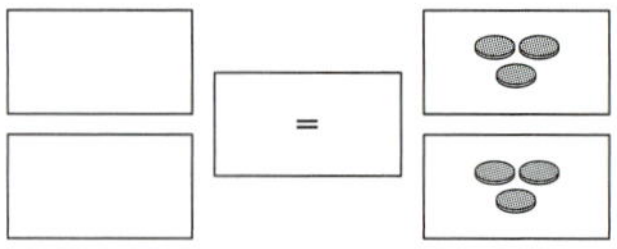

3. Remove all but one blank of paper and one group of counters from each side. What is left? $x =$ 3

4. Fill in the blanks to show what you did.

$2x = 6$

$\frac{2x}{2} = \frac{6}{2}$ Divide both sides by 2.

$x =$ 3

5. Does the value of x you found in Exercise 4 above make the equation $2x = 6$ true? yes

6. Fill in the blanks to solve $\frac{n}{7} = 3$.

$\frac{n}{7} = 3$

$7 \times \frac{n}{7} =$ 7 $\times 3$ Multiply both sides by 7.

$n =$ 21

Interactive Learning

1 Concept Development

Use with Teaching Tool 12.

Purpose

You have learned how to multiply and divide numbers. Today you will learn how to multiply and divide to solve equations.

Pose the Problem

Sam checked out twice as many books as Ray. If Sam checked out 6 books, how many books did Ray check out? Allow time for students to share their ideas.

Model

Distribute 6 counters and 5 index cards per student and copies of Equation Tables (Teaching Tool 12). *How many books did Sam check out?* [6] *What other information are you given in the problem?* [Sam checked out twice as many books as Ray.] *What do we need to find?* [The number of books Ray checked out] *We can use a variable to write an equation and find how many books Ray checked out. Let* r *represent the number of books Ray checked out.*

Name ______________________

Solving Multiplication and Division Equations (continued)

7. Does the value of n you found in Exercise 6 make the equation $\frac{n}{7} = 3$ true? yes

Fill in the blanks to solve each equation.

8. $5b = 400$

$\frac{5b}{\boxed{5}} = \frac{400}{\boxed{5}}$

$b =$ 80

9. $\frac{c}{4} = 19$

$4 \times \frac{c}{4} = 4 \times 19$

$c =$ 76

10. Reasoning Why can you multiply both sides of $\frac{h}{7} = 3$ by 7 and still have a true equation?

Sample answer: Equals multiplied by equals are equal.

Solve each equation.

11. $4a = 16$ $a = 4$

12. $\frac{m}{15} = 2$ $m = 30$

13. $7x = 56$ $x = 8$

14. $16b = 32$ $b = 2$

15. $10y = 40$ $y = 4$

16. $\frac{z}{24} = 3$ $z = 72$

17. $15n = 90$ $n = 6$

18. $\frac{c}{12} = 7$ $c = 84$

19. $\frac{t}{9} = 20$ $t = 180$

20. $19r = 38$ $r = 2$

21. $35s = 140$ $s = 4$

22. $\frac{v}{72} = 4$ $v = 288$

23. Reasoning To solve an equation like $\frac{d}{5} = 7$, you multiply both sides of the equation by 5. Why do you multiply instead of divide?

Sample answer: Since d is divided by 5, do the inverse and multiply by 5 to get the d alone.

Make a table similar to Equation Tables (Teaching Tool 12) on the board. Write $2r = 6$ in the second row. *This equation shows that 6 is the same as 2 times the number of books Ray checked out, r. To solve for r, you will need to use inverse operations. Since division is the inverse operation of multiplication, divide both sides of the equation by 2 to get r by itself.*

Complete the table with the students as shown below. *How many books did Ray check out?* [3 books] *Check your answer. Does the value of r make the equation true?* [Yes; $2 \times 3 = 6$]

	Expression on Left	Inverse Operation	Equal Sign	Expression on Right	Inverse Operation
Equation	$2r$		=	6	
Inverse	$2r$	÷ 2	=	6	÷ 2
Answer	r		=	3	

2 Guided Practice

Use with Exercises 1–7.

For Exercises 1–5, students will solve equations another way using counters and index cards. Point out that $2r = 6$ is the same as $2x = 6$ except the variable is different. Direct students to set up the index cards and counters as shown in Exercises 1 and 2.

Exercises 1 and 2
Why are there two index cards on the left side of the equal sign? [Sample answer: The two index cards show how to represent the $2x$ in the equation $2x = 6$.]

Exercises 6 and 7
Error Intervention

If students have trouble solving for n,

then have them use the table or counters to solve the equation. *What is the inverse operation of dividing by 7?* [Multiplying by 7]

ELL Use Vocabulary

To check understanding, ask a student to repeat and complete this sentence: *The ______ of multiplying by 3 is dividing by 3.* [Inverse operation]

Quick Check Formative Assessment

Solve the equation: $7d = 56$ [$d = 8$]

3 Independent Practice

Use with Exercises 8–23.

Provide copies of Equation Tables (Teaching Tool 12) as needed.

Exercises 11–22
Remind students to multiply or divide both sides of the equation by the same nonzero quantity to maintain equality.

Step **2-1**

Using Models to Find Equivalent Fractions

Objective Students will use models to find equivalent fractions.

Vocabulary Equivalent fractions

Materials Fraction Models: Strips (Teaching Tool 5)

Professional Development

Math Background

- The same fractional amount can be represented by an infinite set of different but equivalent fractions.

Name ______________________ Step **2-1**

Using Models to Find Equivalent Fractions

Find a fraction equivalent to $\frac{3}{4}$ by answering 1 to 3.

1. Show a 1 and $\frac{3}{4}$ with fraction strips.

1		
$\frac{1}{4}$	$\frac{1}{4}$	$\frac{1}{4}$

2. How many $\frac{1}{8}$ strips does it take to equal $\frac{3}{4}$? 6

$\frac{3}{4} = \frac{6}{8}$

3. So, $\frac{3}{4}$ is equal to six $\frac{1}{8}$ strips.

1					
$\frac{1}{4}$		$\frac{1}{4}$		$\frac{1}{4}$	
$\frac{1}{8}$	$\frac{1}{8}$	$\frac{1}{8}$	$\frac{1}{8}$	$\frac{1}{8}$	$\frac{1}{8}$

Find the missing number in $\frac{1}{2} = \frac{?}{10}$, by answering 4 to 7.

The denominators of the fractions tell which fraction strips to use.

4. Show 1 and $\frac{1}{2}$ with fraction strips.

1
$\frac{1}{2}$

5. What is the denominator of the second fraction? 10

6. Since the denominator of the second fraction is 10, find the number of $\frac{1}{10}$ strips equal to $\frac{1}{2}$. 5

1				
$\frac{1}{2}$				
$\frac{1}{10}$	$\frac{1}{10}$	$\frac{1}{10}$	$\frac{1}{10}$	$\frac{1}{10}$

7. So, $\frac{1}{2}$ is equal to five $\frac{1}{10}$ strips.

$\frac{1}{2} = \frac{5}{10}$

12 Using Models to Find Equivalent Fractions

Name ______________________ Teaching Tool 5

Fraction Models: Strips

1											
$\frac{1}{2}$											
$\frac{1}{3}$											
$\frac{1}{4}$											
$\frac{1}{5}$											
$\frac{1}{6}$											
$\frac{1}{8}$											
$\frac{1}{10}$											
$\frac{1}{12}$											

M7

Interactive Learning

1 Concept Development

Use with Teaching Tool 5.

Purpose

You know how to name whole numbers in many different ways. Today you will learn different ways to name the same part of a whole.

Pose the Problem

Distribute copies of Fraction Models: Strips (Teaching Tool 5) and direct students to cut out whole strips. *Erika skipped $\frac{2}{3}$ of the length of the sidewalk in front of her apartment building. Work with a partner to find as many different fractions as you can that name the same part of the sidewalk. Use fraction strips to help you.* Allow student pairs time to work. Invite them to share their solutions.

Model

How can you use a fraction strip to show $\frac{2}{3}$ of the length of Erika's sidewalk? [Use the $\frac{1}{3}$ strip. Color the first 2 parts of it.] Allow time for students to do this.

Name ______________________

Step 2-1

Using Models to Find Equivalent Fractions (continued)

Complete each number sentence.

8.

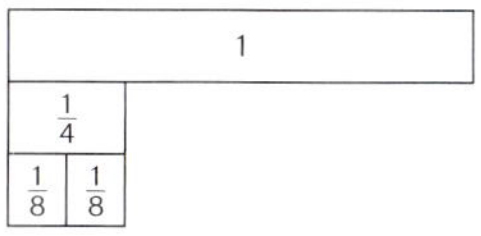

$\frac{1}{4} = \frac{2}{8}$

9.

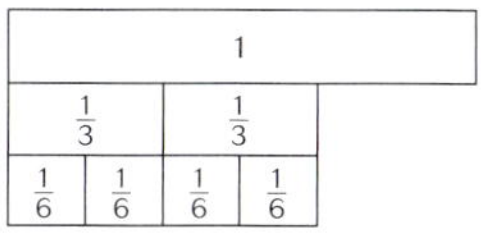

$\frac{2}{3} = \frac{4}{6}$

10.

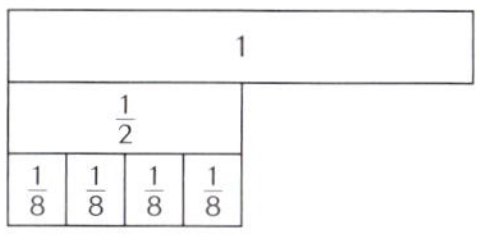

$\frac{1}{2} = \frac{4}{8}$

11.

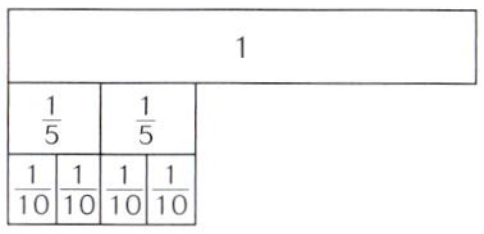

$\frac{2}{5} = \frac{4}{10}$

12.

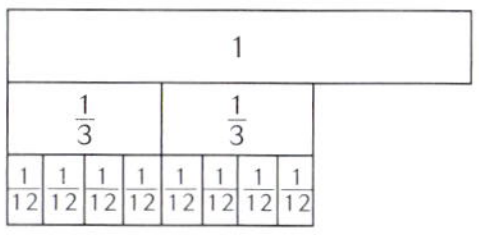

$\frac{2}{3} = \frac{8}{12}$

13.

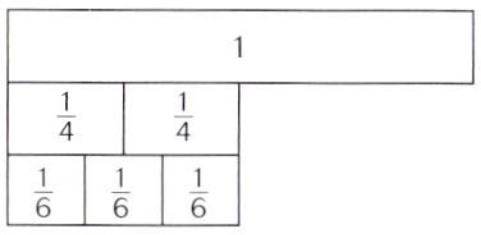

$\frac{2}{4} = \frac{3}{6}$

14. Reasoning On Tuesday, $\frac{2}{3}$ of the class time was spent on math projects. How many *sixths* of the class time was spent on math projects? $\frac{4}{6}$

How could you tell if a fraction with a denominator of 6 could name the same part of the length as $\frac{2}{3}$? [Line up the $\frac{1}{6}$ strip with the strip that shows $\frac{2}{3}$.] *How many sixths have the same length as $\frac{2}{3}$?* [4] *Color them. What fraction with a denominator of 6 names the same length as $\frac{2}{3}$?* [$\frac{4}{6}$] *The fractions $\frac{2}{3}$ and $\frac{4}{6}$ are equivalent fractions. Equivalent fractions name the same part of a whole.*

How can you tell if a fraction with a denominator of 8 could name the same part of a length as $\frac{2}{3}$? [Use the $\frac{1}{8}$ strip to see if a fraction with 8 in the denominator can name the same part of a length as $\frac{2}{3}$.] *Try it. Did you find one?* [No, when the $\frac{1}{8}$ strips are lined up with the $\frac{1}{6}$ strips, there is no number of eighths with the same length as $\frac{2}{3}$.]

2 Guided Practice

Use with Exercises 1–7.

Remind students that the greater the number of equal parts, the smaller the size of one of those parts.

Exercises 4–7

When you look at the fractions $\frac{1}{2}$ and $\frac{5}{10}$ in the number sentence in Exercise 7, $\frac{5}{10}$ may sound like it is more than $\frac{1}{2}$. What does the model show? [It shows that the two fractions are equal.]

Error Intervention

If students have difficulty deciding which fraction strips to use to model the problem,

then remind them that the denominators of the fractions tell which strips to use. The numerator tells the number of parts they will use on the strip.

ELL Use Vocabulary

To check understanding, have a student repeat and complete this sentence: *Fractions that have the same value are ________.* [Equivalent]

Quick Check Formative Assessment

How many twelfths are equivalent to $\frac{1}{3}$? [4 twelfths]

3 Independent Practice

Use with Exercises 8–14.

Be sure that students understand that the models they use must be the same length for the fractions to be equivalent.

For Exercise 14, encourage students to use fraction strips to find how many sixths are equivalent to $\frac{2}{3}$.

Step **2-2**

Greatest Common Factor

Objective Students will determine the greatest common factor of two or more numbers.

Vocabulary Factor, common factor, greatest common factor (GCF)

Materials 12 small pieces of paper in one color and 12 in another color

Professional Development

Math Background

- The number 1 is a common factor of any two counting numbers.
- A prime number has exactly two factors, 1 and itself. Composite numbers have more than two factors.
- The greatest common factor (GCF) of two numbers is the greatest integer that evenly divides both numbers.

Name ______________________ Step **2-2**

Greatest Common Factor

Find the greatest common factor of 72 and 90 by answering 1 to 5.

1. List the factors of 72.
1, 2, 3, 4, 6, 8, 9, 12, 18, 24, 36, 72

There should be 12 factors. Write the factors of 72, one on each piece of paper in one color.

2. List the factors of 90.
1, 2, 3, 5, 6, 9, 10, 15, 18, 30, 45, 90

There should be 12 factors. Write the factors of 90, one on each piece of paper in another color.

3. Group the factors into three groups: factors that appear only on one color of paper; factors that appear only on the other color of paper; and factors that appear on both colors of paper.

Use your groups to fill in the Venn diagram shown. Factors that appear on both colors of paper go in the shaded area on the Venn diagram.

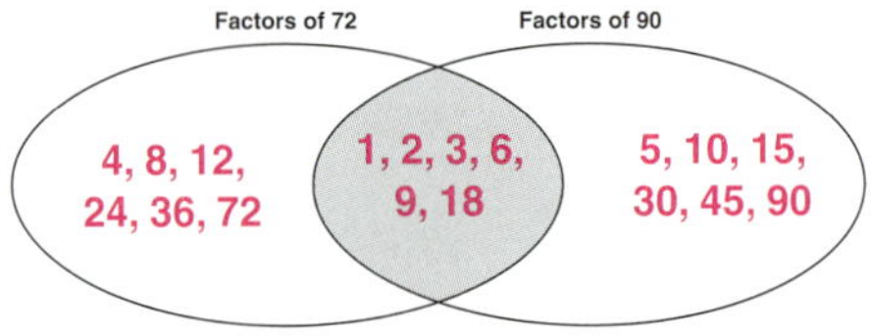

4. Factors in the shaded area are common factors. List the common factors. **1, 2, 3, 6, 9, 18**

5. Which of these common factors is the greatest number? **18**

This is the greatest common factor (GCF) of 72 and 90.

14 Greatest Common Factor

Interactive Learning

1 Concept Development

Purpose

Today you will be learning how to find the greatest common factor of two or more numbers. You will use this skill to better understand how fractions are used as rates and ratios.

Pose the Problem

What is the greatest common factor of 56 and 80? Allow time for students to discuss their ideas.

Model

Make a list of all the multiplication facts that have a product of 56. Begin with 1. What whole number can you multiply by 1 to get 56? [56] Write 1 × 56 on the board. *What whole number can you multiply by 2 to get 56?* [28] Write 2 × 28 below 1 × 56. *Can you multiply a whole number by 3 to get 56?* [No] Have students continue until they have found all of the factors of 56. *In a multiplication sentence, the numbers being multiplied are called factors. What are all of the factors*

Name ______________________ Step 2-2

Greatest Common Factor (continued)

Find the greatest common factor of 12, 18 and 30 by answering 6 to 10.

6. List the factors of 12. 1, 2, 3, 4, 6, 12

7. List the factors of 18. 1, 2, 3, 6, 9, 18

8. List the factors of 30. 1, 2, 3, 5, 6, 10, 15, 30

9. List the common factors of 12, 18 and 30: 1, 2, 3, 6

10. What is the greatest common factor of 12, 18 and 30? 6

Find the greatest common factor (GCF).

11. 9, 21 3	**12.** 15, 20 5	**13.** 15, 45 15	**14.** 27, 90 9
15. 14, 84 14	**16.** 28, 42 14	**17.** 43, 83 1	**18.** 15, 33 3
19. 16, 48 16	**20.** 9, 33, 60 3	**21.** 24, 48, 84 12	**22.** 14, 35, 77 7

23. Reasoning Ruth says the greatest common factor of 14 and 28 is 14. Tom says the greatest common factor is 7. Who is right? How do you know?

Ruth is right. Both 14 and 7 are common factors, but 14 is the greatest common factor.

of 56? [1, 2, 4, 7, 8, 14, 28, 56] Write the factors of 56 on the board.

Next ask students to find the factors of 80. *What are all the factors of 80?* [1, 2, 4, 5, 8, 10, 16, 20, 40, 80] Allow time for students to work. If needed, remind them of the rules for divisibility. Write the factors of 80 on the board.

How can you be sure that your list includes all of the factors of 80? [Sample answer: Start with the factor pair 1 and 80 and continue listing factors in order until they repeat.]

Look at the factors of 56 and 80. Find the numbers that are factors of both 56 and 80. Circle them. [1, 2, 4, 8] *These numbers are common factors of 56 and 80. Which of these factors is the greatest?* [8] *So, 8 is the greatest common factor, or GCF, of 56 and 80.*

2 Guided Practice

Use with Exercises 1–10.

Have students use the pieces of paper to complete this set of exercises. Each student or pair should have 12 pieces of paper in each color.

Exercises 6–10
Some students may not understand that the greatest common factor of three or more numbers is the greatest number that is a factor of all the numbers. They may wish to use three colors of paper and proceed as they did in Exercises 1 through 5.

Error Intervention

If students have difficulty finding the factors,

then have them make a model or draw an array to represent the factors.

ELL Use Vocabulary

To check understanding, have a student repeat and complete this sentence: *The greatest number that evenly divides two or more other numbers is called the ____ of those numbers.* [Greatest common factor]

Quick Check Formative Assessment

What are the common factors of 12 and 20? [1, 2, 4] *What is the greatest common factor of 12 and 20?* [4]

3 Independent Practice

Use with Exercises 11–23.

Remind students that 1 is a factor of every number. Sometimes it is the only common factor of two numbers. If the number is even, 2 is also always a factor.

Exercise 11
Students should identify the factors of 9 as 1, 3, and 9. Remind them that the number 3 does not have to be recorded twice.

Step 2-3

Simplest Form

Objective Students will find the simplest form of a fraction and identify fractions that are in simplest form.

Vocabulary Simplest form, greatest common factor (GCF)

Materials Fractions Models: Strips (Teaching Tool 5)

Professional Development — Math Background

- Equivalent fractions can be found by multiplying the numerator and denominator of a given fraction by the same number.
- Equivalent fractions can also be found by dividing both the numerator and denominator of a given fraction by a common factor.
- If the numerator and denominator of a fraction have no common factors besides 1, the fraction is in simplest form.

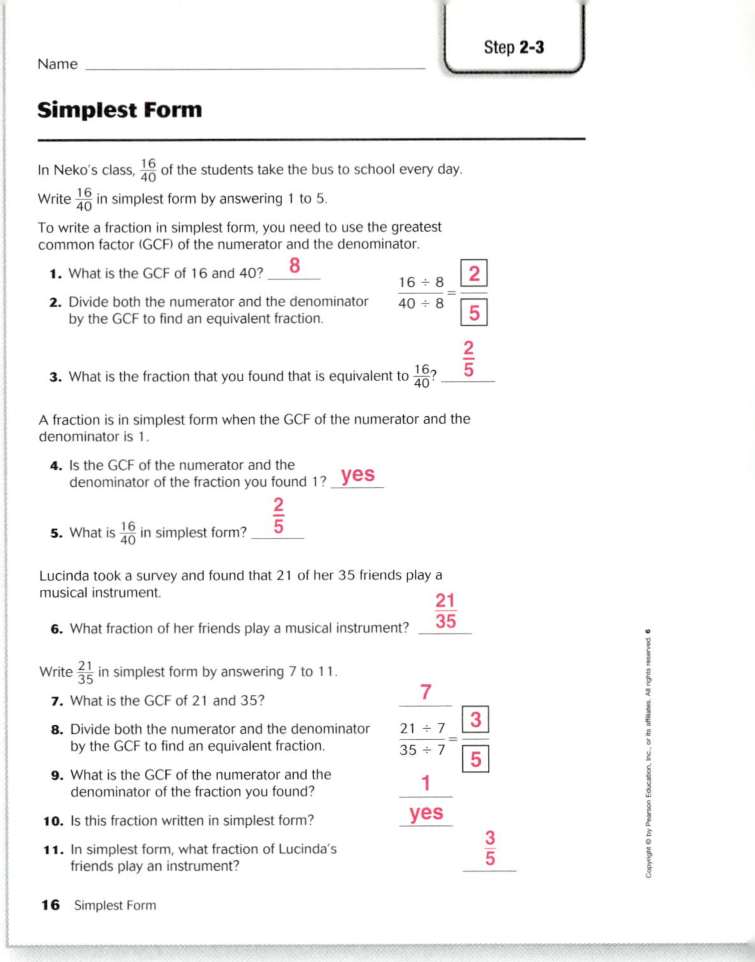

Name ______________________ Step 2-3

Simplest Form

In Neko's class, $\frac{16}{40}$ of the students take the bus to school every day.

Write $\frac{16}{40}$ in simplest form by answering 1 to 5.

To write a fraction in simplest form, you need to use the greatest common factor (GCF) of the numerator and the denominator.

1. What is the GCF of 16 and 40? 8

2. Divide both the numerator and the denominator by the GCF to find an equivalent fraction. $\frac{16 \div 8}{40 \div 8} = \frac{2}{5}$

3. What is the fraction that you found that is equivalent to $\frac{16}{40}$? $\frac{2}{5}$

A fraction is in simplest form when the GCF of the numerator and the denominator is 1.

4. Is the GCF of the numerator and the denominator of the fraction you found 1? yes

5. What is $\frac{16}{40}$ in simplest form? $\frac{2}{5}$

Lucinda took a survey and found that 21 of her 35 friends play a musical instrument.

6. What fraction of her friends play a musical instrument? $\frac{21}{35}$

Write $\frac{21}{35}$ in simplest form by answering 7 to 11.

7. What is the GCF of 21 and 35? 7

8. Divide both the numerator and the denominator by the GCF to find an equivalent fraction. $\frac{21 \div 7}{35 \div 7} = \frac{3}{5}$

9. What is the GCF of the numerator and the denominator of the fraction you found? 1

10. Is this fraction written in simplest form? yes

11. In simplest form, what fraction of Lucinda's friends play an instrument? $\frac{3}{5}$

16 Simplest Form

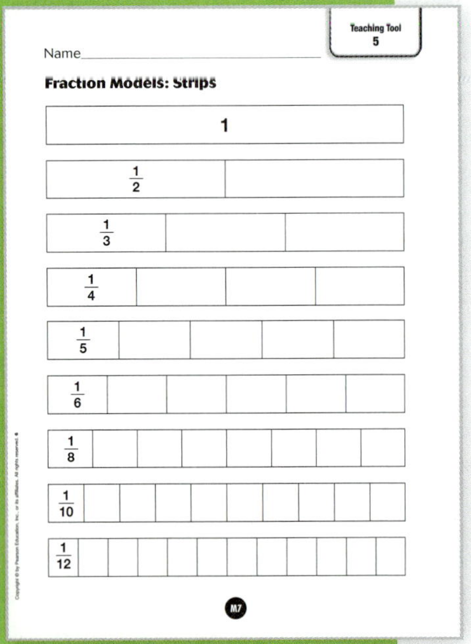

Name ______________________ Teaching Tool 5

Fraction Models: Strips

Interactive Learning 1 Concept Development

Use with Teaching Tool 5.

Purpose

You know how to find equivalent fractions. Today you will learn how to write a fraction in simplest form.

Pose the Problem

How do you write fractions, such as $\frac{6}{10}$, in simplest form? Allow time for students to share their ideas.

Model

Distribute copies of Fraction Models: Strips (Teaching Tool 5). Instruct students to cut out whole strips. *Use your fraction strips to find fractions equivalent to $\frac{6}{10}$.* Give students time to work in pairs. Then ask them to share their results with the class. Write $\frac{3}{5}$ and $\frac{6}{10}$ on the board.

Which fraction do you think is simpler? Why? Students might answer that $\frac{3}{5}$ is simpler because it uses smaller numbers.

Name ______________________

Simplest Form (continued)

Write each fraction in simplest form. If it is in simplest form, write simplest form.

12. $\frac{7}{14}$ — $\frac{1}{2}$	**13.** $\frac{24}{36}$ — $\frac{2}{3}$	**14.** $\frac{28}{35}$ — $\frac{4}{5}$	**15.** $\frac{20}{45}$ — $\frac{4}{9}$
16. $\frac{6}{30}$ — $\frac{1}{5}$	**17.** $\frac{24}{68}$ — $\frac{6}{17}$	**18.** $\frac{15}{23}$ — simplest form	**19.** $\frac{7}{84}$ — $\frac{1}{12}$
20. $\frac{16}{30}$ — $\frac{8}{15}$	**21.** $\frac{56}{72}$ — $\frac{7}{9}$	**22.** $\frac{12}{63}$ — $\frac{4}{21}$	**23.** $\frac{14}{41}$ — simplest form
24. $\frac{28}{84}$ — $\frac{1}{3}$	**25.** $\frac{15}{105}$ — $\frac{1}{7}$	**26.** $\frac{44}{100}$ — $\frac{11}{25}$	**27.** $\frac{8}{64}$ — $\frac{1}{8}$
28. $\frac{19}{49}$ — simplest form	**29.** $\frac{7}{35}$ — $\frac{1}{5}$	**30.** $\frac{23}{43}$ — simplest form	**31.** $\frac{64}{100}$ — $\frac{16}{25}$

32. Reasoning Explain how to tell $\frac{202}{220}$ is not in simplest form without finding all the factors.

202 and 220 are both even, so they can both be divided by 2. So $\frac{202}{220}$ is not in simplest form.

A fraction is in simplest form when the greatest common factor, or GCF, of its numerator and denominator is 1. Look at the fractions $\frac{6}{10}$ and $\frac{3}{5}$. What is the greatest common factor of 6 and 10? [2] *What is the greatest common factor of 3 and 5?* [1] *So, $\frac{3}{5}$ is the simplest form of $\frac{6}{10}$.*

You can find the simplest form of a fraction by dividing the numerator and denominator by their greatest common factor. How could you use the greatest common factor of 6 and 10 to find the simplest form of $\frac{6}{10}$? [Divide both the numerator and denominator by 2.] Write $\frac{6 \div 2}{10 \div 2} = \frac{3}{5}$ on the board. *If the greatest common factor is 1, then the fraction is already in simplest form.*

2 Guided Practice

Use with Exercises 1–11.

Be sure students understand that they can divide the numerator and denominator by any common factor to find an equivalent fraction. Then they might have to divide by another common factor to get the simplest form of the original fraction. However, dividing by the greatest common factor will give the simplest form in one step.

Exercises 1–5
Why are 16 and 40 divided by 8 instead of by 2 or 4? [Dividing by 2 would give $\frac{8}{20}$ and dividing by 4 would give $\frac{4}{10}$. Neither of these is in simplest form.]

Error Intervention

If students have difficulty finding the GCF of the numerator and denominator,

then remind them that they can list all the factors of each number, choose the common factors, and then identify the greatest common factor.

ELL Use Vocabulary

To check understanding, ask a student to repeat and complete this sentence: *If a fraction is not already in simplest form, you can divide the numerator and denominator by the ____ to find the simplest form.* [Greatest common factor]

Quick Check Formative Assessment

How could you show that $\frac{4}{8}$ in simplest form is $\frac{1}{2}$? [Sample answer: Use fraction strips. Line up the $\frac{1}{8}$ strips and the $\frac{1}{2}$ strips. Color 4 of the eighths. Color 1 of the halves and show that they match.]

3 Independent Practice

Use with Exercises 12–32

Exercises 16 and 29
Some students might notice that the answers for these two exercises are the same, $\frac{1}{5}$. Point out that two fractions are equivalent if the simplest form of both fractions is the same.

Step 2-4

Multiplying Two Fractions

Objective Students multiply a fraction by a fraction.

Vocabulary Numerator, denominator

Materials Paper for folding, markers or colored pencils

Math Background

- The algorithm for multiplying fractions is simple: multiply numerators and multiply denominators. $\frac{a}{b} \times \frac{c}{d} = \frac{a \times c}{b \times d}$
- The multiplication of two fractions can be modeled as taking "a part of a part."

Name ________________________ Step **2-4**

Multiplying Two Fractions

Natalia's yard is $\frac{2}{3}$ of an acre. One-third of the yard is a garden. What part of an acre is the garden in Natalia's yard?

Find $\frac{1}{3}$ of $\frac{2}{3}$ or $\frac{1}{3} \times \frac{2}{3}$ by answering 1 to 5.

1. Fold a sheet of paper into 3 equal parts, as shown at the right. Color 2 columns with slanted lines to show $\frac{2}{3}$. Color the rectangle at the right to show what you did.

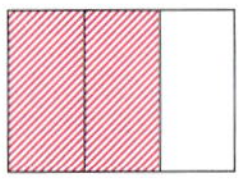

2. Now fold the paper into 3 equal parts the other way. Shade one row with lines slanted the opposite direction of the first set. Color the rectangle at the right to show what you did.

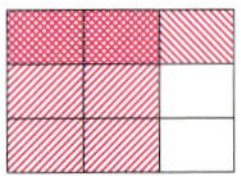

3. What fraction of the paper is shaded with crisscrossed lines? $\frac{2}{9}$

4. The part shaded with crisscrossed lines shows $\frac{1}{3}$ of $\frac{2}{3}$ or $\frac{1}{3} \times \frac{2}{3}$. So, what is $\frac{1}{3} \times \frac{2}{3}$? $\frac{2}{9}$

5. In Natalia's yard, what part of an acre is the garden? $\frac{2}{9}$ acre

6. To find $\frac{1}{3} \times \frac{2}{3}$, how many sections did you divide the paper into? 9

7. What is the product of the denominators in $\frac{1}{3} \times \frac{2}{3}$? $3 \times 3 =$ 9

8. To find $\frac{1}{3} \times \frac{2}{3}$, how many sections did you crisscross? 2

9. What is the product of the numerators in $\frac{1}{3} \times \frac{2}{3}$? $1 \times 2 =$ 2

10. Write the product of the numerators over the product of the denominators. $\frac{1 \times 2}{3 \times 3} = \frac{2}{9}$

11. Is your answer to item 10 the same as item 4? yes

12. Use paper folding to find $\frac{1}{2} \times \frac{2}{3}$. Color the rectangle at the right to show what you did. So, $\frac{1}{2} \times \frac{2}{3} =$ $\frac{2}{6}$.

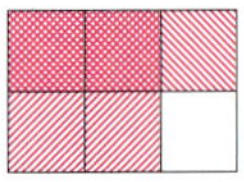

13. To find $\frac{1}{2} \times \frac{2}{3}$, how many sections did you divide the paper into? 6

18 Multiplying Two Fractions

Interactive Learning

1 Concept Development

Use with Exercises 1–11.

Purpose

You have learned how to multiply whole numbers. Today you will learn how to multiply fractions.

Pose the Problem

Natalia's yard is $\frac{2}{3}$ of an acre. One-third of the yard is a garden. What part of an acre is the garden in Natalia's yard? Ask students to share their ideas about this problem.

Model

Distribute a sheet of paper to each student. *Let's say that your piece of paper represents an acre. What part of an acre is Natalia's yard?* [$\frac{2}{3}$] *How many equal parts do you have to divide the paper into to show $\frac{2}{3}$?* [3 equal parts] Ask students to complete Exercise 1 to show the part of an acre that is Natalia's yard.

Name ______________________

Step **2-4**

Multiplying Two Fractions (continued)

14. What is the product of the denominators in $\frac{1}{2} \times \frac{2}{3}$? $2 \times 3 =$ **6**

15. To find $\frac{1}{2} \times \frac{2}{3}$ how many sections did you crisscross? **2**

16. What is the product of the numerators in $\frac{1}{2} \times \frac{2}{3}$? $1 \times 2 =$ **2**

17. Complete: $\frac{1}{2} \times \frac{2}{3} = \frac{1 \times 2}{2 \times 3} = \frac{\boxed{2}}{\boxed{6}}$

To multiply two fractions, you can multiply the numerators and then the denominators. Then simplify, if possible.

$\frac{1}{2} \times \frac{2}{3} = \frac{1 \times 2}{2 \times 3} = \frac{2}{6} = \frac{1}{3}$

18. Reasoning Jack found $\frac{4}{9} \times \frac{3}{4}$ as shown at the right. Why does Jack's method work?

$\frac{4}{9} \times \frac{3}{4} = \frac{\overset{1}{\cancel{4}} \times \overset{1}{\cancel{3}}}{\underset{3}{\cancel{9}} \times \underset{1}{\cancel{4}}} = \frac{1}{3}$

He simplified before multiplying, instead of after.

Multiply. Simplify, if possible.

19. $\frac{1}{4} \times \frac{2}{3} =$ $\frac{1}{6}$ **20.** $\frac{1}{6} \times \frac{3}{4} =$ $\frac{1}{8}$ **21.** $\frac{3}{4} \times \frac{3}{7} =$ $\frac{9}{28}$

22. $\frac{5}{7} \times \frac{1}{3} =$ $\frac{5}{21}$ **23.** $\frac{3}{5} \times \frac{5}{7} =$ $\frac{3}{7}$ **24.** $\frac{2}{5} \times \frac{1}{2} =$ $\frac{1}{5}$

25. $\frac{4}{5} \times \frac{2}{5} =$ $\frac{8}{25}$ **26.** $\frac{1}{3} \times \frac{3}{7} =$ $\frac{1}{7}$ **27.** $\frac{4}{5} \times \frac{3}{4} =$ $\frac{3}{5}$

28. $\frac{3}{8} \times \frac{2}{5} =$ $\frac{3}{20}$ **29.** $\frac{5}{9} \times \frac{2}{7} =$ $\frac{10}{63}$ **30.** $\frac{4}{5} \times \frac{5}{8} =$ $\frac{1}{2}$

31. $\frac{5}{11} \times \frac{4}{5} =$ $\frac{4}{11}$ **32.** $\frac{3}{4} \times \frac{1}{12} =$ $\frac{1}{16}$ **33.** $\frac{5}{12} \times \frac{6}{7} =$ $\frac{5}{14}$

34. One quarter of the classrooms in a school are used for an after-school program. Three quarters of the desks in each classroom are occupied by students. What fraction of the total desks in the school are occupied? $\frac{3}{16}$

The two shaded sections represent Natalia's yard. What part of her yard is a garden? [$\frac{1}{3}$] *How can you divide the paper to show the garden?* [Fold the paper into three equal parts the other way, so that the part that shows Natalia's yard is divided into three.] Ask students to complete Exercise 2.

Think about fractions as part of a whole. If the whole is 3 parts and you have 2 parts, how do you write that as a fraction? [$\frac{2}{3}$] *If the whole is 3 parts and you have 1 part, how do you write that as a fraction?* [$\frac{1}{3}$] *If the whole is 9 parts and you have 2 parts, how do you write that as a fraction?* [$\frac{2}{9}$] Have students complete Exercises 4 and 5.

To multiply fractions, you can follow this simple rule: multiply the numerators and multiply the denominators. Have students complete Exercises 7–11. *So, what part of an acre is the garden in Natalia's yard?* [$\frac{2}{9}$ acre]

2 Guided Practice

Use with Exercises 12–18.

Allow students to continue to use paper for folding. You may wish to have students work in pairs.

Exercises 12–17
Why does it make sense to divide the paper into 6 equal parts? [Sample answer: I know there are going to be 6 parts in the answer because 2 × 3 is 6.]

Exercise 18
Some students may have difficulty understanding that the fractions can be simplified before multiplying. Remind them that multiplying (or dividing) both the numerator and the denominator of a fraction by the same nonzero number is the same as multiplying (or dividing) by one. Point out that multiplication is commutative so the product of the numerators, 4 × 3, is the same as 3 × 4, and $\frac{4 \times 3}{9 \times 4} = \frac{4 \times 3}{4 \times 9}$.

Error Intervention

If students have difficulty understanding why the product of two fractions is less than each factor,

then say: *The paper model shows that the product is "part of a part," so the product will be less than either factor.*

ELL Use Vocabulary

To check understanding, ask a student to repeat and complete this sentence: *The _____ is the number above the fraction bar in a fraction, and it tells the number of objects or equal parts being considered.* [Numerator]

Quick Check Formative Assessment

Find $\frac{3}{5} \times \frac{5}{6}$. [$\frac{1}{2}$]

3 Independent Practice

Use with Exercises 19–34.

Encourage students to simplify before they multiply.

For some exercises, students may want to use models to find the products.

Step 2-5

Multiplying Fractions by Whole Numbers

Objective Students multiply a fraction by a whole number.

Vocabulary Numerator, denominator, common factor

Materials Counters, 18-inch piece of yarn

Math Background

- The multiplication of a fraction by a whole number, such as $\frac{1}{3} \times 6$, can be interpreted *as one third of a group of six.*
- Any whole number, *n*, can be written as a fraction in the form $\frac{n}{1}$. For example, 6 can be written as a fraction as $\frac{6}{1}$.
- The algorithm for multiplying fractions is simple: multiply numerators and multiply denominators. $\frac{a}{b} \times \frac{c}{d} = \frac{a \times c}{b \times d}$

Name ______________________ Step 2-5

Multiplying Fractions by Whole Numbers

Maya has 12 dolls in her collection. Of the 12, $\frac{3}{4}$ are historical dolls. How many of her dolls are historical?

Find $\frac{3}{4}$ of 12 or $\frac{3}{4} \times 12$ by answering 1 to 5.

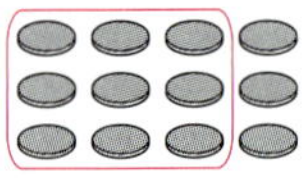

1. Show 12 counters in 4 equal columns.
2. Each column has $\frac{1}{4}$ of the counters. Put the loop of yarn around 3 columns to find $\frac{3}{4}$. Circle 3 columns of counters at the right.
3. How many counters did you circle? 9
4. What is $\frac{3}{4}$ of 12 or $\frac{3}{4} \times 12$? 9
5. How many of Maya's dolls are historical? 9

When you put the 12 counters into 4 columns, you found 12 ÷ 4. This can also be shown as: $\frac{3}{\not{4}_1} \times \frac{\not{12}^3}{1}$.

6. The resulting problem is 3 × 3. What is the product? 9

Find $\frac{3}{5} \times 20$ by answering 7 to 10.

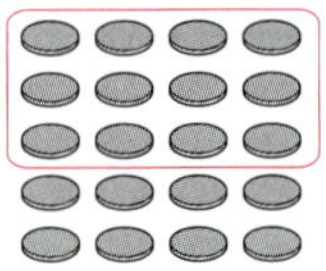

7. Show the product with counters and yarn. Circle the counters at the right.
8. What is 20 ÷ 5? 4
   Show this by crossing out and changing numbers below.
   $\frac{3}{\not{5}_1} \times \frac{\not{20}^4}{1}$
9. Write the new multiplication number sentence.
   3 × 4 = 12
10. What is $\frac{3}{5} \times 20$? 12

20 Multiplying Fractions by Whole Numbers

1 Concept Development

Use with Exercises 1–6.

Purpose

You have learned how to multiply fractions. Today you will multiply a fraction and a whole number.

Pose the Problem

Maya has 12 dolls in her collection. Of the 12 dolls, $\frac{3}{4}$ are historical dolls. How many of Maya's dolls are historical? Ask students to share their ideas about this problem.

Model

Distribute 12 counters and a piece of yarn to each student. *Let's say that each counter represents a doll. Arrange your counters in 4 equal columns. What does your array look like?* [Sample answer: 4 columns of counters with 3 counters in each column]

Now place your piece of yarn around three of the four columns of counters to find $\frac{3}{4}$. Ask students to read and complete Exercises 2 and 3.

Name ____________________

Step 2-5

Multiplying Fractions by Whole Numbers (continued)

Find each product.

11. $\frac{5}{9} \times 36$ 20
12. $42 \times \frac{5}{6}$ 35
13. $\frac{3}{5}$ of 45 27
14. $\frac{5}{11} \times 55$ 25
15. $\frac{1}{2} \times 32$ 16
16. $\frac{2}{5}$ of 95 38
17. $\frac{2}{7} \times 49$ 14
18. $\frac{1}{4} \times 84$ 21
19. $\frac{5}{9}$ of 27 15
20. $\frac{3}{11} \times 88$ 24
21. $\frac{1}{8} \times 56$ 7
22. $\frac{2}{3}$ of 72 48

Use the information in the table for Exercises 23 and 24.

Pie Orders

Flavor	Number	Flavor	Number
Apple	24	Strawberry	3
Cherry	21	Chocolate	8
Blueberry	28	Key Lime	5

23. If $\frac{3}{4}$ of the apple pie orders were from Matt, how many apple pies did Matt order? 18

24. If $\frac{3}{7}$ of the blueberry pie orders were from Jen, how many blueberry pies did Jen order? 12

25. You earned $60 mowing lawns last month. You told your parents that you saved $\frac{2}{5}$ of your earnings. How much did you save last month? $24

26. **Reasoning** If you know that $\frac{2}{3}$ of a number is 8, what is $\frac{1}{3}$ of the same number? 4

When you placed the yarn around three of the four columns, you were finding $\frac{3}{4}$ of the whole group of 12. What is another way of writing $\frac{3}{4}$ of 12? [$\frac{3}{4} \times 12$] Have students complete Exercises 4 and 5.

You can write any whole number as a fraction. The whole number becomes the numerator and the denominator is always 1. How can you write 12 as a fraction? [$\frac{12}{1}$] *What is another way of writing $\frac{3}{4} \times 12$?* [$\frac{3}{4} \times \frac{12}{1}$] Write $\frac{3}{4} \times \frac{12}{1}$ on the board.

You might be able to simplify first by finding a common factor of one of the numerators and one of the denominators. What is a common factor of 12 and 4? [4] *What is 12 ÷ 4?* [3] Cross out the numerator 12 and write 3. *What is 4 ÷ 4?* [1] Cross out the denominator 4 and write 1.

The simplified problem is $\frac{3}{1} \times \frac{3}{1}$. What is another way of writing $\frac{3}{1} \times \frac{3}{1}$? [$3 \times 3$] Have students complete Exercise 6. *So, how many of Maya's dolls are historical?* [9 dolls]

2 Guided Practice

Use with Exercises 7–14.

Allow students to continue to use counters and yarn. You may wish to have pairs of students share counters.

Exercise 7
Why does it make sense to model the problem with an array of 5 rows? [Sample answer: To find $\frac{3}{5}$ of 20, I need to break 20 into 5 equal parts.]

Exercise 13
Remind students that the word "of" used in this way means that they should multiply. *If you are finding $\frac{3}{5}$ of 45, what operation should you use?* [Multiplication]

Error Intervention

If students have difficulty finding the product when the numerator of the fraction is greater than 1,

then explain that they must do two steps to find the answer. First multiply the whole number by the numerator of the fraction. Then divide that product by the denominator. Use Exercise 11 as an example. *For $\frac{5}{9} \times 36$, what operation can you do first?* [$5 \times 36 = 180$] *What operation do you do next?* [Divide 180 by the denominator, $180 \div 9 = 20$.]

ELL Use Vocabulary

To check understanding, ask a student to repeat and complete this sentence: *You can simplify the fractions in a multiplication problem by finding a _____ of the numerator and the denominator.* [Common factor]

Quick Check Formative Assessment

Find $\frac{7}{8}$ of 48. [42]

3 Independent Practice

Use with Exercises 15–26.

Students may have difficulty remembering to multiply the numerators and the denominators. Have them rewrite the problem with the numerators multiplied over the denominators multiplied.

Step 2-6

Dividing Fractions

Objective Students will divide a fraction by a fraction.

Vocabulary Reciprocal, greatest common factor

Materials Index cards (4 blank cards, 1 card with a division symbol on one side and a multiplication symbol on the other side)

Professional Development

Math Background

- Division of fractions requires multiplying by the reciprocal of the divisor.
- When a greater fraction is divided by a lesser fraction, the quotient will be greater than 1.
- When a lesser fraction is divided by a greater fraction, the quotient will be less than 1.

Name ______________________ Step **2-6**

Dividing Fractions

A serving of cheese is $\frac{1}{16}$ of a pound. Answer 1 to 6 to find how many servings of cheese are in $\frac{5}{8}$ of a pound.

Find $\frac{5}{8} \div \frac{1}{16}$.

1. What is the reciprocal of $\frac{1}{16}$? **16**

2. Write $\frac{5}{8} \div \frac{1}{16}$ as $\frac{5}{8}$ times the reciprocal of $\frac{1}{16}$. $\frac{5}{8} \div \frac{1}{16} = \frac{5}{8} \times$ **16**

3. Does $16 = \frac{16}{1}$? **yes**

4. Multiply. Remove common factors first. $\frac{5}{8} \times \frac{16}{1} = \frac{5 \times \overset{2}{\cancel{16}}}{\underset{1}{\cancel{8}} \times 1} = \frac{\boxed{10}}{1}$

5. What is $\frac{5}{8} \div \frac{1}{16}$? $\frac{5}{8} \div \frac{1}{16} = \frac{5}{8} \times 16 =$ **10**

6. How many $\frac{1}{16}$-pound servings are in $\frac{5}{8}$ pound of cheese? **10 servings**

Answer 7 to 11 to find how many $\frac{3}{16}$-pound servings are in $\frac{9}{10}$ pound of fish.

Find $\frac{9}{10} \div \frac{3}{16}$.

7. What is the reciprocal of $\frac{3}{16}$? $\mathbf{\frac{16}{3}}$

8. Write $\frac{9}{10} \div \frac{3}{16}$ as $\frac{9}{10}$ times the reciprocal of $\frac{3}{16}$. $\frac{9}{10} \div \frac{3}{16} = \frac{9}{10} \times$ $\mathbf{\frac{16}{3}}$

9. Multiply. Remove common factors first. $\frac{9}{10} \times \frac{16}{3} = \frac{\overset{3}{\cancel{9}} \times \overset{8}{\cancel{16}}}{\underset{5}{\cancel{10}} \times \underset{1}{\cancel{3}}} = \frac{\boxed{24}}{\boxed{5}}$

10. Write the answer in simplest form. So, $\frac{9}{10} \div \frac{3}{16} = \frac{9}{10} \times \frac{16}{3} =$ $\mathbf{\frac{24}{5}}$ $=$ $\mathbf{4\frac{4}{5}}$

11. How many $\frac{3}{16}$-pound servings are in $\frac{9}{10}$ pound of fish? $\mathbf{4\frac{4}{5}}$ **servings**

12. Fill in the missing numbers to divide. Remove common factors before multiplying.

$\frac{3}{4} \div \frac{7}{12} = \frac{3}{4} \times$ $\mathbf{\frac{12}{7}}$ $= \frac{9}{7} =$ $\mathbf{1\frac{2}{7}}$

Interactive Learning

1 Concept Development

Use with Exercises 1–6.

Purpose

You have learned how to multiply fractions. Today you will learn how to divide a fraction by a fraction.

Pose the Problem

A serving of cheese is $\frac{1}{16}$ of a pound. How many servings of cheese are in $\frac{5}{8}$ of a pound? Allow time for students to discuss their ideas.

Model

Distribute the index cards to each student. Write $\frac{5}{8} \div \frac{1}{16}$ on the board. Direct students to write the numerator and the denominator of each fraction on an index card and use the four numbered cards and the division card to show the problem on the board at their desks.

Dividing by a fraction is the same as multiplying by its reciprocal. The product of a number and its reciprocal is 1. What is the reciprocal of $\frac{1}{16}$? [$\frac{16}{1}$] Point to $\frac{1}{16}$ in the original problem and write $\frac{16}{1}$ directly below it.

Name ____________________

Step **2-6**

Dividing Fractions (continued)

Divide. Simplify, if possible.

13. $\frac{1}{12} \div \frac{4}{9} = \frac{3}{16}$

14. $\frac{5}{12} \div \frac{1}{4} = 1\frac{2}{3}$

15. $\frac{1}{3} \div \frac{4}{5} = \frac{5}{12}$

16. $\frac{3}{7} \div \frac{3}{8} = 1\frac{1}{7}$

17. $\frac{3}{5} \div \frac{3}{10} = 2$

18. $\frac{1}{8} \div \frac{1}{2} = \frac{1}{4}$

19. $\frac{7}{12} \div \frac{1}{2} = 1\frac{1}{6}$

20. $\frac{5}{7} \div \frac{1}{2} = 1\frac{3}{7}$

21. $\frac{2}{9} \div \frac{3}{8} = \frac{16}{27}$

22. $\frac{1}{4} \div \frac{8}{25} = \frac{25}{32}$

23. $\frac{5}{9} \div \frac{3}{7} = 1\frac{8}{27}$

24. $\frac{2}{25} \div \frac{4}{7} = \frac{7}{50}$

25. $\frac{7}{10} \div \frac{2}{7} = 2\frac{9}{20}$

26. $\frac{6}{11} \div \frac{2}{9} = 2\frac{5}{11}$

27. $\frac{1}{16} \div \frac{3}{5} = \frac{5}{48}$

28. $\frac{1}{5} \div \frac{5}{14} = \frac{14}{25}$

29. $\frac{2}{3} \div \frac{3}{4} = \frac{8}{9}$

30. $\frac{2}{5} \div \frac{2}{5} = 1$

31. $\frac{5}{9} \div \frac{4}{5} = \frac{25}{36}$

32. $\frac{7}{10} \div \frac{5}{9} = 1\frac{13}{50}$

33. $\frac{3}{5} \div \frac{5}{12} = 1\frac{11}{25}$

34. **Reasoning** A chef at a restaurant ordered 20 pounds of chicken for soup. If each batch of soup has $\frac{5}{8}$ pound of chicken, how many batches of soup can the chef make? **32 batches**

35. Draw a picture to show $\frac{5}{6} \div \frac{1}{12} = 10$.

Answers will vary. Drawings should show $\frac{5}{6}$ divided into twelfths and that there are 10 twelfths in $\frac{5}{6}$.

Have students switch the numerator and denominator cards at their desk to show the reciprocal of $\frac{1}{16}$. *Now, you can multiply the two fractions. What does the problem become?* [$\frac{5}{8} \times \frac{16}{1}$] On the board, write $\frac{5}{8} \times \frac{16}{1}$. Have students turn the division card over so the problem shown on their desk is $\frac{5}{8} \times \frac{16}{1}$.

You can simplify the fraction multiplication first by finding the greatest common factor for one of the numerators and one of the denominators. What is the greatest common factor of 16 and 8? [8] *What is 16 ÷ 8* [2] Cross out the numerator 16 and write 2. *What is 8 ÷ 8?* [1] Cross out the denominator 8 and write 1. Have students write the new numerators and denominators on the index cards.

The simplified problem is $\frac{5}{1} \times \frac{2}{1}$. What is another way of writing $\frac{5}{1} \times \frac{2}{1}$? [5 × 2] *So, how many $\frac{1}{16}$ pound servings are in $\frac{5}{8}$ pound of cheese?* [10 servings]

2 Guided Practice

Use with Exercises 7–12.

Exercise 9

Why does it help to remove the common factors first? [Sample answer: It's easier to use basic facts or mental math with lesser numbers.]

Exercise 12

Error Intervention

If students have difficulty changing an improper fraction to a mixed number,

then remind them that a mixed number has a whole number part and a fraction part. *What does the fraction $\frac{9}{7}$ mean?* [9 parts in all and 7 parts in each whole] *What is the whole number part of the quotient 9 ÷ 7?* [1] *How many parts are left?* [2]

ELL Use Vocabulary

To check understanding, ask a student to repeat and complete this sentence: *The product of a number and its _____ is 1.* [Reciprocal].

Quick Check Formative Assessment

What is the quotient for $\frac{3}{4} \div \frac{5}{6}$? [$\frac{9}{10}$]

3 Independent Practice

Use with Exercises 13–35.

For more practice, allow students to use index cards to find the reciprocal of the divisors.

For Exercises 13–33, remind students that they cannot remove common factors until they have changed the original division problem to multiplying the dividend by the reciprocal of the divisor.

Exercise 34

How can you write the whole number 20 as a fraction? [$\frac{20}{1}$]

Step 3-1

Understanding Ratios

Objective Students will learn that a ratio is a comparison of two quantities and that a ratio can be written in three ways ($\frac{a}{b}$, *a*:*b*, a to b).

Vocabulary Ratio, term

Materials Two-color counters

Professional Development

Math Background

- A *ratio* is a comparison of two quantities.
- Each quantity in a ratio is a *term*.
- The order in which the terms of a ratio are expressed is important.
- Ratios can compare a part to a whole, a part to a part, a whole to a part, or a whole to another whole.

Name ______________________ Step 3-1

Understanding Ratios

A ratio is a comparison of like or unlike quantities. A ratio of 2 items to 3 items can be expressed in three different ways: 2 to 3, $\frac{2}{3}$ or 2:3.

Answers will vary. Check that ratios match numbers.

Examine ratios in your classroom by answering 1 to 12.

1. How many boys are in the classroom? ________
   How many girls are in the classroom? ________
2. What is the ratio of boys to girls in words? ________ to ________
3. What is the ratio of boys to girls as a fraction? ________
4. Write the ratio of girls to boys using a colon. ________
5. How many students are in the classroom? ________
6. What is the ratio of boys to students in words? ________
7. What is the ratio of students to girls as a fraction? ________
8. Write the ratio of girls to students using a colon. ________
9. **Reasoning** How does the ratio of girls to boys differ from the ratio of boys to girls?
   The numbers will be the same but the order of the numbers will be different.
10. How many students in the classroom have brown hair? ________
    How many students in the classroom have black hair? ________
11. What is the ratio of students with black hair to total students as a fraction? ________
12. Write the ratio of students with brown hair to those with black hair using a colon. ________

Interactive Learning

1 Concept Development

Purpose

You know how to work with fractions. Today you will learn another way to compare numbers, called ratios.

Pose the Problem

A necklace has 2 red beads for every 3 yellow beads. How can you compare the number of red beads to yellow beads for the entire necklace? Students should recognize that this is not a subtraction problem since they do not know the number of beads on the entire necklace.

Model

Distribute 5 counters to each student pair. *How can you model the beads on the necklace?* [Use 2 red counters and 3 yellow counters.] *One way to compare the number of red beads to the number of yellow beads is to use words. The ratio of red beads to yellow beads is 2 to 3.* Write 2 to 3 on the board. *2 and 3 are the terms of the ratio.*

Name ______________________

Step 3-1

Understanding Ratios (continued)

Write each ratio in three different ways.

13. hearts to triangles 5:6, 5 to 6, $\frac{5}{6}$

14. smiley faces to triangles 4:6, 4 to 6, $\frac{4}{6}$

15. squares to all figures 6:21; 6 to 21; $\frac{6}{21}$

16. triangles to squares 6:6, 6 to 6, $\frac{6}{6}$

17. all figures to smiley faces 21:4, 21 to 4, $\frac{21}{4}$

18. triangles to hearts 6:5, 6 to 5, $\frac{6}{5}$

19. hearts and triangles to all figures 11:21, 11 to 21, $\frac{11}{21}$

For Exercises 20–24, use the information in the table to write a ratio for each comparison.

Animals on a Farm

Animals	Number
Chickens	12
Goats	22
Cows	8
Sheep	9
Pigs	15
Rabbits	0

20. chickens to goats 12 to 22; 12:22; $\frac{12}{22}$

21. sheep to chickens 9 to 12; 9:12; $\frac{9}{12}$

22. pigs to cows 15 to 8; 15:8, $\frac{15}{8}$

23. chickens to all animals 12 to 66; 12:66; $\frac{12}{66}$

24. rabbits to goats 0 to 22; 0:22; $\frac{0}{22}$

25. Reasoning Karina's stuffed animals are only teddy bears and dogs. The ratio of teddy bears to dogs is 5:3. What is the ratio of dogs to all stuffed animals? Explain your answer.

3:8; The ratio 5:3 means that for every 5 teddy bears, she has 3 dogs and 8 stuffed animals in all. The ratio of dogs to all stuffed animals is 3 to 8.

Another way to describe the ratio is a fraction. The ratio of red beads to yellow beads is $\frac{2}{3}$. Write $\frac{2}{3}$ below 2 to 3. *A third way to write the ratio is with a colon. The ratio of red beads to yellow beads is 2:3.* Write 2:3 below $\frac{2}{3}$. *What is the ratio of yellow beads to red beads?* [3 to 2] Point out that the order of the numbers has changed. *Write the ratio of yellow beads to red beads as a fraction and with a colon.* [$\frac{3}{2}$, 3:2]

Suppose there are 2 red beads and 3 yellow beads on the necklace. How many beads in all are on the necklace? [5] *So what fraction describes the ratio of red beads to the total number of beads?* [$\frac{2}{5}$] *What is the ratio of the total number of beads to yellow beads?* [5:3]

2 Guided Practice

Use with Exercises 1–9.

If the class has an equal number of male and female students, you might wish to include yourself to get two different terms.

Repeat using the two-color counters to model the number of boys and girls in the classroom. *Suppose you want to use the yellow counters to model the number of boys in our classroom and red counters to model the number of girls.* Have students model the problem and complete Exercise 1. *How does the model show how many students in all are in the classroom?* [The total number of counters used is the total number of students in the classroom.]

Remind students of the three ways to write a ratio: in words, as a fraction, or with a colon. *Use your model to find the ratio of boys to girls and complete Exercises 2–4.*

Exercise 4

Error Intervention

If students don't recognize that the order of the terms has changed,

then ask *In what two ways is Exercise 4 different from Exercise 3?* [The answer in Exercise 4 will have a colon and the ratio compares the number of girls to boys.]

ELL Use Vocabulary

To check understanding, ask a student to repeat and complete this sentence: *A ____ is a comparison of like or unlike quantities.* [Ratio]

Quick Check Formative Assessment

Each desk in the classroom has 4 legs. What ratio compares the number of desks to the number of legs? Write the ratio in three ways. [1 to 4, $\frac{1}{4}$, 1:4]

3 Independent Practice

Use with Exercises 10–25.

Exercises 20–24

Remind students to use the table to find missing information.

Step **3-2**

Equal Ratios and Proportions

Objective Students will find equal ratios and determine if two ratios form a proportion.

Vocabulary Proportion

Materials Centimeter Grid Paper (Teaching Tool 10), green and blue markers or colored pencils

Professional Development

Math Background

- Proportionality involves a relationship in which the ratio of two quantities remains constant as the corresponding values of the quantities change
- Two equal ratios form a proportion.
- There is an infinite number of ratios equal to any given ratio.

Name ______________________ Step **3-2**

Equal Ratios and Proportions

Equal ratios can be found by multiplying or dividing both terms of the ratio by the same number except zero.

Rectangle *A* has a length of 10 centimeters and a width of 8 centimeters. The ratio of the length to the width is $\frac{10}{8}$. Find two ratios equal to $\frac{10}{8}$ by answering 1 to 4.

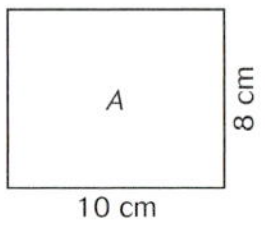

1. Try multiplying by 5. length → width → $\frac{10}{8} = \frac{10 \times \boxed{5}}{8 \times 5} = \frac{\boxed{50}}{\boxed{40}}$

2. What is one ratio that is equal to $\frac{10}{8}$? $\frac{50}{40}$

3. Try dividing by 2. length → width → $\frac{10}{8} = \frac{10 \div \boxed{2}}{8 \div 2} = \frac{\boxed{5}}{\boxed{4}}$

4. What is another ratio equal to $\frac{10}{8}$? $\frac{5}{4}$

5. Reasoning How many ratios are equal to $\frac{10}{8}$? Explain.
There is an unlimited number because you can multiply or divide both terms by any number except zero.

Rectangle *B* has a length of 60 cm and a width of 48 cm. Are the sides of Rectangle *B* proportional to the sides of Rectangle *A*? Find out by answering 6 to 8.

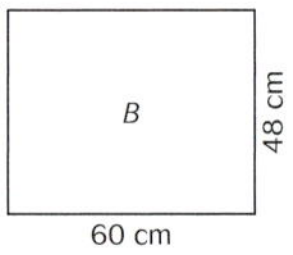

6. What is the ratio of the length to the width in Rectangle B? $\frac{60}{48}$

7. The sides of Rectangle *B* are proportional to the sides of Rectangle *A* if $\frac{10}{8}$ is equal to $\frac{60}{48}$. Try to multiply both terms of $\frac{10}{8}$ by the same number to get $\frac{60}{48}$.

$\frac{10}{8} = \frac{10 \times \boxed{6}}{8 \times \boxed{6}} = \frac{\boxed{60}}{\boxed{48}}$

8. Are the sides of Rectangle A proportional to the sides of Rectangle *B*? yes

---

Name ______________________ Teaching Tool **10**

Centimeter Grid Paper

M12

Interactive Learning **1**

Concept Development

Use with Teaching Tool 10.

Purpose

You have learned how to write and find ratios. Today you will learn about equal ratios and proportions.

Pose the Problem

How can you find equal ratios? Have students share their ideas.

Model

Distribute copies of Centimeter Grid Paper (Teaching Tool 10). *Use your green marker to color 5 squares in the top row on the left side of the paper. Use your blue marker to color 3 squares in the second row.* Allow time for students to work. *What is the ratio of green squares to blue squares?* [$\frac{5}{3}$] *Color 5 more green squares next to the green squares and 3 more blue squares next to the blue squares. What is the ratio of green squares to blue squares now?* [$\frac{10}{6}$] *How do the fractions $\frac{5}{3}$ and $\frac{10}{6}$ compare?* [They are equal.] Write $\frac{5}{3} = \frac{10}{6}$ on the board. *An equation formed by two equal ratios is a **proportion**. $\frac{5}{3} = \frac{10}{6}$ is a proportion.*

Name ______________________

Equal Ratios and Proportions (continued)

Rectangle *C* has a width of 24 cm. The ratio of the length to the width of Rectangle *C* is the same as Rectangle *A*. Find the length of Rectangle *C* by answering 9 to 11.

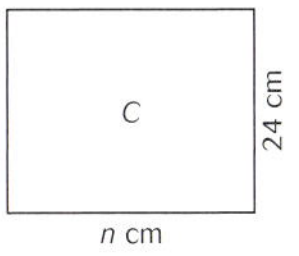

9. Set the ratio of the sides in Rectangle *A* equal to the ratio of the sides in Rectangle *C*. Use *n* to represent the length of Rectangle *C*. What is the proportion? $\frac{10}{8} = \frac{n}{24}$

10. Complete to find the value of *n*. $\frac{10}{8} = \frac{10 \times \boxed{3}}{8 \times \boxed{3}} = \frac{\boxed{30}}{24}$

11. What is the length of Rectangle *C*? 30 cm

Write three ratios that are equal to each of the following. Sample answers shown:

12. $\frac{5}{10}$ $\frac{1}{2}, \frac{10}{20}, \frac{15}{30}$

13. $\frac{8}{12}$ $\frac{4}{6}, \frac{2}{3}, \frac{16}{24}$

14. $\frac{8}{6}$ $\frac{4}{3}, \frac{16}{12}, \frac{24}{18}$

Tell whether each pair of ratios can form a proportion.

15. $\frac{5}{6}, \frac{15}{18}$ yes

16. $\frac{8}{14}, \frac{4}{7}$ yes

17. $\frac{5}{6}, \frac{30}{42}$ no

18. $\frac{6}{15}, \frac{30}{25}$ no

19. $\frac{5}{8}, \frac{25}{45}$ no

20. $\frac{16}{20}, \frac{4}{5}$ yes

21. $\frac{27}{30}, \frac{9}{10}$ yes

22. $\frac{16}{18}, \frac{2}{9}$ no

Find the missing number in each proportion.

23. $\frac{2}{5} = \frac{18}{n}$ 45

24. $\frac{48}{64} = \frac{n}{4}$ 3

25. $\frac{24}{n} = \frac{3}{7}$ 56

26. $\frac{10}{45} = \frac{2}{n}$ 9

27. You use a photocopy machine to enlarge a paper for school. The original is 4 inches wide and 5 inches long. The enlarged copy has a width of 12 inches. What is the length? 15 inches

Color 5 more green and 3 more blue squares. What is the ratio of green squares to blue squares? [$\frac{15}{9}$] *Write a proportion using $\frac{15}{9}$ and another ratio.* [$\frac{15}{9} = \frac{5}{3}$ or $\frac{15}{9} = \frac{10}{6}$] *Equal ratios can be found by multiplying or dividing both terms of the ratio by the same nonzero number.*

Suppose you color 5 green and 3 blue squares once more. How many green squares in all are colored? [20] *How many blue squares?* [12] *Is the ratio $\frac{12}{20}$ equivalent to $\frac{15}{9}$? Why or why not?* [No, the order of the terms has been changed.]

2 Guided Practice

Use with Exercises 1–8.

Remind students that there are many possibilities for ratios equivalent to a given ratio.

Exercise 6

Error Intervention

If students have difficulty writing the ratio of length to width of Rectangle B,

then ask: *how many centimeters long is Rectangle B?* [60] *How many centimeters wide is Rectangle B?* [48] *Write the ratio of the length to the width as a fraction.* [$\frac{60}{48}$]

ELL Use Vocabulary

To check understanding, have a student repeat and complete this sentence: *Two equal ratios form a _____.* [Proportion]

Quick Check Formative Assessment

What are two ratios that are equal to $\frac{18}{24}$? [Sample answer: $\frac{3}{4}$, $\frac{36}{48}$]

3 Independent Practice

Use with Exercises 9–27.

Exercises 12–14
Some students may write ratios in word form or with a colon. Explain that this is correct, but the fraction form is easier to use in a proportion.

Exercises 23–26
Suggest that students look at the ratio that has numbers for both terms. Then have them notice which term is given in the other ratio. *Look at Exercise 25. You know both terms in one ratio and the numerators of both ratios. Compare the numerators. What number do you multiply or divide 3 by to get 24?* [Multiply by 8.] *So multiply the denominator in that ratio by 8 to find the missing term.* [$7 \times 8 = 56$.]

Step 3-3

Solving Proportions

Objective Students will solve a proportion by finding the unit rate for a given rate.

Vocabulary Proportion, rate, unit rate

Materials Function Tables (Teaching Tool 13)

Math Background

- Two equal ratios form a proportion.
- A rate is a special ratio that compares two quantities with different units.
- A unit rate is a rate that compares a quantity to one unit of another quantity.

Name ______________________

Teaching Tool 13

Function Tables

Rule: ______________

Rule: ______________

Rule: ______________

Rule: ______________

M15

Name ______________________

Step 3-3

Solving Proportions

When thawing a turkey, it can take 12 hours of thawing time for every 3 pounds of turkey. How many hours should be allowed to thaw a 15 pound turkey? You can use a table or a proportion to find the answer.

1. Complete the ratio table to find the number of hours.

Hours of Thawing Time	12	24	36	48	60
Pounds of Turkey	3	6	9	12	15

2. How many hours of thawing time should be allowed for a 15 pound turkey? **60 hours**

3. You can also use a proportion to find the number of hours. Set the ratio 12 hours to 3 pounds equal to a ratio of *n* hours to 15 pounds.

Write the proportion. $\frac{12 \text{ hours}}{3 \text{ pounds}} = \frac{n \text{ hours}}{15 \text{ pounds}}$

4. What is the unit rate for thawing? **4 hours per pound**

5. Multiply 15 by the unit rate to find the number of hours.

What is 15×4? **60**

6. How many hours of thawing time should be allowed for a 15 pound turkey? **60 hours**

How many hours of thawing time should be allowed for a 20 pound turkey?

7. Can the answer be found in the ratio table above? **no**

8. So, use a proportion to find the number of hours. Set the ratio 12 hours to 3 pounds equal to a ratio of *n* hours to 20 pounds.

Write the proportion. $\frac{12 \text{ hours}}{3 \text{ pounds}} = \frac{n \text{ hour}}{20 \text{ pounds}}$

9. What is the unit rate for thawing? **4 hours per pound**

28 Solving Proportions

Interactive Learning 1

Concept Development

Use with Teaching Tool 13.

Purpose

You have learned how to find equal ratios. Today you will learn about a special ratio, called a rate, and learn how to find a unit rate. Then you will solve a proportion using the unit rate.

Pose the Problem

If you walk 885 feet in 5 minutes, how many feet do you walk in 1 minute? Have students share their ideas on how to solve the problem.

Model

Distribute copies of Function Tables (Teaching Tool 13). *The ratio $\frac{885}{5}$ compares the number of feet walked to the number of minutes. This ratio is a rate because the terms have different units.* Draw a table on the board and have students complete their Function Tables as follows: *Write Feet as the title of the left column and Minutes as the title of the right column. Then write 885 and 5 in the first row.*

Name ______________________

Step **3-3**

Solving Proportions (continued)

10. Multiply 20 by the unit rate to find the number of hours.
What is 20 × 4? **80**

11. How many hours of thawing time should be allowed for a 20 pound turkey? **80 hours**

12. Rachel is paid $13 for 2 hours of babysitting. Complete the ratio table and use the table to answer 13 to 15.

Dollar amount	13	26	39	52	65
Hours of Babysitting	2	4	6	8	10

13. How much money does Rachel make for 4 hours of babysitting? **$26**

14. How much money does Rachel make for 8 hours of babysitting? **$52**

15. How long does Rachel have to baby sit to make $65? **10 hours**

Use unit rates to solve the proportions.

16. $\frac{21\text{ people}}{\text{class}} = \frac{x\text{ people}}{3\text{ classes}}$ $x =$ **63**

17. $\frac{36\text{ feet}}{12\text{ sec}} = \frac{n\text{ feet}}{20\text{ sec}}$ $n =$ **60**

18. $\frac{9\text{ fouls}}{3\text{ games}} = \frac{f\text{ fouls}}{9\text{ games}}$ $f =$ **27**

19. $\frac{16\text{ pages}}{4\text{ hours}} = \frac{m\text{ pages}}{24\text{ hours}}$ $m =$ **96**

20. $\frac{10\text{ points}}{2\text{ items}} = \frac{p\text{ points}}{18\text{ items}}$ $p =$ **90**

21. $\frac{8\text{ pictures}}{\text{day}} = \frac{a\text{ pictures}}{7\text{ days}}$ $a =$ **56**

22. The average snow fall in a town is 22 inches per year. How much snow would be expected to fall in this town in 4 years?
88 inches

23. Reasoning Do unit rates have an advantage over ratio tables when finding an unknown in a proportion? Explain.
Yes, unit rates work for any values while ratio tables only contain values that are multiples of the original ratio.

How can you find a ratio that is equal to $\frac{885}{5}$? [Sample answer: multiply each term by 2.] *In the second row, write a ratio that is equal to $\frac{885}{5}$.*

A unit rate is a rate in which the comparison is to one unit, so the second term is always 1. How can you find a ratio equal to $\frac{885}{5}$ with 1 as the second term? [Divide each term by 5.] *Find the first term and write the ratio with 1 as the second term.* [$\frac{885}{5} = 177$; $\frac{177}{1}$] *So the rate is equal to the unit rate $\frac{177}{1}$.* On the board, write 177 and 1 in the next row of the table and have students add it to their tables.

Write 30 in the bottom row of the right column. *How can you find how far you could walk in 30 minutes at this rate?* [Find an equal ratio with 30 as the second term.] Write $\frac{177}{1} = \frac{?}{30}$ on the board. *Write a proportion using the unit rate and the ratio with the missing term. How can you find the missing term?* [Multiply each term in the second ratio by 30.] *How many feet could you walk in 30 minutes?* [177 × 30 or 5,310 feet] Write 5,310 in the bottom row of the left column.

2 Guided Practice

Use with Exercises 1–11.

Remind students that the second term in a unit rate is always 1. That means the order of the terms in the ratio determines what the unit rate describes. *The ratio 12 hours of thawing time per 3 pounds of turkey is equal to a unit rate of 4 hours per 1 pound. The ratio describing pounds of turkey to thawing time is equal to the unit rate $\frac{1}{4}$ pound per 1 hour.* Point out that the word *per* is often used in unit rates. Ask the students for examples.

Use with Exercises 8 and 9.

Error Intervention

If students write a proportion with pounds as the first term (the numerator) and hours as the second term (the denominator),

then, ask *What unit rate are you trying to find?* [The number of hours to thaw 1 pound of turkey] *So when you write your ratios, the number of pounds is the second term – the denominator.*

ELL Use Vocabulary

To check understanding, have a student repeat and complete this sentence: *A _____ is a special ratio that compares quantities with two different units.* [Rate]

Quick Check Formative Assessment

A car uses 18 gallons of gas to travel 414 miles. What unit rate is equal to the ratio 414 miles/18 gallons? [$\frac{23\text{ miles}}{1\text{ gallon}}$]

3 Independent Practice

Use with Exercises 12–23.

For Exercises 12–15, students may have difficulty finding and multiplying with the unit rate, $6.50 per hour. Point out that they can use the given rate and multiply each term by the same number to complete the table.

For Exercise16 and 21, some students may think that a number is missing in the denominator of the first ratio. Point out that 21 people/class is a rate of 21 people per class, or 21 people in each class. The ratio is $\frac{21}{1}$.

Step **3-4**

Solving Proportions Using Cross Products

Objective Students will use cross products to solve proportions.

Vocabulary Proportion, cross product

Professional Development

Math Background

- Proportions can be solved using cross multiplication.
- Cross multiplication is a shortcut for multiplying both sides of a proportion by the product of the second terms and simplifying.
- Two ratios are equal if their cross products are equal.

Name ______________________ Step **3-4**

Solving Proportions Using Cross Products

The Cougars scored 5 touchdowns during the first 4 football games of the season. At this rate, how many touchdowns should the team score in a 12-game season?

Write a proportion and solve to find the number of touchdowns, by answering 1 to 5.

1. Write a proportion.

Touchdowns scored → $\frac{\boxed{5}}{\boxed{4}} = \frac{n}{\boxed{12}}$ ← Touchdowns for season
Number of games → ← Games in season

2. Find the cross products.

$\frac{5}{4} \times \frac{n}{12}$ $4 \times n =$ **4n**
$5 \times 12 =$ **60**

3. Set the cross products equal. $4n =$ **60**

4. Solve $4n = 60$.

$n =$ **15**

5. How many touchdowns should the Cougars score in a 12-game season? **15** touchdowns

The Rodriguez family is taking a 40 mile biking trip. After 3 hours they traveled a distance of 15 miles. At this rate, how many total hours will they need to travel to complete the trip? Find out by answering 6 to 11.

6. Write a proportion. Use h to represent the hours needed to complete the trip.

Distance traveled → $\frac{\boxed{15}}{\boxed{3}} = \frac{\boxed{40}}{h}$ ← Total Distance
Hours traveled → ← Total hours

7. What is one cross product? **15 × h**

8. What is the other cross product? **3 × 40**

Interactive Learning

1 Concept Development

Purpose

You have already learned how to solve proportions using equal ratios and unit rates. Today you will use cross products to solve a proportion.

Pose the Problem

Five out of every seven flowers in the garden are red. If the garden has 49 flowers, how many are red? Solve this using any method you've already used. Have students share their solution methods.

Model

How can you write a proportion to help find the number of red flowers? After students respond, write the proportion on the board, $\frac{5 \text{ red flowers}}{7 \text{ flowers}} = \frac{n \text{ red flowers}}{49 \text{ flowers}}$. Then write $\frac{5}{7} = \frac{n}{49}$ under it.

Name ______________________

Step 3-4

Solving Proportions Using Cross Products (continued)

9. Write an equation using the cross products. $15h = 120$

10. Solve $15h = 120$. $h =$ 8

11. How long will it take to complete the trip? 8 hours

Write the cross products for each proportion.

12. $\frac{5}{10} = \frac{12}{n}$ $5n = 120$

13. $\frac{1}{12} = \frac{n}{9}$ $12n = 9$

14. $\frac{n}{15} = \frac{10}{6}$ $6n = 150$

Find the missing number in each proportion.

15. $\frac{6}{8} = \frac{n}{20}$ 15

16. $\frac{n}{5} = \frac{27}{45}$ 3

17. $\frac{9}{8} = \frac{81}{n}$ 72

18. $\frac{5}{n} = \frac{10}{12}$ 6

19. $\frac{6}{7} = \frac{n}{56}$ 48

20. $\frac{n}{12} = \frac{3}{36}$ 1

21. $\frac{66}{n} = \frac{11}{12}$ 72

22. $\frac{3.5}{4} = \frac{n}{8}$ 7

23. $\frac{n}{0.5} = \frac{0.4}{0.1}$ 2

24. $\frac{20}{18} = \frac{30}{n}$ 27

25. $\frac{3}{2} = \frac{n}{6}$ 9

26. $\frac{25}{n} = \frac{15}{12}$ 20

27. Five bags of rice weigh 70 ounces. How much do four bags of rice weigh? 56 ounces

28. If 15 pieces of gum cost $0.90, how much do 12 pieces of gum cost? $0.72

29. A babysitter earns $51 for working 8 hours. How much does the sitter earn for working 40 hours? $255

30. **Reasoning** When solving a proportion involving the lengths and widths of two rectangles, does it matter whether you put length or width in the top of the ratio?

No, as long as you put them in the same order in both ratios.

There is another way to solve proportions. Write $7 \times \frac{5}{7} = \frac{n}{49} \times 7$ on the board. *Will the value of n be the same? Explain.* [Yes, both sides were multiplied by 7.] Write $49 \times 7 \times \frac{5}{7} = \frac{n}{49} \times 7 \times 49$ on the board. Show how to simplify the 7s on the left and the 49s on the right so the equation is $49 \times 5 = n \times 7$.

Finding cross products is a shortcut for what we just did. Show students how to use cross multiplication. *What do you get when you cross multiply?* [$245 = 7n$] *If 7 times n is 245, how can you find n?* [Divide 245 by 7.] *What is the quotient?* [35] *So if there are 49 flowers, how many flowers are red?* [35]

2 Guided Practice

Use with Exercises 1–11.

Point out to students that not every proportion with a missing term has a whole number solution. Remind them that a ratio shows a relationship.

Use with Exercises 6–11.

Error Intervention

If students have trouble deciding which cross product to write first,

then, remind them that the cross products in a proportion are equal, so it doesn't matter which product is on the left side of the equation and which is on the right side.

ELL Use Vocabulary

To check understanding, have a student repeat and complete this sentence: *To solve a proportion, you can multiply the ______.* [Cross products]

Quick Check — Formative Assessment

Write the cross products and then solve the equation to find the missing term in the following proportion: $\frac{65 \text{ songs}}{5 \text{ CDs}} = \frac{s \text{ songs}}{7 \text{ CDs}}$.
[$65 \times 7 = 5s$; $s = 91$]

3 Independent Practice

Use with Exercises 12–30.

If a ratio is not in simplest form, suggest students write an equivalent ratio with numbers that are easier to work with. *In Exercise 26, what fraction is equal to $\frac{15}{12}$?* [$\frac{5}{4}$] *Write the proportion using $\frac{5}{4}$ instead of $\frac{15}{12}$.* [$\frac{25}{n} = \frac{5}{4}$] *What are the cross products?* [$25 \times 4 = 5n$] *Use mental math to solve.* [$100 = 5n$; $n = 20$]

Step 3-5

Write to Explain

Objective Students will explain solutions to word problems.

Vocabulary Proportion

Materials Crayons, markers, or colored pencils

Professional Development — Math Background

- Mathematical explanations can be given using words, pictures, numbers, or symbols.
- A good explanation is correct, simple, complete, and easy to understand. It includes known information and how that information is used to find the solution.
- There can be more than one good explanation as to how to solve a math problem.

Name ______________________ **Step 3-5**

Write to Explain

A student's work is shown at the right. Is the answer correct? Draw a picture to explain why or why not.

Solve by answering 1 and 2.

1. Color the counters below to represent the DVDs paid for in one color and the free ones in another color.

> Max's Media gives six DVD rentals for the price of 5. If Anna Maria pays for 15 rentals, how many rentals does she get in all?
>
> 15 − 5 = 10
> 6 + 10 = 16
> She gets 16 rentals.

2. Repeat the set of counters until there are 15 DVDs paid for.

If Anna Maria pays for 15 rentals, how many rentals does she get in all?

She gets **18** rentals in all.

The answer 16 rentals is not correct.

3. Fill in the blanks to explain how to write and solve a proportion to solve the problem.

Let r be the **number of rentals** Anna Maria gets.

Then $\frac{5}{6} = \frac{15}{r}$.

Using cross products, $5r =$ **90**.

$r =$ **18**

Anna Maria gets **18** rentals in all.

---

1 Concept Development

Interactive Learning

Purpose

You have already learned how to solve problems using a variety of strategies. Today you will learn how to write a good explanation for the solution to a mathematical problem.

Pose the Problem

Jess walks 1 mile every 16 minutes. Today she walked for 40 minutes. Explain how to find the number of miles she walked. Give students time to formulate their solution methods and record their explanations. Invite volunteers to share their explanations.

Model

What are you being asked? [To explain how to find the number of miles Jess walked in 40 minutes] *How can you solve this problem?* Discuss students' suggestions.

Name ______________________

Write to Explain (continued)

Explain your solution to each problem. Show your work.

4. Manuel went on a 400-mile trip with his friend Julio. If Manuel drove $\frac{3}{5}$ of the trip, how far did he drive?

   You need to find how far Manuel drove; $400 \times \frac{3}{5} = 240$ miles

5. Sliced turkey cost \$2.89 per pound. Sliced beef costs \$3.11 per pound. Majorie buys 2 pounds of turkey and 1 pound of beef. Estimate the total cost of the meat. Explain how you made your estimate. If she pays with a \$10 bill, will she get change?

   Sample answer: Yes; I rounded \$2.89 to \$3 and \$3.11 to \$3. The cost of 2 lbs of turkey and 1 lb of beef is \$6 + \$3 = \$9. She will get change.

6. Mrs. Barker is making chocolate chip cookies. Her recipe calls for $\frac{3}{4}$ cup of sugar. She does not have enough sugar for a full recipe. Write and explain how you would find how many cups of sugar are needed to make only half the recipe.

   Divide $\frac{3}{4}$ cup by 2. $\frac{3}{4} \div 2 = \frac{3}{4} \times \frac{1}{2} = \frac{3}{8}$.
   Mrs. Barker would need $\frac{3}{8}$ cup of sugar.

7. How many square feet of roofing paper does Joe need in order to put a new roof on his dog house? The roof has 2 rectangular sides, and each side of the roof measures 3 feet by 2 feet.

   12 ft²; Sample answer: The area of each side of the roof is $3 \times 2 = 6$.
   The area of the two sides is $2 \times 6 = 12$.

Write to Explain **33**

One way to solve this problem is to write a proportion and find the cross products. What ratios form the proportion? [$\frac{1}{16}$, $\frac{x}{40}$] *Use the cross products to solve.* [$1 \times 40 = 16x$; $40 = 16x$; $x = 2.5$ miles] Write the solution only on the board. Point out that the solution can also be expressed as $2\frac{1}{2}$ miles.

If you said that Jess walked 2.5 miles, is that a good explanation? Explain why or why not. [No; it gives the answer, but it doesn't explain how to solve the problem.] *What explanation could be included to complete the answer?* [Sample answer: Since Jess walks 1 mile in 16 minutes, I can write a proportion to find how many miles she walks in 40 minutes. $\frac{1}{16} = \frac{x}{40}$, so Jess walked 2.5 miles.]

2 Guided Practice

Use with Exercises 1–3

Point out to students that it is easier to see a ratio by using the same coloring scheme in each row.

Exercise 3

Error Intervention

If students have trouble understanding why the second term of the ratio is 6,

then ask *What information do you know?* [If Anna Maria pays for 5 DVD rentals, she gets 1 free DVD rental.] *How many DVDs in all does she get?* [6] *What ratio describes the number of paid rentals to the number of DVD rentals in all?* [$\frac{5}{6}$]

ELL Use Vocabulary

To check understanding, have a student repeat and complete this sentence: *A _____ shows that two ratios are equal.* [Proportion]

Quick Check Formative Assessment

The cost of 9 tickets is \$30. Explain how to find the cost of 12 tickets. [Sample answer: The ratios of tickets to cost are $\frac{9}{30}$ and $\frac{12}{c}$. I write the proportion $\frac{9}{30} = \frac{12}{c}$ and use cross products to solve it. $9c = 30 \times 12$; $9c = 360$; $c = 40$; the cost of 12 tickets is \$40.]

3 Independent Practice

Use with Exercises 4–7

Remind students that using words is not the only way to explain how to solve a math problem. Diagrams, illustrations, or drawings can be used in an explanation.

In Exercise 6, what are you trying to find? [How many cups are half of $3\frac{1}{2}$ cups] *How can you model $3\frac{1}{2}$?* [Draw 3 identical squares and half of a 4th square.] *How can you find half of the squares in your drawing?* [Divide each into 2 equal parts and then add the parts: $\frac{1}{2} + \frac{1}{2} + \frac{1}{2} + \frac{1}{4} = 1\frac{3}{4}$.]

Step 3-6

Similar Figures and Proportions

Objective Students write and solve proportions to find lengths of sides of similar figures.

Vocabulary Similar figures, proportional

Materials Centimeter Grid Paper (Teaching Tool 10)

Professional Development

Math Background

- Similar figures have the same shape but may or may not have the same size.
- Corresponding sides of similar polygons are proportional and corresponding angles are congruent.
- All circles are similar.
- Regular polygons with the same number of sides are similar.

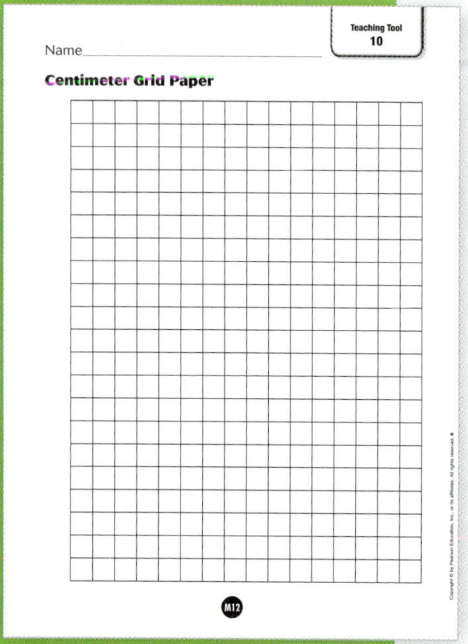

Teaching Tool 10

Name

Centimeter Grid Paper

M12

Name ______________________ Step 3-6

Similar Figures and Proportions

Similar figures have the same shape, but not necessarily the same size. The lengths of the sides of similar figures are proportional.

In the similar trapezoids below, $\frac{8}{15} = \frac{16}{30}$.

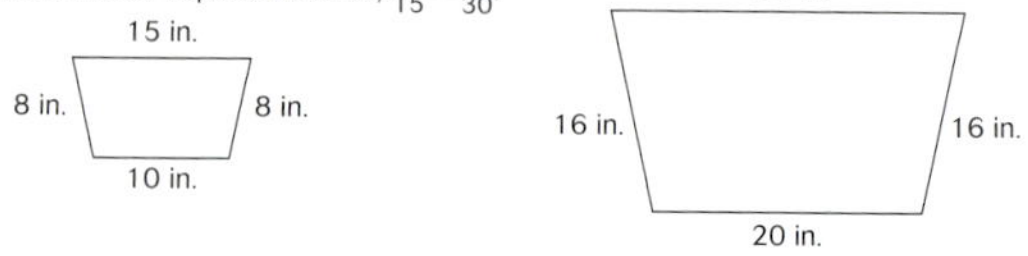

1. Complete the proportion for the trapezoids above.

$\frac{10}{8} = \frac{\boxed{20}}{16}$

Mrs. King drew the trapezoid below. Each leg is 3 inches long, and the other sides are 6 inches and 4 inches long. She wants a similar trapezoid with the length of the longest side 24 inches for a bulletin board. Find the lengths of the legs and the other side of the bulletin board trapezoid by answering 2 to 10.

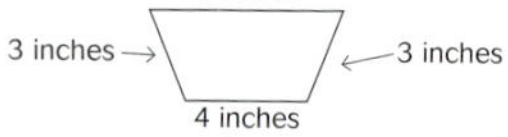

2. Write a proportion to find the legs of the trapezoid. Use n to represent the length of the legs of the trapezoid on the bulletin board.

legs in model → $\frac{3 \text{ in.}}{\boxed{6} \text{ in.}} = \frac{n \text{ in.}}{\boxed{24} \text{ in.}}$ ← legs on bulletin board
longest side in model → ← longest side on bulletin board

3. Write an equation using the cross products. $6n = 72$

4. Solve $6n = 72$. What is the value of n? $n =$ 12

5. What is the length of each leg of the bulletin board trapezoid? 12 inches

34 Similar Figures and Proportions

Interactive Learning

1 Concept Development

Use with Teaching Tool 10.

Purpose

You have already learned how to solve proportions. Today you will learn to find missing dimensions of proportional figures.

Pose the Problem

On the board, draw a rectangle and label its side lengths 2 feet and 4 feet. ***Sam's family is building a garden with the same shape as the rectangle on the board. The length of the longer side of the garden will be 18 feet. How long will the shorter side be?*** Have copies of Centimeter Grid Paper (Teaching Tool 10) available for students to draw Sam's garden. Provide time for students to complete and record their work. Invite volunteers to share their solutions with the class.

Name ______________________

Similar Figures and Proportions (continued)

6. Write a proportion to find the remaining side. Use *b* to represent the length of the remaining side of the bulletin board trapezoid.

remaining side in model → $\frac{4 \text{ in.}}{6 \text{ in.}} = \frac{b \text{ in.}}{24 \text{ in.}}$ ← remaining side on bulletin board
longest side in model → ← longest side on bulletin board

7. Write an equation using the cross products. $6b = 96$

8. Solve the equation. What is the value of *b*? $b =$ 16

9. What is the length of the remaining side of the bulletin board trapezoid? 16 inches

10. Fill in the measurements for the bulletin board trapezoid:

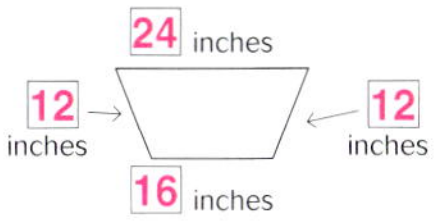

The figures shown below are similar. Find the missing sides. Show the proportion you use and the equation using the cross products.

11.

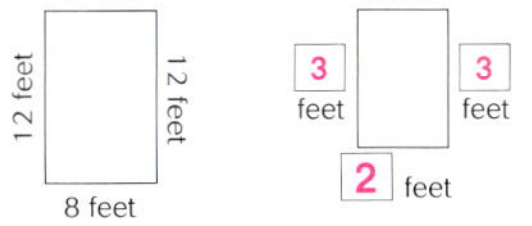

Proportion: $\frac{8}{12} = \frac{2}{n}$

Equation: $8n = 24$

Solution: $n = 3$

12.

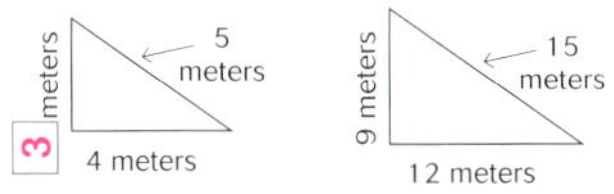

Proportion: $\frac{9}{12} = \frac{n}{4}$

Equation: $12n = 36$

Solution: $n = 3$

13. Reasoning Why are all squares similar?
Sample answer: All squares are the same shape.

2 Guided Practice

Use with Exercises 1–10.

Remind students that there is more than one way to find the missing term in a proportion. They can use cross products or find a ratio equivalent to the given ratio.

Point out that it may be easier to identify corresponding sides of similar figures if one figure is turned so it has the same orientation as the other. Drawing figures to scale on grid paper will help students see proportionality that may not be obvious from labeled dimensions.

Exercise 2

Error Intervention

If students have trouble finding corresponding sides of similar figures,

then suggest they think of sliding one figure on top of the other.

ELL Use Vocabulary

To check understanding, have a student repeat and complete this sentence: *Similar figures are the same shape and their corresponding sides are _____.* [Proportional]

Quick Check Formative Assessment

The ratio of the width to length in a rectangle is $\frac{3}{4}$. The width of a similar rectangle is 36 inches. What is the length of that rectangle? Show how you solved. [48 inches; $\frac{3}{4} = \frac{36}{x}$; $4 \times 36 = 3x$; $144 = 3x$; $x = 48$.]

3 Independent Practice

Use with Exercises 11–13.

Remind students that the inverse relationship of multiplication and division can be used to solve equations. The equation $8n = 24$ can be rewritten as $24 \div 8 = n$.

Model

Draw a larger, similar rectangle next to the existing drawing. *The larger rectangle represents Sam's garden. The two rectangles are similar figures. The rectangles are not the same size, but they are the same shape and their sides are proportional. What dimension of the larger rectangle do you know?* [The longer side is 18 feet.] *What do you need to find?* [The length of the shorter side] *How can you find the length of the missing side?* [Accept all reasonable answers.]

One way to find the missing side is to write and solve a proportion for the side lengths. What ratios form the proportion? [$\frac{2}{4}$, $\frac{x}{18}$] *How can you solve the proportion?* [Find the cross products: $2 \times 18 = 4x$; $36 = 4x$; $x = 9$ feet] *What will be the length of the shorter side of Sam's garden?* [9 feet]

Step **4-1**

Rates and Unit Rates

Objective Students will use division to find the unit rate for a given rate.

Vocabulary Rate, unit rate

Professional Development

Math Background

- A rate is a special kind of ratio.
- A rate compares quantities or measurements having different units.
- If the second term of a rate is 1, the rate is a unit rate.

Name ______________________ Step **4-1**

Rates and Unit Rates

A rate is a special type of ratio that compares quantities with unlike units, such as hits per game.

The table shows the number of hits for some members of a baseball team. Use the table for 1 to 7.

Name	Number of Hits	Number of Games
Maurice	20	10
Wade	24	8
Alfonso	30	15

1. What is Maurice's rate of hits to games? **20** hits in **10** games

2. To find Maurice's unit rate, divide the number of hits by the number of games.

20 ÷ **10** = **2** hits per game

At this rate, Maurice gets 2 hits per game.

3. What is Wade's rate of hits to games? **24 hits in 8 games**

4. At this rate, how many hits per game does Wade get?

24 ÷ **8** = **3** hits per game

5. What is Alfonso's rate of hits to games? **30 hits in 15 games**

6. At this rate, how many hits per game does Alfonso get?

30 ÷ **15** = **2** hits per game

7. Reasoning Although Alfonso had the most hits, he did not have the greatest unit rate. Why not?

Alfonso played in more games than the others, so his number of hits was divided by a greater number.

Interactive Learning 1

Concept Development

Use with Exercises 1–4.

Purpose

You have learned that a ratio is a comparison. Today you will learn about a special ratio, called a rate, and how to find a unit rate.

Pose the Problem

If you know how many hits a baseball player had in a given number of games, how could you find the average number of hits per game for that player? Have students share their ideas.

Model

A rate is a special ratio. It compares quantities that have different units. The table on page 36 lists three baseball players, the number of hits each one had, and the number of games they played. You can use the numbers in the table to find each player's rate of hits to games.

Name ______________________

Rates and Unit Rates (continued)

Find the unit rate.

8. 525 points in 15 games

35 points per game

9. 54 teachers for 6 schools

9 teachers per school

10. 33 apples for 11 fruit baskets

3 apples per basket

11. $1.77 for 3 pounds of bananas

$0.59 per lb of bananas

12. 312 miles every 12 gallons

26 miles per gallon

13. 185 feet in 37 seconds

5 feet per second

14. 42 tennis balls in 14 cans

3 tennis balls per can

15. 120 calories in 4 servings

30 calories per serving

16. $1.50 for 3 snack bars

$0.50 per snack bar

17. 1,530 miles in 6 hours

255 miles per hour

18. $48 in 8 hours

$6 per hour

19. 96 feet in 12 seconds

8 feet per second

20. Samantha scored a total of 6 goals in 6 soccer games. What units would you use to describe her unit rate? What is her unit rate?

Goals per game; 1 goal per game

21. A light bulb manufacturer claims that each bulb lasts at least 480 hours. Suppose you get 3,000 hours of use from 6 light bulbs. Write this information as a unit rate.

500 hours per light bulb

Notice that they did not all play the same number of games. Maurice had 20 hits and played in 10 games. His rate of hits to games is 20 hits in 10 games. Have students complete Exercise 1.

A unit rate is a rate in which the second term is 1. For example, a unit rate for Maurice's hits to games would be the average number of hits he had per game. The unit rate can be found by dividing the first term of the rate by the second term. In this case, divide the number of hits by the number of games. Have students complete Exercise 2. Be sure students understand that Maurice did not necessarily get 2 hits in every game. This unit rate is an *average* number of hits per game.

In a similar manner, discuss Wade's rate of hits to games and his unit rate. Have students complete Exercises 3 and 4.

2 Guided Practice

Use with Exercises 5–7.

Remind students that a unit rate always has 1 as its second term. In the case of hits to games, the unit rate is the average number of hits per game.

Exercise 7

Error Intervention

If students have difficulty explaining why Alfonso's unit rate was not the highest,

then ask: *What numbers do you need to use to find the unit rate?* [The number of hits and the number of games] *Did all three team members play in the same number of games?* [No] *Who played in the most games?* [Alfonso]

ELL Use Vocabulary

To check understanding, ask a student to repeat and complete this sentence: *A rate in which the second term is 1 is called a ________.* [Unit rate]

Quick Check Formative Assessment

What is the unit rate for traveling 200 miles in 4 hours?
[50 miles per hour]

3 Independent Practice

Use with Exercises 8–21.

If students have difficulty organizing their work, provide copies of Division Templates (Teaching Tool 11). Check to see that they are aligning the digits correctly.

Be sure students remember to include units when they give the unit rate. For example, in Exercise 8, the answer "35" or "35 points" would not be complete. The unit rate is 35 points per game.

For Exercises 13, 17, and 19, point out to students that speed is an example of a unit rate they are familiar with.

Step **4-2**

Comparing Rates

Objective Students will use unit rates to compare rates.

Vocabulary Unit price

Math Background

- Rates can be compared when they are written as unit rates.
- To find the unit rate, divide the first term by the second term.
- The unit price is the cost of one of an item.

Name ______________________

Step **4-2**

Comparing Rates

Larry's Market sells 6 bagels for $2.28. Sal's Convenience Mart sells the same bagels but charges $3.50 for 10 bagels. Find which store has the better buy by answering 1 to 8.

1. What is the rate of the cost of bagels at Larry's? $ 2.28 per 6 bagels

To compare two prices to find which is the better buy, find the unit price for each. The unit price is the same as the unit rate.

2. To find the unit price, divide the price by the number of bagels. 2.28 ÷ 6 = 0.38

3. What is the unit price for bagels at Larry's? $ 0.38 per bagel

4. What is the rate of the cost of bagels at Sal's? $ 3.50 per 10 bagels

5. To find the unit price, divide the price by the number of bagels. 3.50 ÷ 10 = 0.35

6. What is the unit price for bagels at Sal's? $ 0.35 per bagel

7. Compare. Write > or <. $0.38 (>) $0.35

8. Which store has the better buy? Sal's

The Thompson family drove 5 hours and traveled a total of 275 miles. The Gonzalez family drove 8 hours and traveled a total of 400 miles. Find which family traveled at a faster rate by answering 9 to 14.

To find the unit rate, divide the miles by the number of hours.

9. Divide total miles by hours to find the Thompson family's unit rate of speed. 275 ÷ 5 = 55

10. What was the Thompson family's unit rate of speed? 55 miles per hour

11. Divide to find the Gonzalez family's unit rate of speed. 400 ÷ 8 = 50

1 Concept Development

Use with Exercises 1–8.

Purpose

You have learned how to find a unit rate. Today you will learn how to compare two rates by using unit rates.

Pose the Problem

Two stores are advertising a sale on bagels. If you know the sale price for each store, how can you decide which store has the better buy? Allow time for students to share their ideas.

Model

Review with students the difference between a rate and a unit rate. *What information are you given?* [Larry's Market is selling 6 bagels for $2.28; Sal's Convenience Mart is selling 10 bagels for $3.50] Have students complete Exercises 1 and 4.

Name ______________________

Comparing Rates (continued)

12. What was the Gonzalez family's unit rate of speed? **50** miles per hour

13. Compare. Write > or <. 55 miles per hour (**>**) 50 miles per hour

14. Which family traveled at a faster rate? **Thompsons**

Find each unit price. Determine the better buy.

15. \$3 for 4 baseballs or \$4 for 5 baseballs
\$0.75; \$0.80; \$3 for 4 baseballs

16. 6 wristbands for \$1.68 or 9 wristbands for \$2.43
\$0.28; \$0.27; 9 wristbands for \$2.43

17. \$64 for 2 wallets or \$93 for 3 wallets
\$32; \$31; \$93 for 3 wallets

Find each unit rate and determine which rate is greater.

18. 12 runs in 4 games or 20 runs in 5 games
3 runs per game; 4 runs per game; 20 runs in 5 games is greater

19. 8 feet in 4 seconds or 15 feet in 5 seconds
2 feet per second; 3 feet per second; 15 feet in 5 seconds is greater

20. 9 strikeouts in 3 innings or 4 strikeouts in 2 innings
3 strikeouts per inning; 2 strikeouts per inning; 9 strikeouts in 3 innings is greater

21. Your pulse rate is the number of times your heart beats per minute. Betty counted 130 beats in 2 minutes and Sarah counted 204 beats in 3 minutes. Who had the higher pulse rate? **Sarah**

22. Reasoning At Store A, 28 pencils cost \$7.50, and at Store B, 29 pencils cost \$7.25. Explain without doing any calculations why Store B has the better buy. **Sample answer: Store B has more pencils for less money.**

To find which store has the better buy, you need to compare unit rates. A unit rate that deals with the cost per item is called a unit price. How can you find the unit price of the bagels at Larry's Market? [Divide: \$2.28 ÷ 6 = \$0.38] Have students solve the division and complete Exercises 2 and 3.

How can you find the unit price of the bagels at Sal's Convenience Mart? [Divide: \$3.50 ÷ 10 = \$0.35] Have students solve the division and complete Exercises 5 and 6.

Now you can compare the unit prices. How do you decide which store has the better buy? [The rate with the lower unit price is the better buy.] Have students complete Exercises 7 and 8.

2 Guided Practice

Use with Exercises 9–14.

Remind students to find the unit rate by dividing the first term by the second term.

Exercise 13
Error Intervention

If students have trouble deciding which family traveled at a faster rate,

then remind them that *faster* means a *greater* number of miles per hour.

ELL Use Vocabulary

To check understanding, ask a student to repeat and complete this sentence: *The cost for one item is called the ______.* [Unit price]

Quick Check Formative Assessment

Which rate is the better buy: 2 t-shirts for \$22 or 3 t-shirts for \$30? [3 t-shirts for \$30]

3 Independent Practice

Use with Exercises 15–22.

If students have difficulty organizing their work, provide copies of Division Templates (Teaching Tool 11). Check to see that they are aligning the digits correctly.

Remind students that the better buy is the item with the *lower* unit price.

For Exercises 18–22, however, they will be looking for the *greater* unit rate.

Step 4-3

Distance, Rate, and Time

Objective Students will use a formula to find distance, rate, and time.

Vocabulary Formula

Math Background

- A formula is a rule that uses symbols to relate quantities.
- The formula $d = r \times t$ shows the relationship between distance, rate, and time.

Name ______________________ Step 4-3

Distance, Rate, and Time

The formula $d = r \times t$ relates distance, d, rate, r and time, t. In this formula, rate means average speed.

The table shows the results of practice races run by some members of a track team. Rates written as 6 meters/second are read 6 meters per second.

Complete the table by answering 1 to 13.

Name	Distance	Rate	Time
Hannah	600 meters	6 meters/second	100 seconds
Mya	800 meters	5 meters/second	160 seconds
Adrienne	600 meters	5 meters/second	120 seconds

1. What is the formula that relates distance, rate and time? $d = r \times t$
2. For Hannah, what is the value of r in meters/second? 6
3. For Hannah, how many seconds is the value of t? 100
4. For Hannah, what information is unknown? distance
5. Substitute Hannah's values for r and t in the formula.

$d = r \times t$

$d = 6 \times 100$

6. Find the distance. Show your work.

$d = 600$

7. How far did Hannah run? Write this distance in the table. 600 meters
8. Substitute Mya's values for r and t in the formula.

$d = r \times t$

$d = 5 \times 160$

1 Concept Development

Use with Exercises 1–7.

Purpose

You have learned about ratios and proportion. Today you will learn about a special proportional relationship involving distance, rate, and time.

Pose the Problem

Three members of a track team recorded the results of their practice races. Using the table on page 40, how can you identify who ran the longest race? Have students share their ideas.

Model

A formula can be used to show the relationship between distance, rate, and time. Write the formula $d = r \times t$ on the board and have students complete Exercise 1. *How do you read this formula as a sentence?* [Distance equals rate times time]

Name ______________________

Distance, Rate, and Time (continued)

9. Find the distance. Show your work.

$d =$ 800

10. How far did Mya run? Write this distance in the table. 800 meters

11. Substitute Adrienne's values for r and t in the formula.

$d = r \times t$

$d = 5 \times 120$

12. Find the distance. Show your work.

$d =$ 600

13. How far did Adrienne run? Write this distance in the table. 600 meters

Use the formula $d = r \times t$ to find the distance.

14. r = 55 miles/hour, t = 7 hours

$d =$ 385 miles

15. r = 15 feet/second, t = 20 seconds

$d =$ 300 feet

Complete the table.

	Distance	Rate	Time
16.	200 meters	2 meters/second	100 seconds
17.	8 miles	2 miles/hour	4 hours
18.	80 yards	8 yards/minute	10 minutes

19. Reasoning Two people run the same distance but one person takes less time than the other. How do their rates compare?

The person who takes less time has a higher rate.

Look at the table on page 40. What does the distance, or d, represent? [The length of the race; how far the runner ran] *What does rate, or r, represent?* [The runner's average speed] *What does time, or t, represent?* [How long it took the runner to complete the race]

Look at Hannah's results. What information do you know? [The rate and time] Have students complete Exercises 2 and 3. *The distance Hannah ran is missing information.* Have students complete Exercise 4. *To find the distance Hannah ran, use the formula d = r × t.*

Have students complete Exercise 5. *To find the distance Hannah ran, multiply the rate, 6 meters/second, by the time, 100 seconds.* Have students complete Exercises 6 and 7. *What were Hannah's running results?* [Distance = 600 meters; rate = 6 meters/second; time = 100 seconds]

2 Guided Practice

Use with Exercises 8–13.

Point out to students that they are multiplying the rate by the time to find the distance.

Exercise 13

Error Intervention

If students have difficulty remembering the formula $d = r \times t$,

then say: *The "d" in distance, the "r" in rate, and the "t" in time are written in alphabetical order when written correctly in the formula.*

ELL Use Vocabulary

To check understanding, ask a student to repeat and complete this sentence: *d = r × t is a ______ that shows the relationship between distance, rate, and time.* [Formula]

Quick Check Formative Assessment

Michelle bikes 9 miles per hour for 3 hours. How many total miles does she ride? [27 miles]

3 Independent Practice

Use with Exercises 14–19.

Students should write each distance with a label. Point out that the rate will help them determine the label for the distance.

Exercise 19

If students do not understand how to compare the rates of the two runners, have them use the completed table on page 40 as a reference. Point out that Hannah and Adrienne ran the same distance, but in different times.

Grade 6 NCTM Focal Point

Algebra: Writing, interpreting, and using mathematical expressions and equations

BOOK C

Algebra

Step 1-1

Adding Two-Digit Numbers

Objective Students will find the sum of two-digit numbers.

Vocabulary Sum, regroup

Materials Addition/Subtraction Templates (Teaching Tool 9), place-value blocks

Math Background

Professional Development

- Place-value blocks can be used to model two-digit addition.
- The ones are added first, and then the tens.
- Each group of 10 ones can be regrouped as 1 ten.

Step 1-1

Name ______________________

Adding Two-Digit Numbers

There are 25 boys and 38 girls at the library. What is the total number of children at the library?

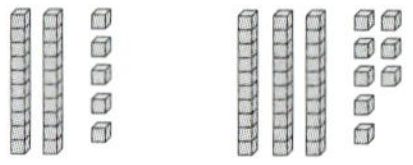

1. Show 25 using place-value blocks.
2. Show 38 using place-value blocks.
3. Add 25 + 38 to find the total.

   Add the ones. 5 + 8 = 13
4. Do you have more than 10 ones? yes
5. Since you have 13 ones, regroup them into tens and ones.

   13 ones = 1 ten and 3 ones
6. Record the 3 ones at the bottom of the ones column of the Tens and Ones chart. Record the 1 ten at the top of the tens column.

	Tens	Ones
	1	
	2	5
+	3	8
	6	3

7. Add the tens. Add the 1 ten that you regrouped, the 2 tens from the 25, and the 3 tens from the 38.

   1 ten + 2 tens + 3 tens = 6 tens
8. Record the tens at the bottom of the tens column of the Tens and Ones chart.
9. So, 25 + 38 = 63

   How many children are at the library? 63
10. Use place value-blocks and the Tens and Ones chart to add 46 + 29.

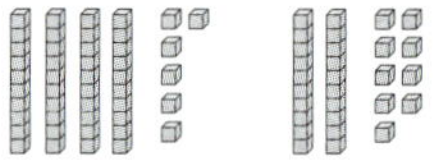

	Tens	Ones
	1	
	4	6
+	2	9
	7	5

2 Adding Two-Digit Numbers

Teaching Tool 9

Name ______________________

Addition/Subtraction Templates

A: Tens | Ones (three charts)

B: Tens | Ones | . | Tenths | Hundredths (two charts)

C: Hundreds | Tens | Ones | . | Tenths | Hundredths | Thousandths (two charts)

M11

1 Concept Development

Interactive Learning

Use with Teaching Tool 9.

Purpose

There is a standard way to find the sum of two numbers. Today you will learn how to add and record two-digit numbers using place value.

Pose the Problem

Jean collected 18 seashells. Her brother collected 24 seashells. How many seashells in all did they collect? Have students share their ideas. They should recognize that this is an addition problem.

Model

Distribute place-value blocks and copies of Addition/Subtraction Templates (Teaching Tool 9). Explain that students will use the place-value blocks to model addition and use the charts to record their work.

Name ____________________

Adding Two-Digit Numbers (continued)

Add.

11.

	Tens	Ones
	1	
	1	3
+	2	8
	4	1

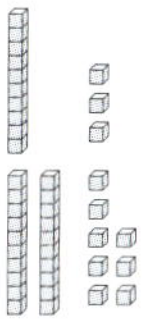

12.

	Tens	Ones
	1	
	2	4
+	2	9
	5	3

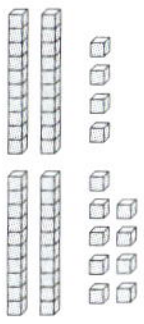

Add. Use a tens and ones chart if you like.

13. 58 + 17 = 75 **14.** 56 + 11 = 67 **15.** 18 + 19 = 37 **16.** 20 + 28 = 48

17. 46 + 45 = 91 **18.** 36 + 17 = 53 **19.** 17 + 49 = 66 **20.** 45 + 14 = 59

21. 32 + 66 = 98 **22.** 26 + 37 = 63 **23.** 22 + 65 = 87 **24.** 33 + 33 = 66

25. 21 + 39 = 60 **26.** 17 + 29 = 46 **27.** 36 + 16 = 52 **28.** 64 + 27 = 91

29. A puppy weighs 15 pounds. His mother weighs 65 pounds. How much do the puppy and his mother weigh together? 80 pounds

30. Reasoning What number do you add to 19 to get 30? 11

Write 18 + 24 in vertical form on the board. *Write this addition problem in the "A" chart. Place each digit in the correct place-value column. How many tens and ones do I need to show 18 using place-value blocks? 24 using place-value blocks?* [1 ten 8 ones; 2 tens 4 ones] Have students show 18 and 24 on their desks. *Add the ones.* Have students combine the ones blocks. *How many ones are there?* [12 ones] *How can you regroup 12 ones so you use fewer blocks?* [Exchange 10 ones for 1 ten.] *There are 2 ones blocks left. Record a 2 in the bottom of the ones column and a 1 at the top of the tens column of your chart. Use your blocks to add the tens.* Have students combine the tens blocks. *How many tens are there?* [4 tens] *Record a 4 in the bottom of the tens column. So, how many seashells in all did Jean and her brother collect?* [42 seashells]

2 Guided Practice

Use with Exercises 1–10.

Remind students that they can regroup 10 ones as 1 ten.

Exercise 3
Point out to students that adding two or more numbers gives a total.

Exercise 10
Error Intervention

If students forget to add the regrouped ten,

then have them add the regrouped ten first. *What is 1 ten + 4 tens + 2 tens?* [7 tens]

ELL Use Vocabulary

To check understanding, ask a student to repeat and complete this sentence: *19 ones can be ____ into 1 ten and 9 ones.* [Regrouped]

Quick Check Formative Assessment

Find the sum: 28 + 63. [91]

3 Independent Practice

Use with Exercises 11–30.

Provide extra copies of Addition/Subtraction Templates (Teaching Tool 9) to help students align each place value correctly. Student may also use place-value blocks to solve the problems.

Exercises 13–28
Point out to students that some problems do not require any ones to be regrouped.

Exercise 30
Students may use mental math to solve. *Count on from 19. 19 plus what number equals 20?* [1] *20 plus what number equals 30?* [10]

Step 1-2

Subtracting Two-Digit Numbers

Objective Students will use models to subtract two-digit numbers with regrouping.

Vocabulary Difference, regroup

Materials Addition/Subtraction Templates (Teaching Tool 9), place-value blocks

Math Background

- Place-value blocks can be used to model two-digit subtraction.
- The ones are subtracted first, and then the tens.
- Sometimes it is necessary to rename 1 ten as 10 ones.

Name ____________________ Step 1-2

Subtracting Two-Digit Numbers

There are 34 kittens and 16 puppies. How many more kittens than puppies are there?

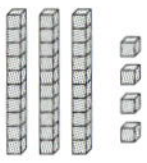

1. Show 34 with place-value blocks.
2. Do you have enough ones to take away 6 ones? no
3. Regroup 1 ten into 10 ones. Show this with your place-value blocks.

   3 tens and 4 ones = 2 tens and 14 ones.

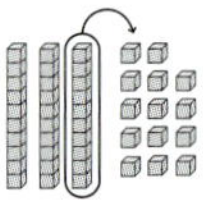

4. Cross out the 3 tens in the Tens and Ones chart and write 2 above it. Cross out the 4 ones and write 14 above it.
5. Now, take away 6 ones and write the difference at the bottom of the ones column.

   14 ones − 6 ones = 8 ones
6. Subtract the tens and write the difference at the bottom of the tens column.

   2 tens − 1 ten = 1 ten
7. So, 34 − 16 = 18

   How many more kittens than puppies are there? 18
8. Use place-value blocks and the Tens and Ones chart to subtract 56 − 27.

	Tens	Ones
	2	14
	~~3~~	~~4~~
−	1	6
	1	8

	Tens	Ones
	4	16
	~~5~~	~~6~~
−	2	7
	2	9

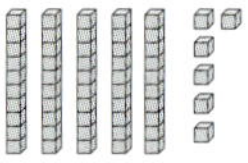

4 Subtracting Two-Digit Numbers

1 Concept Development

Interactive Learning

Use with Teaching Tool 9.

Purpose

You have learned how to find the sum of two-digit numbers. Today you will learn how to find and record the difference of two-digit numbers using place value.

Pose the Problem

Pine Trails is 29 miles long. Meadow Trails is 44 miles long. How many more miles longer is Meadow Trails? Have students work with a partner to solve the problem. They should recognize that this is a subtraction problem.

Model

Distribute place-value blocks and copies of Addition/Subtraction Templates (Teaching Tool 9). Explain that students will use the place-value blocks to model subtraction and use the charts to record their work. *When you want to find the difference between two numbers, what operation do you use?* [Subtraction]

Name ____________________ Teaching Tool 9

Addition/Subtraction Templates

A

Tens	Ones

A

Tens	Ones

A

Tens	Ones

B

Tens	Ones	.	Tenths	Hundredths

B

Tens	Ones	.	Tenths	Hundredths

C

Hundreds	Tens	Ones	.	Tenths	Hundredths	Thousandths

C

Hundreds	Tens	Ones	.	Tenths	Hundredths	Thousandths

M11

Name ______________________________

Subtracting Two-Digit Numbers (continued)

Subtract.

9.

	Tens	Ones
	3	12
	~~4~~	~~2~~
−	1	9
	2	3

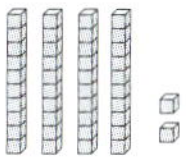

10.

	Tens	Ones
	4	10
	~~5~~	~~0~~
−	2	4
	2	6

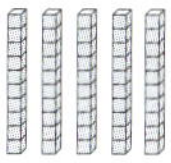

Subtract. Use a Tens and Ones chart if you like.

11. 35 − 17 = 18
12. 80 − 38 = 42
13. 45 − 39 = 6
14. 61 − 13 = 48

15. 74 − 45 = 29
16. 22 − 18 = 4
17. 50 − 32 = 18
18. 48 − 20 = 28

19. 95 − 69 = 26
20. 34 − 7 = 27
21. 61 − 26 = 35
22. 90 − 74 = 16

23. Thompson has 32 flowers. If he plants 18 flowers in the front yard, how many will he have left? 14

24. Reasoning In which problem do you need to regroup to subtract, 53 − 28 or 58 − 23? Explain.

53 − 28; There are not enough ones in 53 to take away the 8 ones in 28. However, there are enough ones in 58 to take away the 3 ones in 23.

Write 44 − 29 in vertical form on the board. *Write this subtraction problem in the "A" chart. Place each digit in the correct place-value column. How many tens and ones do you need to show 44 using place-value blocks?* [4 tens 4 ones] *Start with the ones place. Do you have enough ones to take away 9 ones?* [No] *Look at the tens place. How many tens are there?* [4] *Regroup 1 ten into 10 ones. How many tens and ones are there now?* [3 tens and 14 ones] Explain to students that renaming 44 into 3 tens and 14 ones is equal to 4 tens and 4 ones. *What is 14 − 9?* [5] Record the regrouping on the board. *Now, use the blocks to subtract the tens. Take away 2 tens from 3 tens. How many tens are left?* [1 ten] *Record a 1 at the bottom of the tens column. How many miles longer is Meadow Trails?* [15 miles longer]

2 Guided Practice

Use with Exercises 1–8.

Remind students that they can regroup 1 ten as 10 ones if they do not have enough ones to do the subtraction.

Exercise 7

Error Intervention

If students want to check their solution,

then remind them that addition and subtraction have an inverse relationship. *Add 18 + 16. Does the answer check?* [Yes; 18 + 16 = 34]

ELL Use Vocabulary

To check understanding, ask a student to repeat and complete this sentence: *The _____ is the answer to a subtraction problem.* [Difference]

Quick Check

Formative Assessment

Find the difference: 74 − 28. [46]

3 Independent Practice

Use with Exercises 9–24.

Exercises 11–22
Provide extra copies of Addition/Subtraction Templates (Teaching Tool 9) to help students align each place value correctly. Students may also use place-value blocks to solve the problems.

For Exercise 18, point out to students that this problem does not require any tens to be regrouped.

Exercise 23
Have students look for words or phrases that will help them decide what operation to use to solve the problem.

Step **1-3**

Adding Decimals to Hundredths

Objective Students will add decimals to hundredths.

Vocabulary Tenth, hundredth

Materials Addition/Subtraction Templates (Teaching Tool 9), place-value blocks

Professional Development

Math Background

- To add decimals, write the decimals with the decimal points aligned. Add as with whole numbers, and bring the decimal point straight down.
- Regrouping involves place value. 10 hundredths = 1 tenth, and 10 tenths = 1 one.

Name ______________________ Step **1-3**

Adding Decimals to Hundredths

It rained 2.36 inches in May and 1.57 inches in June. Answer 1 to 11 to find the total amount of rainfall in May and June.

Find 2.36 + 1.57.

Let the block at the right represent one unit, or 1.0.

1.0

So, ▯ represents one tenth, or 0.1 and ▫ represents one hundredth or 0.01.

1. Show 2.36 and 1.57 using place-value blocks.

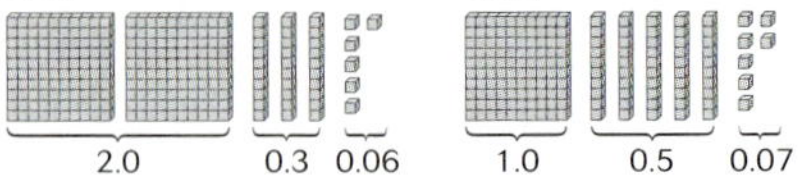

2. To add the hundredths, combine the small cubes.

6 hundredths + 7 hundredths = __13__ hundredths

3. Trade 10 hundredths for 1 tenth.

13 hundredths = __1__ tenth and __3__ hundredths

4. Record the 3 hundredths in the hundredths column of the place-value chart. Record the 1 tenth at the top of the tenths column.

	Ones		Tenths	Hundredths
			1	
	2	.	3	6
+	1	.	5	7
		.		3

Interactive Learning

1 Concept Development

Use with Teaching Tool 9.

Purpose

You know how to add whole numbers. Today you will learn how to add decimals.

Pose the Problem

Lydia bought 1.38 pounds of cashews and 2.47 pounds of walnuts. How can you find the total weight of the nuts Lydia bought? Discuss students' ideas about how to solve the problem. They should recognize that this is an addition problem.

Model

Distribute copies of Addition/Subtraction Templates (Teaching Tool 9) and 3 ones, 9 tenths, and 15 hundredths blocks per student. Explain that students will use the place-value blocks to model addition and use the charts to record their work. Write 1.38 + 2.47 in vertical form on the board. *Write these decimals in the middle row of a "B" chart. Be careful to place each digit in the correct place-value column. Be sure to write the decimal points and a plus sign.*

Name ______________________ Teaching Tool 9

Addition/Subtraction Templates

A

Tens	Ones

A

Tens	Ones

A

Tens	Ones

B

Tens	Ones	.	Tenths	Hundredths

B

Tens	Ones	.	Tenths	Hundredths

C

Hundreds	Tens	Ones	.	Tenths	Hundredths	Thousandths

C

Hundreds	Tens	Ones	.	Tenths	Hundredths	Thousandths

M11

Name ______________________ Step 1-3

Adding Decimals to Hundredths (continued)

5. Combine the tenths.
1 tenth + 3 tenths + 5 tenths =
9 tenths

6. Record the 9 tenths in the tenths column of the place-value chart.

7. Add the ones.
2 ones + 1 one = 3 ones

	Ones	.	Tenths	Hundredths
			1	
	2	.	3	6
+	1	.	5	7
	3	.	9	3

8. Record the 3 ones in the ones column of the place-value chart.

9. So, what is 2.36 + 1.57? 3.93

10. What was the total rainfall in May and June? 3.93 inches

11. **Reasoning** Estimate 2.36 + 1.57 and use the estimate to explain why the sum 3.93 is reasonable.

2.36 + 1.57 is about 2 + 2 = 4. Since 3.93 is close to 4, it is reasonable.

Add.

12. 6.28 + 1.47 = 7.75

13. 3.55 + 4.69 = 8.24

14. 8.6 + 2.7 = 11.3

15. 5.4 + 3.3 = 8.7

16. 2.6 + 3.1 = 5.7

17. 0.58 + 6.13 = 6.71

18. 5.1 + 3.97 = 9.07

19. 8.9 + 2.2 = 11.1

20. 5.18 + 3.24 = 8.42

21. 9.37 + 0.44 = 9.81

22. 13.8 + 5.71 = 19.51

23. \$1.75 + 5.15 = \$6.90

24. Ramon bought 2.4 yards of blue fabric and 3.25 yards of red fabric for a craft project. How many total yards of fabric did he buy? 5.65 yards

We can use these place-value blocks to model decimals. Hold up a flat block. *How many little cubes make up this block?* [100] *If this block represents one whole, then which block represents one tenth?* [The rod] *Which block represents one hundredth?* [The cube]

Which place-value blocks can you use to show 1.38? [1 flat, 3 rods, 8 cubes] *How can you show 2.47?* [2 flats, 4 rods, 7 cubes]

Start with the hundredths. Combine all the cubes. How many hundredths in all did you get? [15] *Trade 10 hundredths for 1 tenth, so you have 5 hundredths and 1 tenth.* Show students how to record the 5 hundredths at the bottom of the hundredths column and the 1 tenth at the top of the tenths columns. *Next, combine all the tenths. How many tenths in all did you get?* [8] *Record that in the chart. Combine all the ones. How many ones in all did you get?* [3] *Record that in the chart. Be sure to write the decimal point in the answer. So, what was the total weight of the nuts?* [3.85 pounds]

2 Guided Practice

Use with Exercises 1–11.

Remind students that they should begin adding hundredths first, then tenths, and then ones.

Exercises 2 and 3
What can 10 hundredths be regrouped as? [1 tenth]

Exercise 11
Error Intervention

If students have difficulty estimating the sum,

then say: *Suppose these decimals are money amounts. If you have \$2.36, is that closer to \$2 or to \$3?* [\$2] *Is \$1.57 closer to \$1 or to \$2?* [\$2] *So, you have about \$4 in all. Is that close to \$3.93?* [Yes]

ELL Use Vocabulary

To check understanding, ask a student to repeat and complete this sentence: *10 _____ equal 1 one, and 10 _____ equal 1 tenth.* [Tenths; hundredth]

Quick Check — Formative Assessment

Find 4.23 + 1.29. [5.52]

3 Independent Practice

Use with Exercises 12–24.

Provide extra copies of Addition/Subtraction Templates (Teaching Tool 9) as needed. Students can also use place-value blocks to help them find the sum.

Exercises 18, 22
Draw students' attention to how the decimal points are lined up, not the digits along the right side.

Step 1-4

Subtracting Decimals to Hundredths

Objective Students will subtract decimals to hundredths.

Vocabulary Tenth, hundredth

Materials Addition/Subtraction Templates (Teaching Tool 9), place-value blocks

Math Background

- To subtract decimals, write the decimals with the decimal points aligned. Subtract as with whole numbers, and bring the decimal point straight down.
- Regrouping involves place value. 1 one = 10 tenths, and 1 tenth = 10 hundredths.

Name ______________________ Step 1-4

Subtracting Decimals to Hundredths

Cable jumped 2.15 meters and Pedro jumped 1.72 meters. Answer 1 to 11 to find how much farther Cable jumped than Pedro.

Find 2.15 − 1.72.

Let the block at the right represent one unit, or 1.0.

1.0

So, ▯ represents one tenth, or 0.1 and ▫ represents one hundredth or 0.01.

1. Show 2.15 using place-value blocks.

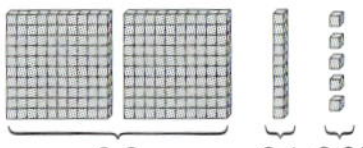

2. Do you have enough hundredths to take away 2 hundredths? **yes**

3. Subtract the hundredths.
5 hundredths − 2 hundredths = **3** hundredths
Write 3 in the hundredths column of the place-value chart.

	Ones	.	Tenths	Hundredths
	2	.	1	5
−	1	.	7	2
		.		**3**

4. Do you have enough tenths to take away 7 tenths? **no**

5. Regroup. Trade 1 one for 10 tenths.

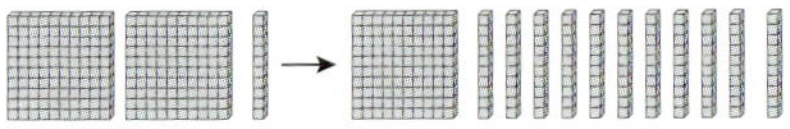

Name ______________________ Teaching Tool 9

Addition/Subtraction Templates

A

Tens	Ones

A

Tens	Ones

A

Tens	Ones

B

Tens	Ones	.	Tenths	Hundredths

B

Tens	Ones	.	Tenths	Hundredths

C

Hundreds	Tens	Ones	.	Tenths	Hundredths	Thousandths

C

Hundreds	Tens	Ones	.	Tenths	Hundredths	Thousandths

1 Concept Development

Interactive Learning

Use with Teaching Tool 9.

Purpose

You know how to add decimals. Today you will learn how to subtract decimals.

Pose the Problem

Alicia lives 3.64 miles from school. Samir lives 1.27 miles from school. How can you find how much farther Alicia lives from school than Samir? Be sure students understand that this is a subtraction problem.

Model

Distribute copies of Addition/Subtraction Templates (Teaching Tool 9) and 3 ones, 11 tenths, and 14 hundredths blocks per pair. Explain that students will use the place-value blocks to model subtraction and use the charts to record their work. Write 3.64 − 1.27 in vertical form on the board. *Write these decimals in the middle row of a "B" chart. Be careful to place each digit in the correct place-value column. Be sure you write the decimal points and a minus sign.*

Name ______________________

Subtracting Decimals to Hundredths (continued)

6. How many ones do you have left? Record this value in the chart. Cross out the 2 ones and write 1 above it. __1__

7. How many tenths do you have now? Record this value in the chart. Cross out the 1 tenth and write 11 above it. __11__

	Ones		Tenths	Hundredths
	1		11	
	~~2~~	.	~~1~~	5
−	1	.	7	2
	0	.	4	3

8. Subtract the tenths. 11 tenths − 7 tenths = __4__ tenths
Write 4 in the tenths column of the chart.

9. Subtract the ones. 1 one − 1 one = __0__ ones
Write 0 in the ones column of the chart.

10. So, what is 2.15 − 1.72? __0.43__

11. How much farther did Cable jump than Pedro? __0.43__ meter

Subtract.

12. 7.34 − 2.18 = **5.16**

13. 5.27 − 4.58 = **0.69**

14. 6.7 − 1.5 = **5.2**

15. 9.2 − 2.7 = **6.5**

16. 7.4 − 3.8 = **3.6**

17. 3.68 − 1.93 = **1.75**

18. 3.4 − 2.2 = **1.2**

19. 5.69 − 4.35 = **1.34**

20. Paulie caught two fish. One weighed 1.43 pounds and the other weighed 5.7 pounds. Janice caught one 7.09 pound fish. Who caught more pounds of fish? __Paulie;__

How much more? __0.04 lb more__

21. Reasoning What regrouping do you need to do to subtract 8 − 5.43?
Trade 1 one for 10 tenths and then trade one of those tenths for 10 hundredths.

Review how to use place-value blocks to model decimals. Hold up the flat block. *If this block represents one whole, then which block represents one tenth?* [The rod] *Which block represents one hundredth?* [The cube]

Which place-value blocks can you use to show 3.64? [3 flats, 6 rods, 4 cubes] *We need to take away 1.27.*

Start with the hundredths. Do you have enough hundredths to take away 7 hundredths? [No] *Trade 1 tenth for 10 hundredths. So now, instead of 6 tenths you have 5 tenths, and instead of 4 hundredths you have 14 hundredths.* Show students how to cross out the 6 in the tenths column and write 5 above it, and cross out the 4 in the hundredths column and write 14 above it.

Take away the 7 hundredths and record the difference in the chart. Then take away the 2 tenths and record the result. Take away the 1 one and record the result. Be sure to write the decimal point in the answer. So, how much farther does Alicia live from school than Samir? [2.37 miles]

2 Guided Practice

Use with Exercises 1–11.

Review with students what each place-value block represents.

Exercise 1
After students show 2.15 using place-value blocks, ask: *What number do you need to subtract?* [1.72] *How many ones are in that number?* [1] *How many tenths?* [7] *How many hundredths?* [2] *What should you subtract first?* [2 hundredths]

Exercises 5–7
Error Intervention

If students have difficulty recording the regrouped numbers,

then explain that 1 one and 11 tenths is the same as 2 ones and 1 tenth.

ELL Use Vocabulary

To check understanding, ask a student to repeat and complete this sentence: *You can trade 1 one for 10 _____, and you can trade 1 tenth for 10 _____.* [Tenths; hundredths]

Quick Check Formative Assessment

Find 4.38 − 1.57. [2.81]

3 Independent Practice

Use with Exercises 12–21.

Provide extra copies of Addition/Subtraction Templates (Teaching Tool 9) and place-value blocks as needed.

Exercise 20
This is a multiple-step problem. Students must first find the total weight of the fish Paulie caught before comparing that weight to the weight of Janice's fish.

Exercise 21
Point out that students should begin by writing 8 as 8.00.

Step 1-5

Adding and Subtracting Decimals to Thousandths

Objective Students will add and subtract decimals to thousandths.

Vocabulary Thousandths

Materials Addition/Subtraction Templates (Teaching Tool 9)

Professional Development

Math Background

- To add or subtract decimals to thousandths, write the decimals with the decimal points aligned. Add or subtract as with whole numbers, and bring the decimal point straight down.

Teaching Tool 9

Name

Addition/Subtraction Templates

A

Tens	Ones

B

Tens	Ones	.	Tenths	Hundredths

C

Hundreds	Tens	Ones	.	Tenths	Hundredths	Thousandths

M11

Step 1-5

Name

Adding and Subtracting Decimals to Thousandths

At a gymnastics competition Claudia earned a score of 7.75 on the uneven parallel bars. She scored 1.465 points higher on the beam. Answer 1 to 9 to find how many points she earned on the beam.

Find 7.75 + 1.465.

	Ones		Tenths	Hundredths	Thousandths
	1		1		
	7	.	7	5	
+	1	.	4	6	5
	9	.	2	1	5

1. How many thousandths are in 7.75? 0

2. Add 0 thousandths and 5 thousandths and record the value in the place-value chart.

3. Add the hundredths. 5 hundredths + 6 hundredths = 11 hundredths

4. Regroup the hundredths. 11 hundredths = 1 tenth and 1 hundredth

Record the 1 hundredth at the bottom of the hundredths column and the 1 tenth at the top of the tenths column.

5. Add the tenths. 1 tenth + 7 tenths + 4 tenths = 12 tenths

6. Regroup the tenths. 12 tenths = 1 one and 2 tenths

Record the 2 tenths at the bottom of the tenths column and the 1 one at the top of the ones column.

7. Add the ones and record. 1 one + 7 ones + 1 one = 9 ones

8. So, what is 7.75 + 1.465? 9.215

9. How many points did Claudia earn on the beam? 9.215 points

Claudia also earned a score of 6.825 on her floor routine. How many more points did she earn on the uneven parallel bars than the floor routine?

Find 7.75 − 6.825 by answering 10 to 18.

10. Since 7.75 has 0 thousandths, write a zero in the place-value chart on the next page, to change 7.75 to 7.750.

10 Adding and Subtracting Decimals to Thousandths

Interactive Learning

1 Concept Development

Use with Teaching Tool 9.

Purpose

You know how to add and subtract decimals to hundredths. Today you will learn how to add and subtract decimals to thousandths.

Pose the Problem

A grocer sold 5.47 kilograms of potatoes and 3.625 kilograms of onions. How many more kilograms of potatoes did she sell than onions? Students should recognize that this is a subtraction problem.

Model

Distribute copies of Addition/Subtraction Templates (Teaching Tool 9). Explain that students will use the "C" charts to record their work. Write 5.47 − 3.625 in vertical form on the board. *Write these decimals in the middle row of the chart. Be careful to place each digit in the correct place-value column. Remember to show the decimal points and a minus sign.*

Name ______________________

Adding and Subtracting Decimals to Thousandths (continued)

11. Regroup. Trade 1 hundredth for 10 thousandths. In the chart, cross out the 5 hundredths and write 4 above it. Cross out the 0 thousandths and write 10 above it.

	Ones		Tenths	Hundredths	Thousandths
	6		17	4	10
	~~7~~	.	~~7~~	~~5~~	~~0~~
−	6	.	8	2	5
	0	.	9	2	5

12. Subtract the thousandths. 10 thousandths − 5 thousandths = __5__ thousandths

Record the 5 in the thousandths column.

13. Subtract the hundredths. 4 hundredths − 2 hundredths = __2__ hundredths

Record the 2 in the hundredths column.

14. Regroup. Trade 1 one for 10 tenths. Cross out the 7 ones and write 6 above it. Cross out the 7 tenths and write 17 above it.

15. Subtract the tenths. 17 tenths − 8 tenths = __9__ tenths

Record the 9 in the tenths column.

16. Subtract the ones and record the value in the ones column.

17. So, what is 7.75 − 6.825? __0.925__

18. How many more points did Claudia earn on the uneven parallel bars than the floor routine? __0.925__ point

Find each sum or difference.

19. 43.72 − 18.68 = **25.04**

20. 25.83 + 14.76 = **40.59**

21. 75.77 − 64.89 = **10.88**

22. 865.80 + 74.95 = **940.75**

23. 0.951 − 0.678 = **0.273**

24. 0.810 + 0.125 = **0.935**

25. 7.618 − 4.909 = **2.709**

26. 6.234 + 5.195 = **11.429**

27. Bart is 1.486 meters tall and Sergio is 1.817 meters tall. What is the difference in their heights? __0.331 meter__

Discuss the place values of 5.47. *How many ones are there?* [5] *How many tenths?* [4] *How many hundredths?* [7] *Does 5.47 have any thousandths?* [No] *Write a zero in the thousandths place.*

Record the calculations on the board as you discuss the problem. *As with whole numbers, you start subtracting on the right. Do you have enough thousandths to take away 5 thousandths?* [No] *Regroup 7 hundredths as 6 hundredths and 10 thousandths.* Students should cross out the 7 in the hundredths column and write 6 above it, and cross out the 0 in the thousandths column and write 10 above it.

Subtract the thousandths, and then the hundredths. Record each digit in the correct column. What do you need to do to subtract the tenths? [Regroup the 5 ones as 4 ones and 10 tenths to make a total of 14 tenths.] Check to be sure students correctly record this regrouping. Then have them complete the subtraction. *Remember to write the decimal point in the answer. So, how many more kilograms of potatoes did the grocer sell than onions?* [1.845 kilograms]

2 Guided Practice

Exercises 1–18

Review how adding and subtracting decimals compares to adding and subtracting whole numbers. *How is adding and subtracting decimals similar to adding and subtracting whole numbers?* [Sample answers: You add or subtract from right to left. You regroup the same way. You add or subtract one place at a time.] *How is it different?* [Sample answer: You have to line up the decimal points and include a decimal point in the answer.]

Exercises 1–9

Error Intervention

If students have difficulty adding the decimals because the digits do not align on the right,

then have them write a zero in the thousandths place first.

ELL Use Vocabulary

To check understanding, ask a student to repeat and complete this sentence: *You can regroup 1 hundredth as 10 ____.* [Thousandths]

Quick Check Formative Assessment

Find 6.72 − 3.208. [3.512]

3 Independent Practice

Exercises 19–27

Remind students that they need to keep the decimal points lined up when they add or subtract decimals. Provide extra copies of Addition/Subtraction Templates (Teaching Tool 9) as needed.

Exercise 27

When you need to find the difference, what operation do you use? [Subtraction]

Step **2-1**

Multiplying Two-Digit Numbers

Objective Students will multiply two-digit numbers by one-digit numbers.

Vocabulary Tens, ones

Materials Multiplication Charts (Teaching Tool 4), place-value blocks

Professional Development

Math Background

- The standard multiplication algorithm uses simpler calculations by breaking apart numbers into their place values.
- Making an array with place-value blocks provides a way to visualize and find products.

Name ______________________ Step **2-1**

Multiplying Two-Digit Numbers

A small auditorium has 4 rows of seats. Each row can seat 23 people. Answer 1 to 7 to find the number of seats there are in the auditorium.

Find 4 × 23.

1. Show 4 groups of 23 using place-value blocks.

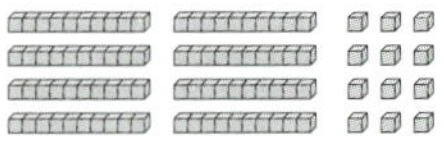

2. Multiply the ones. 4 × 3 ones = __12__ ones

3. Regroup the ones. Trade groups of ten ones for tens.

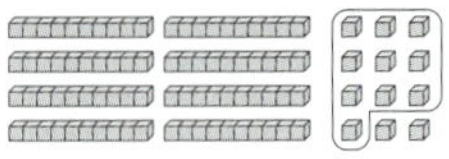

4. 12 = 1 ten and __2__ ones. Record the ones in the ones column of the Tens and Ones chart. Record the tens at the top of the tens column of the chart.

5. Multiply the tens. 4 × 2 tens = __8__ tens

6. Add the regrouped tens to the 8 tens and record this value in the tens column of the chart.

8 tens + 1 ten = __9__ tens

7. So, 4 × 23 = __92__. How many seats does the small auditorium have in all? __92__

	Tens	Ones
	1	
	2	3
×		4
	9	2

Interactive Learning

1 Concept Development

Use with Teaching Tool 4.

Purpose

You have learned how to add and subtract numbers. Today you will learn how to multiply a two-digit number by a one-digit number.

Pose the Problem

Milo purchased 3 boxes of envelopes. Each box had 25 cards. How many envelopes did Milo buy in all? Have students share their ideas. They should recognize that this is a multiplication problem.

Model

Distribute 7 tens blocks and 15 ones blocks and a copy of Multiplication Charts (Teaching Tool 4) to each student. Explain that students will use the place-value blocks to model multiplication and use the charts to record their work. Write 3 × 25 in vertical form on the board. *Write this multiplication problem in the "A" chart. Place each digit in the correct place-value column.*

Name ______________________ Teaching Tool 4

Multiplication Charts

A
Thous	Hunds	Tens	Ones

A
Thous	Hunds	Tens	Ones

B
Thous	Hunds	Tens	Ones

B
Thous	Hunds	Tens	Ones

C
Ten Thous	Thous	Hunds	Tens	Ones

C
Ten Thous	Thous	Hunds	Tens	Ones

M6

Name ______________________________

Multiplying Two-Digit Numbers (continued)

Multiply.

8. 14×6 = 84

9. 21×5 = 105

10. 32×2 = 64

11. 18×9 = 162

12. 31×6 = 186

13. 52×4 = 208

14. 27×4 = 108

15. 43×3 = 129

16. 22×6 = 132

17. 15×2 = 30

18. 36×4 = 144

19. 26×5 = 130

20. 21×7 = 147

21. 53×2 = 106

22. 63×2 = 126

23. 38×2 = 76

24. 28×3 = 84

25. 56×3 = 168

26. 64×3 = 192

27. 41×3 = 123

28. Jack is 14 years old. His mother is 3 times his age. How old is his mother? 42 years

29. Julie scored 16 points in each of her last 3 basketball games. How many points did she score in all? 48 points

30. Reasoning Write a two-digit number multiplied by a one-digit number that requires regrouping.

Answers will vary. Sample answer: 6×24

How many tens and ones do I need to show 25? [2 tens, 5 ones] Have students show 25 at their desks. *How many groups of 25 do I need to show for the number of boxes?* [3] Have students show three groups of 25 at their desks with the tens on the left and the ones on the right.

Hold up a cube. *Start with the ones. How many ones are there?* [15] *Since there are more than 10 ones, you need to regroup. Trade groups of ten ones for tens. How many tens and how many ones is that?* [1 ten, 5 ones] *On your chart, record the 5 ones at the bottom of the ones column, and the 1 ten in the box at the top of the tens column.*

Hold up a rod. *Next, find how many tens there are. Combine the 3 groups of 2 tens. Then add the 1 ten from the regrouping. How many tens in all did you get?* [7] *Record the 7 tens at the bottom of the tens column on your chart. What is the product?* [75] *So, how many envelopes did Milo buy in all?* [75 envelopes]

2 Guided Practice

Use with Exercises 1–7.

Place-value blocks can be used to model two-digit numbers. The number 23 is shown with 2 tens and 3 ones.

Exercise 4

Error Intervention

If students forget how to regroup the ones,

then say: *How many groups of 10 can you make with 12 ones?* [1] *How do you record the regrouped 1 ten?* [Write a 1 at the top of the tens column.]

ELL Use Vocabulary

To check understanding, ask a student to repeat and complete this sentence: *Ten_____ can be regrouped as one _____* [Ones; ten].

Quick Check Formative Assessment

Find the product: 6×16. [96]

3 Independent Practice

Use with Exercises 8–30.

Provide students with extra copies of Multiplication Charts (Teaching Tool 4) as needed. Students will need to use the hundreds column when they record the product if the problem requires regrouping groups of tens to hundreds.

For Exercise 30, students may have trouble writing a multiplication problem that uses regrouping. Have students use their knowledge of basic facts to help them.

Step 2-2

Multiplying Three-Digit Numbers

Objective Students will multiply three-digit numbers by one-digit multipliers.

Vocabulary Hundreds, tens, ones

Materials Multiplication Charts (Teaching Tool 4)

Math Background

- A three-digit number can be represented as the sum of hundreds, tens, and ones. For example, 235 = 2 hundreds + 3 tens + 5 ones.
- To multiply three-digit numbers, the ones are multiplied first, then the tens, and then the hundreds.
- Each group of 10 ones can be regrouped as 1 ten, and each group of 10 tens can be regrouped as 1 hundred.

Name ______________________ Teaching Tool 4

Multiplication Charts

A

Thous	Hunds	Tens	Ones
×			

A

Thous	Hunds	Tens	Ones
×			

B

Thous	Hunds	Tens	Ones
×			
+			

B

Thous	Hunds	Tens	Ones
×			
+			

C

Ten Thous	Thous	Hunds	Tens	Ones
×				
+				

C

Ten Thous	Thous	Hunds	Tens	Ones
×				
+				

M6

Name ______________________ Step 2-2

Multiplying Three-Digit Numbers

A parking garage has 6 different levels. There are 128 parking spots on each level. Answer 1 to 13 to find the total number of parking spots.

Find 6 × 128.

1. 128 = __1__ hundred + __2__ tens + __8__ ones
2. Multiply the ones. 6 × 8 ones = __48__ ones
3. Do you need to regroup the ones? __yes__
4. 48 ones = __4__ tens + __8__ ones
5. Record the ones in the ones column of the chart at the right. Record the regrouped tens at the top of the tens column.
6. Multiply the tens.
   6 × 2 tens = __12__ tens

	Hundreds	Tens	Ones
	1	4	
	1	2	8
×			6
	7	6	8

7. Now, add the regrouped tens.
   __12__ tens + __4__ tens = __16__ tens = __160__
8. Do you need to regroup the tens? __yes__
9. 160 = __1__ hundred + __6__ tens
10. Record the tens in the tens column. Record the regrouped hundreds at the top of the hundreds column.
11. Multiply the hundreds. 6 × 1 hundred = __6__ hundreds
12. Now add the regrouped hundreds and record in the hundreds column.
    __6__ hundreds + __1__ hundred = __7__ hundreds = __700__
13. So, 6 × 128 = __768__.
    How many parking spots are in the garage? __768__

14 Multiplying Three-Digit Numbers

Interactive Learning 1

Concept Development

Use with Teaching Tool 4.

Purpose

You know how to multiply a two-digit number by a one-digit number. Today you will learn how to multiply a three-digit number by a one-digit number.

Pose the Problem

Nellie has 4 memory cards for her camera. Each card can hold 235 pictures. How many pictures can the 4 cards hold? Students should recognize that this is a multiplication problem.

Model

Distribute copies of Multiplication Charts (Teaching Tool 4). Write 4 × 235 in vertical form on the board. *Write this multiplication problem in an "A" chart. Place each digit in the correct place-value column. How many hundreds, tens, and ones are there in 235?* [2 hundreds, 3 tens, 5 ones] *In which column should you write the 4?* [Ones]

Name ______________________

Multiplying Three-Digit Numbers (continued)

Multiply.

14.

	Th	H	T	O
	1	1	2	
		4	5	7
×				3
	1	3	7	1

15.

	Th	H	T	O
	3	1	4	
		5	2	6
×				7
	3	6	8	2

16. 223 × 4 = **892**

17. 246 × 7 = **1,722**

18. 117 × 5 = **585**

19. 434 × 4 = **1,736**

20. 519 × 2 = **1,038**

21. 327 × 3 = **981**

22. 572 × 5 = **2,860**

23. 357 × 8 = **2,856**

24. 323 × 4 = **1,292**

25. 351 × 5 = **1,755**

26. 217 × 7 = **1,519**

27. 352 × 2 = **704**

28. A company makes 352 boxes of cereal each day. How many boxes are made in 7 days? **2,464** boxes

29. Reasoning Is 2,124 a reasonable product for 3 × 78? Use estimation to explain why or why not.

No; 3 × 78 is close to 3 × 80 = 240, and 2,124 is much greater than 240.

Start with the ones. Multiply 4 × 5 ones. How many ones do you get? [20] *You need to regroup the 20 ones as tens and ones. How many tens and how many ones is it?* [2 tens, 0 ones] Guide students as they record the 0 ones at the bottom of the ones column and the 2 tens in the box at the top of the tens column.

Next, multiply 4 × 3 tens. How many tens do you get? [12 tens] *Add the 2 tens that resulted from the regrouping. How many tens do you have in all?* [14] *Regroup 14 tens as hundreds and tens. How many hundreds and how many tens is that?* [1 hundred, 4 tens] Have students record the 4 tens at the bottom of the tens column and the 1 hundred in the box at the top of the hundreds column.

Now multiply 4 × 2 hundreds. How many hundreds do you get? [8 hundreds] *Add the 1 hundred from the regrouping. How many hundreds do you have in all?* [9] Have students record the 9 hundreds at the bottom of the hundreds column. *What is the product?* [940] *So, how many pictures can the 4 cards hold?* [940 pictures]

2 Guided Practice

Use with Exercises 1–13.

Remind students that they should begin multiplying the ones, then the tens, and then the hundreds.

Whenever you get 10 ones, what can you trade that for? [1 ten] *Whenever you get 10 tens, what can you trade that for?* [1 hundred]

Exercises 3, 4, 8, and 9

Error Intervention

If students have difficulty regrouping,

then have them use place-value blocks to verify that 10 ones = 1 ten and 10 tens = 1 hundred. Then they can use the place-value blocks to model 48 ones = 4 tens 8 ones, and 16 tens = 1 hundred 6 tens.

ELL Use Vocabulary

To check understanding, ask a student to repeat and complete this sentence: *When you multiply three-digit numbers, first multiply the _____, then the _____, and then the _____.* [Ones; tens; hundreds]

Quick Check Formative Assessment

Find 176 × 5. [880]

3 Independent Practice

Use with Exercises 14–29.

Provide extra copies of Multiplication Charts (Teaching Tool 4) as needed. Remind students that today they are using the "A" charts. Point out that some of the products will have four digits, so they will need to use the thousands column when they record the product.

Exercises 29

Remind students that an estimate is an approximate number or answer. They can use either rounding or compatible numbers to estimate.

Step 2-3

Dividing Three-Digit Numbers

Objective Students will divide three-digit numbers by one-digit divisors.

Vocabulary Hundreds, tens, ones

Materials Division Templates (Teaching Tool 11), place-value blocks, 6 half sheets of paper

Professional Development

Math Background

- The division algorithm involves these steps: divide, multiply, subtract, compare, and bring down the next number.
- Divide the hundreds first if there are enough hundreds to do so. If not, regroup the hundreds as tens, and divide the tens.

Name ______________________ Step 2-3

Dividing Three-Digit Numbers

There are 324 baseball players at camp. If the camp counselors put them into 9 equal-sized groups, how many players are in each group?

Find 324 ÷ 9 by answering 1 to 17.

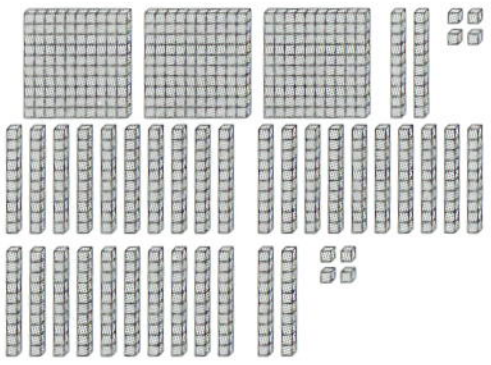

1. The place-value blocks at the right show 324. Are there enough hundreds in 324 to put one in each of 9 groups? __no__

2. Regroup the hundreds.

3 hundreds + 2 tens = __32__ tens

3. How many tens can go into each of 9 groups? __3__

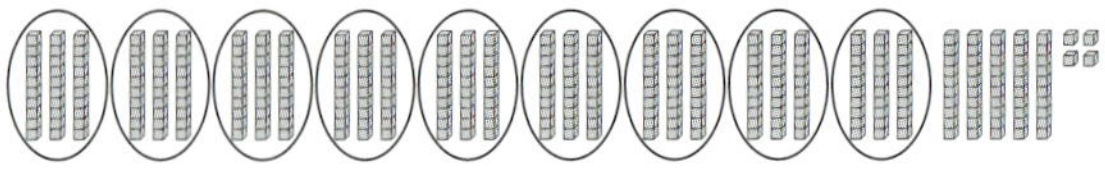

4. Record the 3 above the 2 in 324, at the right.

5. How many tens were used?

9 × 3 tens = __27__ tens

6. Record the tens used below the 32 in 324, at the right.

7. How many tens are left over?

32 − 27 = __5__ tens

$$\begin{array}{rl} & 36 \\ 9\overline{)324} & \\ 9 \times 3 \rightarrow & 27 \\ 32 - 27 \rightarrow & 54 \\ 9 \times 6 \rightarrow & 54 \\ 54 - 54 \rightarrow & 0 \end{array}$$

8. Record the tens left below the 27 and the line.

9. Regroup the tens into ones and add the other 4 ones. Bring down the 4 to show the total ones.

5 tens + 4 ones = __54__ ones

16 Dividing Three-Digit Numbers

Name ______________________ Teaching Tool 11

Division Templates

A B C C

M13

Interactive Learning 1 Concept Development

Use with Teaching Tool 11.

Purpose

You have learned how to multiply three-digit numbers. Today you will learn how to divide three-digit numbers.

Pose the Problem

There are 144 sixth-grade students at Williams School. There are 6 classrooms each with the same number of students. How many students are in each room? Ask students to discuss their ideas and explain why this is a division problem.

Model

Distribute 1 hundreds block, 14 tens blocks, and 24 ones blocks per pair and copies of Division Templates (Teaching Tool 11). Write $6\overline{)144}$ on the board. *Write this division problem in the "A" chart. How many hundreds, tens, and ones are in 144?* [1 hundred, 4 tens, 4 ones] *Use your blocks to model 144.*

How many equal groups are we making? [6] Have students place 6 half sheets of paper on their desks. *How many hundreds can you put in each group?* [None]

Name ______________________

Dividing Three-Digit Numbers (continued)

10. How many of the 54 ones can go in each of the 9 groups? __6__ ones

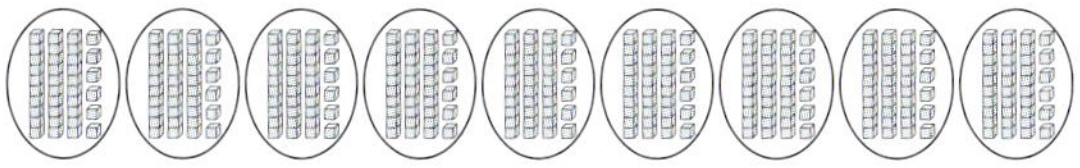

11. Record the 6 above the 4 in 324.

12. How many ones were used? 9 × 6 ones = __54__ ones

13. Record the ones used below the 54 regrouped ones.

14. How many ones are leftover? 54 − 54 = __0__ ones

15. Record the ones left below the 54 and the line.

16. What is 324 ÷ 9? __36__

17. How many players are in each group? __36__ players

Find each quotient.

18. $8\overline{)656}$ **82** **19.** $2\overline{)304}$ **152** **20.** $9\overline{)828}$ **92**

21. $5\overline{)465}$ **93** **22.** $7\overline{)238}$ **34** **23.** $3\overline{)639}$ **213**

24. Nine friends are sharing a box of crackers. The box contains 135 crackers. How many crackers will each friend get if the crackers are divided evenly? **15 crackers**

25. Reasoning In the division problem 432 ÷ 5, should the first step be to divide the hundreds or to regroup the hundreds to tens? Explain your reasoning.

Begin by regrouping because 4 hundreds are not enough to put one hundred in each of 5 groups.

There are not enough hundreds in 144 to put one hundred in each group, so regroup the hundreds as tens. How can you regroup 1 hundred and 4 tens? [14 tens] *How many tens can you put in 6 equal groups?* [2] Have students move 2 tens blocks onto each sheet and record the 2 in the quotient as you record it at the board.

You put 2 tens in each group. How many tens did you use? [12] Remind students to think "6 × 2" as they record the 12 under the 14. *How many tens are left?* [2] Remind students to think "14 − 12" as they record the 2 at the bottom of the tens column.

Regroup the leftover tens as ones so we can divide all of the ones into the 6 groups. How many ones do you have in all? [24] Show students how to bring down the 4 and write it to the right of the 2. *How many ones can you put in each of the 6 equal groups?* [4] Have students move 4 ones onto each sheet and record the 4 in the quotient as you record it at the board.

How many students are in each classroom? [144 students]

2 Guided Practice

Use with Exercises 1–17.

To help students complete the calculations, emphasize the four steps of the division algorithm: (1) Divide, (2) Multiply, (3) Subtract, and (4) Bring down.

Remind students that sometimes there are not enough hundreds to divide them into equal groups. In that case, they must regroup the hundreds as tens and the division process will begin with the tens rather than the hundreds. Some students may benefit from writing 0 in the hundreds place of the quotient before they regroup and divide.

Exercise 4

Error Intervention

If students do not understand why the 3 in the quotient is written above the 2 and not above the 3,

then ask: *Were there enough hundreds to divide into 9 groups?* [No] *Were you able to divide the tens?* [Yes] *Then you need to record how many tens are in each group.*

ELL Use Vocabulary

To check understanding, ask a student to repeat and complete this sentence: *If there are not enough ________ when you are dividing a three-digit number, regroup and divide the _____* [Hundreds; tens].

Quick Check Formative Assessment

Find 426 ÷ 6. [71]

3 Independent Practice

Use with Exercises 18–25.

Provide students with extra copies of Division Templates (Teaching Tool 11) as needed. Alternatively, students may do their work on Centimeter Grid Paper (Teaching Tool 10) to help them keep the digits correctly aligned.

For Exercise 19, point out to students that a zero in the dividend does not change the steps in the division algorithm.

Step 2-4

One- and Two-Digit Quotients

Objective Students will divide a three-digit number by a two-digit divisor to find a one- or two-digit quotient.

Vocabulary Remainder

Materials Division Templates (Teaching Tool 11)

Professional Development

Math Background

- Dividing by two-digit divisors is just an extension of the steps for dividing by one-digit divisors.
- An estimate can help determine where to place the first digit in the quotient.

Name ______________________ Step 2-4

One- and Two-Digit Quotients

Joel wants to buy a camera which costs $985. With his part-time job, he can save $46 a week. How many weeks does he need to save to have enough money to buy the camera?

Find 985 ÷ 46 by answering 1 to 11.

1. Begin by estimating the quotient.
1,000 ÷ 50 = **20**

Since the estimate has two digits, begin by dividing the tens.

2. Write the first digit of the estimate in the tens place of the quotient.

3. What is 46 × 2 tens? **92** tens
Write the product below the 98.

4. What is 98 tens − 92 tens? **6** tens
Write the difference below the 92 and the line.

$46\overline{)985}$: quotient **2**; below: **9 2**; **6**

5. Bring down the ones. Regroup to show the total ones.
6 tens and 5 ones = **65** ones

6. How many groups of 46 are there in 65? **1**
Write this number in the ones place of the quotient.

7. What is 46 × 1? **46** Write the product below the 65.

8. What is 65 − 46? **19**
Write the difference below the 46 and the line.

$46\overline{)985}$: quotient 2 **1**; below: 9 2; 6 **5**; **4 6**; **1 9**

9. Compare the remainder to the divisor. Write > or <.
19 (<) 46

Since the remainder is less than the divisor, the division is finished.

10. 985 ÷ 46 = **21** R **19**

11. Reasoning How many weeks does Joel need to save to have enough money to buy the camera? Explain.
Joel needs to save 21 weeks and part of another week. After 22 weeks, he will have enough money.

18 One and Two-Digit Quotients

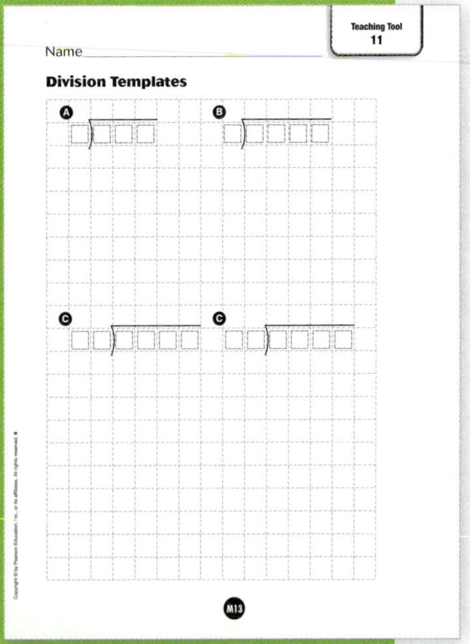

1 Concept Development

Interactive Learning

Use with Teaching Tool 11.

Purpose

You have learned how to divide three-digit numbers. Today you will learn how to find the quotient when you divide by a two-digit divisor.

Pose the Problem

A carpenter cut a board that is 189 inches long. He cut pieces 15 inches long. How many pieces did he cut? Allow time for students to estimate the answer and share their ideas.

Model

Distribute copies of Division Templates (Teaching Tool 11). Write $15\overline{)189}$ on the board. *Write this division problem in the "C" chart. An estimate can help you decide where to place the first digit of the quotient. How can you estimate the answer?* [Sample answer: Use compatible numbers; 200 ÷ 20 = 10 pieces] *So, it looks like the quotient will have 2 digits. Write the first digit of the estimate in the tens place of the quotient.* At the board, write a 1 above the 8 in the dividend.

Name ______________________________

One- and Two-Digit Quotients (continued)

Find 348 ÷ 49 by answering 12 to 17.

12. Begin by estimating the quotient: 350 ÷ 50 = __7__

Since the estimate has one digit, begin by dividing the ones.

13. Write the estimate in the ones place of the quotient.

14. What is 49 × 7? __343__
Write the product below the 348.

15. What is 348 − 343? __5__
Write the difference below the 343 and the line.

$$\begin{array}{r} 7 \\ 49\overline{)348} \\ 343 \\ \hline 5 \end{array}$$

16. Compare the remainder to the divisor. Write > or <.

5 (<) 49

Since the remainder is less than the divisor, the division is finished.

17. 348 ÷ 49 = __7__ R __5__

Divide.

18. 46)254 — 5 R24 **19.** 29)105 — 3 R18 **20.** 57)629 — 11 R2

21. 38)812 — 21 R14 **22.** 21)712 — 33 R19 **23.** 26)985 — 37 R23

24. 13)234 — 18 **25.** 24)195 — 8 R3 **26.** 33)471 — 14 R9

27. Records indicate that 726 people participated in the Greenview City guided tours in May. There were 33 guided tours and each tour had the same number of people. How many people were on each tour? __22__

28. Reasoning Is 23 R28 a reasonable answer for the problem 511 ÷ 21? Why or why not?
No, the remainder is greater than the divisor.

Multiply 15 × 1 ten and compare the product to the dividend. How does it compare? [The product, 15 tens, is less than the dividend, 189.] Explain that if the product was greater than the dividend, then the estimate was too high. On the board, write 15 under the 18, subtract to get 3 tens, and bring down the 9 ones.

There are 3 tens and 9 ones. That's 39 ones. Now you need to divide the ones: 39 ÷ 15. Guide students as they repeat the division process to find the second digit of the quotient.

What is the remainder? [9] *Is the remainder less than the divisor?* [Yes] *The division is finished. 189 ÷ 15 = 12 R9. How many 15-inch pieces did the carpenter cut?* [12] *Explain.* [The carpenter cut 12 pieces with 9 inches left over.]

2 Guided Practice

Use with Exercises 1–11.

Remind students that estimating helps determine the place of the first digit of the quotient and check the reasonableness of their answer.

Exercise 1

Error Intervention

If students have difficulty estimating the quotient,

then remind them to round the divisor to the nearest ten, and then use compatible numbers to estimate the quotient.

ELL Use Vocabulary

To check understanding, ask a student to repeat and complete this sentence: *The ____ is the number that is left over after the division is complete.* [Remainder]

Quick Check Formative Assessment

Find 429 ÷ 37. [11 R22]

3 Independent Practice

Use with Exercises 12–28.

Provide extra copies of Division Templates (Teaching Tool 11) as needed. Alternatively, students may do their work on grid paper (Teaching Tool 10) to help them keep the digits correctly aligned.

Exercise 24
Point out to students that if the dividend is a multiple of the divisor, the quotient is the exact number of equal groups with none left. The "R0" does not need to be written.

For Exercise 28, remind students that the remainder should have a value that is less than the divisor.

Step 2-5

Multiplying with Decimals and Whole Numbers

Objective Students will find the product of a decimal and a whole number.

Vocabulary Decimal point, decimal places

Materials Addition/Subtraction Templates (Teaching Tool 9), place-value blocks

Math Background

- Multiplication of whole numbers and decimals is similar to multiplication of two whole numbers.
- The number of decimal places in the product is equal to the sum of the number of decimal places in each factor.

Name ______________ Teaching Tool 9

Addition/Subtraction Templates

A

Tens	Ones

A

Tens	Ones

A

Tens	Ones

B

Tens	Ones	.	Tenths	Hundredths

B

Tens	Ones	.	Tenths	Hundredths

C

Hundreds	Tens	Ones	.	Tenths	Hundredths	Thousandths

C

Hundreds	Tens	Ones	.	Tenths	Hundredths	Thousandths

M11

Name ______________ Step 2-5

Multiplying with Decimals and Whole Numbers

A bottle of water costs $0.63. What is the cost of four bottles?

Find 4 × 0.63 by answering 1 to 10.

Let the block at the right represent one unit, or 1.0.

So, [rod] represents one tenth, or 0.1 and [cube] represents one hundredth or 0.01.

1. Show four groups of 0.63 using place-value blocks.

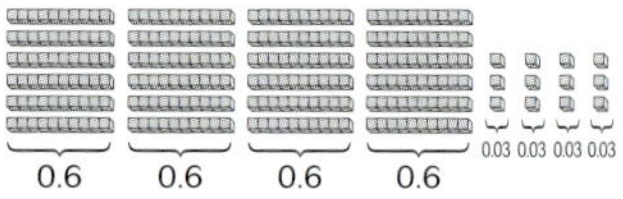

2. Multiply the hundredths.

4 × 3 hundredths = 12 hundredths

3. Trade 10 hundredths for 1 tenth.

12 hundredths = 1 tenth

and 2 hundredths

Record the 2 in the answer and write the 1 above the 6 tenths to show the regrouping.

$$\begin{array}{r} {}^{2}{}^{1} \\ 0.63 \\ \times\ 4 \\ \hline 2.52 \end{array}$$

0.63 ← 2 decimal places
× 4 ← 0 decimal places
2.52 ← 2 decimal places

4. Multiply the tenths. 4 × 6 tenths = 24 tenths

5. Add the regrouped tenth. 24 tenths + 1 tenth = 25 tenths

6. Trade groups of 10 tenths for 1 one.
25 tenths = 2 ones and 5 tenths

Record the 5 in the answer and write the 2 above the 0 to show the regrouping.

1 Concept Development

Interactive Learning

Use with Teaching Tool 9.

Purpose

You have learned how to multiply whole numbers. Today you will learn how to multiply a decimal and a whole number.

Pose the Problem

Marie bought 3 packages of beads. Each package was on sale for $0.59. How much did Marie pay for the packages of beads? Have students share their ideas before modeling the solution. They should recognize that this is a multiplication problem.

Model

Distribute the Addition/Subtraction Templates (Teaching Tool 9). Write 3 × 0.59 vertically on the board and show 3 groups of 0.59 with the place-value blocks. *Multiplying with a decimal is similar to multiplying whole numbers. What do you do first?*

Name ______________________

Step 2-5

Multiplying with Decimals and Whole Numbers (continued)

7. Multiply the ones. 4×0 ones = 0 ones

8. Add the regrouped ones. 0 ones + 2 ones = 2 ones

Record the 2 in the answer.

9. What is 4×0.63? 2.52

10. What is the cost of four bottles? $2.52

11. How many decimal places are there in 0.63? 2

12. How many decimal places are there in 4? 0

13. How many decimal places are there in both factors combined? 2

14. How many decimal places are in the product $0.63 \times 4 = 2.52$? 2

The total number of decimal places in the factors always equals the number of decimal places in the product.

15. Reasoning If $3 \times 56 = 168$, what is 3×0.56? Explain.

1.68; 3×0.56 has two decimal places.

Find each product.

16. 3.8×7 = 26.6

17. 23×1.5 = 34.5

18. 21.3×4 = 85.2

19. 8.17×6 = 49.02

20. Randy bought 6 erasers that cost $0.33 each. How much did he pay for them? $1.98

21. A small bottle of lotion holds 0.4 ounce. How many ounces would 12 of these bottles hold? 4.8 ounces

[Multiply each digit in 0.59 by 3 from right to left.] *Look at the hundredths blocks. How many hundredths are in 3×0.09?* [27 hundredths] *Trade groups of 10 hundredths for 1 tenth. So, 27 hundredths is equal to 2 tenths and 7 hundredths.* Record the 7 at the bottom of the hundredths column and the 2 at the top of the tenths column. *Look at the tenths blocks.* Continue to model how to multiply the tenths and the ones. *What do you get after you multiply each digit?* [177]

Place a decimal point in the product to get the correct answer. How many decimal places are in the first factor? [2] *How many decimal places are in the second factor?* [0] *Add the number of decimal places in each factor to find the number of decimal places in the product. How many decimal places are there in all?* [2] Have students demonstrate how to place the decimal point in the product. *How much did Marie pay for the packages of beads?* [$1.77]

2 Guided Practice

Use with Exercises 1–14.

Allow students to use place-value blocks as needed to help with regrouping.

Remind students to add the number of decimal places in both factors to correctly place the decimal point in the product.

Exercises 1–10
Why does multiplication begin with the hundredths place instead of the ones place? [You multiply from right to left.]

Exercises 11, 12
Error Intervention

If students have difficulty counting the number of decimal places in each factor,

then remind them to count from the place that is farthest right.

ELL Use Vocabulary

To check understanding, ask a student to repeat and complete this sentence: *There are three _____ in the number 23.985.* [Decimal places]

Quick Check — Formative Assessment

Find the product: 1.26×7. [8.82]

3 Independent Practice

Use with Exercises 15–21.

Encourage students to cross out the regrouped numbers when they are added. Have students check their work to see that all of the regrouped numbers have been crossed out.

For Exercise 17, explain to students that having the decimal as the multiplier does not change the way to find the product. Since they will need to record partial products on more than one row, you may want to have students use Teaching Tool 4, Multiplication Charts, or Teaching Tool 10, Centimeter Grid Paper.

Step **2-6**

Dividing with Decimals and Whole Numbers

Objective Students will divide a decimal by a whole number.

Vocabulary Decimal point, tenths, hundredths

Materials Division Templates (Teaching Tool 11), place-value blocks

Professional Development

Math Background

- Division of a decimal by a whole number uses the same steps as division of whole numbers.
- When the divisor is a whole number, the decimal point in the quotient is placed directly above the decimal point in the dividend.

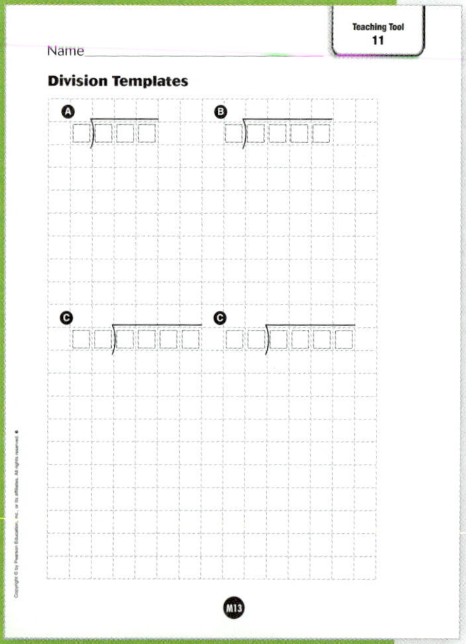

Name ______________________ Step **2-6**

Dividing with Decimals and Whole Numbers

Roben has 3.56 feet of wrapping paper to wrap 2 identical boxes. If he cuts the paper into 2 equal pieces, how long is each piece?

Find 3.56 ÷ 2 by answering 1 to 20 and completing the division problem below.

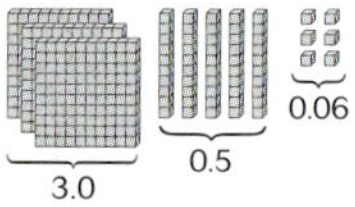

1. Use place-value blocks to show 3.56.
2. Divide the 3 ones into 2 equal groups.
3. How many ones are in each group? __1__
4. Write the 1 above the 3 in 3.56, at the right.
5. How many ones were used? __2__ ones
6. Write the 2 below the 3 in 3.56, at the right.
7. How many ones are leftover? 3 − 2 = __1__ one
8. Write the 1 below the 2 and the line.
9. Regroup the one into tenths and add the 5 tenths from the dividend.
   __1__ one + 5 tenths = __15__ tenths
10. Bring down the 5 next to the 1, to show the 15 tenths.
11. Divide the 15 tenths into 2 groups. How many tenths are in each group? __7__
12. Write the 7 above the 5 in 3.56.
13. How many tenths were used? 7 × 2 tenths = __14__ tenths
14. Write the 14 below the 15. Subtract to find how many tenths are left. How many tenths are left? __1__ tenth

```
   1.78
2)3.56
  2       ← 2 × 1
  15
  14      ← 2 × 7
   16
   16     ← 2 × 8
    0
```

Interactive Learning **1**

Concept Development

Use with Teaching Tool 11.

Purpose

You have learned how to divide whole numbers. Today you will learn how to divide a decimal by a whole number.

Pose the Problem

A fruit market had a sale on grapes. Joy bought 3 pounds of grapes and spent $4.65. What was the price per pound of the grapes? Allow time for students to solve and share their ideas.

Model

Distribute copies of Division Templates (Teaching Tool 11). Explain to students that the grid lines will help keep each place value aligned correctly. ***How much did Joy spend?*** [$4.65] Show 4 ones, 6 tenths, and 5 hundredths with the place-value blocks. ***To find the price per pound of the grapes, you can divide.*** Write 3)$4.65 on the board.

Name ______________________ Step 2-6

Dividing with Decimals and Whole Numbers (continued)

15. Regroup the leftover tenth into hundredths and add the 6 hundredths from the dividend.

__1__ tenth + 6 hundredths = __16__ hundredths

16. Bring down the 6 next to the 1, to show the 16 hundredths. Divide the 16 hundredths into 2 groups. How many hundredths are in each group? __8__

17. Write the 8 above the 6 in 3.56.

18. How many hundredths were used? 2 × 8 hundredths = __16__ hundredths

How many hundredths are left? __0__ hundredths

19. What is 3.56 ÷ 2? __1.78__

20. How long is each piece of Roben's wrapping paper? __1.78 feet__

21. **Reasoning** Where is the decimal point placed in the quotient when a decimal is divided by a whole number?

The decimal point is placed above the decimal point in the dividend.

Find each quotient.

22. 4)24.08 — 6.02
23. 8)26.16 — 3.27
24. 5)36.05 — 7.21
25. 6)35.22 — 5.87

26. 9)7.47 — 0.83
27. 5)57.85 — 11.57
28. 3)38.61 — 12.87
29. 4)38.88 — 9.72

30. Four friends are equally dividing a bill for $49.88. How much will each person pay? __$12.47__

Dividing with Decimals and Whole Numbers **23**

Have students write the problem in the "B" chart and record the calculations as you model the division. *When the divisor is a whole number, dividing a decimal is similar to dividing a whole number. First, place a decimal point in the quotient directly above the decimal point in the dividend.* Explain to students that they can avoid forgetting the decimal point in the quotient by placing it before they divide.

Use the blocks to show how to divide 4 ones into 3 groups. How many ones go in each group? [1] Record the 1 in the ones place of the quotient and the product 3 below the 4. *Are there any ones left? How many?* [Yes; 1 one is left.] Record the 1. *What do you do next?* [Bring down the 6 tenths, regroup the 1 one into 10 tenths, and add them to the 6 tenths.] *How many tenths go in each group?* [5] Continue using the blocks to model how to divide the tenths and the hundredths.

What is the quotient? [1.55] *So, what is the price per pound of the grapes?* [$1.55]

2 Guided Practice

Use with Exercises 1–20.

Remind students that regrouping requires groups of 10.

Exercise 20
Error Intervention

If students forget to place the decimal point in the quotient,

then encourage them to write the decimal point in the quotient before dividing.

ELL Use Vocabulary

To check understanding, ask a student to repeat and complete this sentence: *In the number 6.3, the____ separates the ones and tenths.* [Decimal point]

Quick Check Formative Assessment

Find the quotient: 56.28 ÷ 6 [9.38]

3 Independent Practice

Use with Exercises 21–30.

Provide extra copies of Division Templates (Teaching Tool 11) as needed. Assist students in recording each digit in the appropriate column to find the quotient.

For Exercise 22, remind students to write a 0 in the quotient when there are not enough to divide into equal groups.

Input/Output Tables

Objective Students will complete tables and write rules to show how pairs of numbers are related.

Vocabulary Input, output

Materials Function Tables (Teaching Tool 13)

Math Background

Professional Development

- The relationships between some pairs of real-world quantities represent functions.
- The value of one quantity can be found if you know the value of the other quantity and a rule that relates them.

Name ______________________ Step 3-1

Input/Output Tables

1. There are 5 pennies in a nickel. In the table below, draw two sets of 5 pennies next to the row with 2 nickels.

Nickels	Pennies
1	5
2	10
3	15
4	20
5	25
7	35
8	40

2. How many pennies equal 2 nickels? Write your answer in the table.
3. Complete the table. Draw pennies, if necessary.
4. What is a rule for the table? Multiply the number of nickels by 5.
5. **Reasoning** How can you find the number of pennies in 9 nickels? Multiply 9 by 5.
6. How many pennies are in 9 nickels? 45
7. How many pennies are in 10 nickels? 50

24 Input/Output Tables

Name ______________________ Teaching Tool 13

Function Tables

Rule: ____________

Rule: ____________

Rule: ____________

Rule: ____________

M15

Interactive Learning 1 Concept Development

Use with Teaching Tool 13.

Purpose

You have added, subtracted, multiplied, and divided pairs of numbers. Today you will use all four operations and tables to show how certain pairs of numbers are related.

Pose the Problem

A truck weighs 12 tons when it is empty. What is the total weight of the truck and a 6-ton load of gravel? What if the gravel weighs 10 tons? 12 tons? 15 tons? 18 tons? Ask students to share their ideas and discuss an organized way to show the results.

Model

We can use a table to organize our work in this problem. Draw a blank, vertical function table on the board. Discuss how to record the information in the table. As you do so, label the top of the left column "Gravel Weight (tons)," and label the top of the right column "Total Weight (tons)." In the left column,

Name ______________________________ Step 3-1

Input/Output Tables (continued)

Complete the table. Write a rule. **Sample rules are given.**

8.

Number of Ants	Number of Legs
1	6
2	12
3	**18**
4	24
5	30

Rule: **Multiply Number of Ants by 6.**

9.

Regular Price	Sale Price
$5	$3
$7	$5
$8	$6
$12	$10
$17	$15

Rule: **Subtract $2 from Regular Price.**

10.

My Age	My Brother's Age
9	12
10	13
12	15
15	**18**
20	23

Rule: **Add 3 to My Age.**

11.

Number of Packages	Number of Pencils
1	8
3	24
5	40
6	**48**
8	64

Rule: **Multiply Number of Packages by 8.**

12.

Loaves of Bread	2	4	5	**7**	10
Number of Eggs Used	8	**16**	20	28	40

Rule: **Multiply Loaves by 4.**

13.

Total Weight of Suitcase and Contents in Pounds	5	7	9	**11**	14
Content of Suitcase in Pounds	3	**5**	7	9	12

Rule: **Subtract 2 pounds from Total Weight.**

write the weights of the gravel given in the problem. Distribute copies of Function Tables (Teaching Tool 13). Have students copy the table shown on the board.

What is the total weight of the truck and the 6-ton load of gravel? [18 tons] *How do you know?* [12 + 6 = 18.] *Write 18 in the right column in the same row as the 6.*

What is the total weight of the truck and the 10-ton load of gravel? [22 tons] *How do you know?* [12 + 10 = 22.] Write 22 in the right column in the same row as the 10.

Have students complete the rest of the table. *What rule describes how you figured out the total weight each time?* [Add 12 to the weight of the gravel.] Have students write a rule for the table.

Each number you listed in the left column of the table is called an input number. After you apply a rule to that number, you get the output number, which you write in the right column. Suppose you wrote another input number, 8. What is the output number? [20]

2 Guided Practice

Use with Exercises 1–7.

Remind students that a rule for a table must work for every pair of input and output numbers.

Exercise 4
Error Intervention

If students have difficulty finding a rule for the table,

then have them write a number sentence to show how they completed each row of the table. For example, $2 \times 5 = 10$, $3 \times 5 = 15$, $4 \times 5 = 20$, and so on. *What do you notice that is the same in each number sentence?* [Each number sentence includes times 5.] *Then that's your rule: Multiply the input number by 5.*

ELL Use Vocabulary

To check understanding, ask a student to repeat and complete this sentence: *After you apply a rule to the input number, you get the _____ number.* [Output]

Quick Check Formative Assessment

The input column is labeled "Number of Nickels." The output column is labeled "Number of Pennies." If 20 is in the input number, what is the output number? [100]

3 Independent Practice

Use with Exercises 8–13.

Remind students that they should use the given input/output pairs to determine a rule. Then they should complete the table.

Explain that when the input numbers are missing, students need to use their rule and work backward from the output number to find the missing input number.

Exercises 12–13
Point out that in a horizontal table, the input numbers are in the top row, and the output numbers are in the bottom row.

Step 3-2

Expressions with Addition and Subtraction

Objective Students will complete tables and write addition and subtraction rules to show how pairs of numbers are related.

Vocabulary Variable, algebraic expression

Materials Function Tables (Teaching Tool 13)

Professional Development Math Background

- A variable is a symbol that stands for a number. One or more variables can be used in an algebraic expression or in a rule that shows how quantities are related.
- In an addition or subtraction pattern, the same number is added to or subtracted from the input number to produce the output number.

Name ____________ Teaching Tool 13

Function Tables

Rule: ____________

Rule: ____________

Rule: ____________

Rule: ____________

M15

Name ____________ Step 3-2

Expressions with Addition and Subtraction

1. Complete to find a pattern in the table.

Total Number of Students	Number of Students Going to Picnic
30	25
36	31
42	37
50	45
54	49

Think:
30 − 5 = 25
36 − 5 = 31
42 − 5 = 37
50 − 5 = 45

2. What is a rule for the table above, in words? Subtract 5 from the Total Number of Students.

3. Let *t* equal the total number of students. The rule, in symbols, for the table is $t - 5$. Use the rule to complete the table above.

4. Complete to find a pattern in the table.

Input	Output
12	14
15	17
18	20
22	24
26	28

Think:
12 + 2 = 14
15 + 2 = 17
22 + 2 = 24
26 + 2 = 28

5. What is the rule for the table, in words? Add 2 to the Input.

6. Let *b* equal the input. What is the rule for the table, in symbols? $b + 2$

7. Use the rule to complete the table.

26 Expressions with Addition and Subtraction

Interactive Learning 1 Concept Development

Use with Teaching Tool 13.

Purpose

You have used rules to describe how pairs of numbers are related. Today you will learn another way to write rules that involve addition and subtraction.

Pose the Problem

Write the following table on the board.

Class Size	Number of Pictures
22	24
25	27
26	28
28	30
31	33

This table shows how many pictures a photographer takes in each classroom on Picture Day. What is a rule for the table? Ask students to share their ideas.

Name

Step 3-2

Expressions with Addition and Subtraction (continued)

Find a rule for each table. Write the rule in symbols. Let *n* equal the input. Then use the rule to complete the table.

8.

Input	Output
27	24
20	17
18	15
12	9
9	6

$n - 3$

9.

Input	Output
7	15
10	18
11	19
15	23
18	26

$n + 8$

10.

Input	Output
7	5
9	7
15	13
16	14
20	18
25	23

$n - 2$

11.

Input	Output
3	20
5	22
7	24
12	29
25	42
32	49

$n + 17$

12. Reasoning How can you tell an addition pattern in an input/output table from a subtraction pattern?

The output values are greater than the input values for an addition pattern, but are less for a subtraction pattern.

Model

Distribute copies of Function Tables (Teaching Tool 13). Have students copy the table shown on the board. *How many pictures does the photographer take in a class of 22 students?* [24] *The input number is 22. What number sentence shows how to get the output number?* [22 + 2 = 24] *What are the number sentences for the other rows in the table?* [25 + 2 = 27; 26 + 2 = 28; 28 + 2 = 30; 31 + 2 = 33] Have students write each number sentence to the right of the corresponding row as you do the same at the board.

What is the rule for the table? [Add 2 to the class size.] *Another way to write this rule is to use a variable. A variable is a symbol that stands for a number. In each of your number sentences, circle the input number.* Do the same at the board. *I can use* n *to represent the input number.* Write *n* under the 31 in the last number sentence. *Then* n + 2 *shows how to get the output number.* Have students write *n* + 2 on the "Rule" line for the table. *n + 2 is an algebraic expression. It is a mathematical phrase that contains numbers or variables and at least one operation.*

2 Guided Practice

Use with Exercises 1–7.

Remind students that the variable in their rule represents the input number.

Exercise 6
Error Intervention

If students have difficulty using a variable to write the rule for the table,

then have them circle the input number in one of the number sentences in Exercise 4. *You are going to write* b *in place of the input number. Instead of 12 + 2, you write* b + 2. *This shows that you have to add 2 to the input number to get the output number.*

ELL Use Vocabulary

To check understanding, ask a student to repeat and complete this sentence: *A _____ is a symbol that stands for a number.* [Variable]

Quick Check Formative Assessment

Suppose a rule for a table is Subtract 8. How can you write that rule using the variable c? [c − 8]

3 Independent Practice

Use with Exercises 8–12.

Remind students that their rule should contain a variable and one operation. For some students, it might be a good idea to first write number sentences for the rows of the table. Other students might be able to give their rule in words and then give the rule as an algebraic expression.

Exercises 8–11
Suggest that students make sure that their rule works for every row of the table.

Step 3-3

Expressions with Multiplication and Division

Objective Students will complete tables and write multiplication and division rules to show how pairs of numbers are related.

Vocabulary Variable, algebraic expression

Materials Function Tables (Teaching Tool 13)

Professional Development

Math Background

- In a multiplication or division pattern, the input number is multiplied or divided by the same number to produce the output number.

Teaching Tool 13

Name ____________

Function Tables

Rule: ____________

Rule: ____________

Rule: ____________

Rule: ____________

M15

Step 3-3

Name ____________

Expressions with Multiplication and Division

1. Complete to find a pattern in the table.

Number of Kittens	Total Number of Paws
3	12
4	16
6	24
8	32
9	36

Think:

3 × 4 = 12

4 × 4 = 16

4 × 8 = 32

4 × 9 = 36

2. What is a rule for the table, in words? Multiply Number of Kittens by 4.

3. Let *k* equal the number of kittens. The rule, in symbols, for the table is 4 × *k*. Use the rule to complete the table.

4. Complete to find a pattern in the table.

Input	Output
6	2
9	3
15	5
18	6
24	8

Think:

6 ÷ 3 = 2

9 ÷ 3 = 3

15 ÷ 3 = 5

24 ÷ 3 = 8

5. What is the rule for the table, in words? Divide Input by 3.

6. Let *c* equal the input. What is the rule for the table, in symbols? $c \div 3$

7. Use the rule to complete the table.

28 Expressions with Multiplication and Division

Interactive Learning

1 Concept Development

Use with Teaching Tool 13.

Purpose

You have used addition and subtraction rules to describe how pairs of numbers are related. Today you will learn to write rules that involve multiplication and division.

Pose the Problem

Write the following table on the board.

Number of Markers	Number of Packages
12	2
18	3
24	4
42	7
54	9

What is a rule for this table? Ask students to share their ideas. They may recognize that this is not an addition or subtraction pattern.

Name ______________________

Step 3-3

Expressions with Multiplication and Division (continued)

Find a rule for each table. Write the rule in symbols. Let *n* equal the input. Then use the rule to complete the table.

8.

Input	Output
24	12
20	10
16	8
14	7
10	5

$n \div 2$

9.

Input	Output
2	8
4	16
5	20
7	28
9	36

$4 \times n$

10.

Input	Output
0	0
8	2
12	3
20	5
28	7
40	10

$n \div 4$

11.

Input	Output
0	0
1	9
4	36
5	45
7	63
10	90

$n \times 9$

12. **Reasoning** How can you tell an addition pattern in an input/output table from a multiplication pattern?

Sample Answer: In an addition pattern, the same number is added to each input number. In a multiplication pattern, the same number is multiplied by each input.

Model

Distribute copies of Function Tables (Teaching Tool 13). Have students copy the table shown on the board. *What are some number sentences that show how 12 and 2 are related?* [Sample answers: 12 − 10 = 2; 12 ÷ 6 = 2] *Does subtracting 10 work for the next row of the table?* [No] *Does dividing by 6 work for the next row of the table?* [Yes] *Does dividing by 6 work for the other rows of the table?* [Yes] Have students write the division sentences to the right of the corresponding rows as you do the same at the board.

What is the rule for the table? [Divide the number of markers by 6.] *In each of your number sentences, circle the input number.* Do the same at the board. *Let's use the variable* n *to represent the input number.* Write *n* below the 54 in the last number sentence. *Then* n ÷ 6 *shows how to get the output number.* Have students write *n* ÷ 6 on the Rule line for the table. *Remember,* n ÷ 6 *is an algebraic expression. It is a mathematical phrase that contains numbers or variables and at least one operation.*

2 Guided Practice

Use with Exercises 1–7.

Remind students that a variable represents a number. Its value can *vary*, or change, in different situations.

Exercise 6

Error Intervention

If students have difficulty using a variable to write the rule for the table,

then have them circle the input number in one of the number sentences in Exercise 4. *You are going to write* c *in place of the input number. Instead of 6 ÷ 3, you write* c *÷ 3. This shows that you divide the input number by 3 to get the output number.*

ELL Use Vocabulary

To check understanding, ask a student to repeat and complete this sentence: *An _____ is a mathematical phrase that contains numbers or variables and at least one operation.* [Algebraic expression]

Quick Check Formative Assessment

Using words, a rule for a table is Multiply by 7. How can you write that rule using the variable g*?* [$g \times 7$]

3 Independent Practice

Use with Exercises 8–12.

Remind students that their rule must work for every row of the table.

Exercises 8–11

Some students might find it helpful to begin by writing number sentences for each row of the table. Other students might be able to describe a rule in words and then write it as an algebraic expression.

Variables and Expressions

Objective Students will evaluate algebraic expressions using substitution.

Vocabulary Evaluate, substitute

Materials Function Tables (Teaching Tool 13)

Professional Development Math Background

- The value of an algebraic expression can be found by replacing the variable(s) with given number(s) and doing the calculation(s).

Name ____________________ Step 3-4

Variables and Expressions

1. Complete the table.

Number	Number + 5
2	2 + 5 = 7
8	8 + 5 = 13
10	10 + 5 = 15
15	15 + 5 = 20
21	21 + 5 = 26

You can use n for the number and $n + 5$ as the rule. The n is called a variable, because its value varies, or changes, to represent different numbers.

2. To find $n + 5$, when $n = 4$, substitute 4 for n and then add.

n + 5
↓
4 + 5 = 9

3. Find $3 \times n$, when $n = 7$.

$3 \times n$
↓
$3 \times$ 7 = 21

4. Find $30 - 6 + q$, when $q = 8$.

$30 - 6 + q$
↓
$30 - 6 +$ 8
= 24 + 8
= 32

30 Variables and Expressions

Name ____________________ Teaching Tool 13

Function Tables

Rule: ____________

Rule: ____________

Rule: ____________

Rule: ____________

M15

Interactive Learning 1 Concept Development

Use with Teaching Tool 13.

Purpose

You have learned how to use variables to write expressions. Today you will learn how to find the value of an expression containing a variable when you are given the value of the variable.

Pose the Problem

Write the following table on the board.

Number	Number × 3
2	6
4	12
5	
10	

The table shows the input numbers and a rule. How can you find the numbers that are missing in the second column? Ask students to share their ideas.

Name ______________________ Step 3-4

Variables and Expressions (continued)

Evaluate each expression for $b = 6$.

5. $b - 4$ 2 **6.** $3 + b$ 9 **7.** $8 - b$ 2 **8.** $13 + b - 1$ 18

Evaluate each expression for $c = 11$.

9. $c + 10$ 21 **10.** $14 - 5 + c$ 20 **11.** $11 - c$ 0 **12.** $15 - c$ 4

Evaluate each expression for $x = 3$.

13. $2x$ 6 **14.** $\frac{x}{6}$ $\frac{1}{2}$ **15.** $7x$ 21 **16.** $\frac{18}{x}$ 6

Complete each table.

17.

x	$x - 4$
4	0
9	5
15	11
21	17

18.

n	$7 + n$
6	13
15	22
20	27
50	57

19.

x	$5x$
3	15
7	35
12	60
20	100

20.

y	$\frac{56}{y}$
2	28
7	8
14	4
56	1

21. Jeff is three years younger than Steve. Complete the table to show Jeff's age.

Steve's age	n	10	15	21	35
Jeff's age	$n - 3$	7	12	18	32

22. Reasoning Using the table in Exercise 21, if Jeff is 45, how old is Steve? 48 years old

Model

Distribute copies of Function Tables (Teaching Tool 13). Have students copy and complete the table shown on the board. Be sure that students complete the table correctly.

How do you write the rule for the table using the variable n? [$n \times 3$] *Each time you found the output number you were finding the value of the expression n × 3. When you evaluate an expression, you substitute a number for the variable and then do the calculations.*

You can also evaluate expressions that are not in a table. Suppose you need to evaluate the expression k + 7 when k is equal to 6. Here's how to show your work. Write the following on the board as you explain the steps.

$k + 7$

↓

$6 + 7 = 13$

When k = 6, the value of the expression is 13.

2 Guided Practice

Use with Exercises 1–4.

Remind students that to evaluate an expression, they should substitute the value they are given for the variable.

Exercise 4
Error Intervention

If students have difficulty evaluating the expression,

then remind them that a variable stands for a number. *In this problem, what value should you use for q?* [8] *Write the 8 under the arrow. Then compute 30 − 6 + 8.* Point out that they should do the subtraction first in this problem.

ELL Use Vocabulary

To check understanding, ask a student to repeat and complete this sentence: *To find the value of an expression, you _____ a number for the variable and then do the calculations.* [Substitute]

Quick Check Formative Assessment

What is the value of h − 10 when h = 24? [14]

3 Independent Practice

Use with Exercises 5–22.

Remind students to rewrite the expression, replacing the variable with the given value for the variable. Then they should perform the calculation(s).

Exercises 8, 10
For expressions with addition and subtraction, remind students to compute from left to right.

Exercise 14
After students replace the variable in the numerator of the fraction, they should simplify the fraction.

Exercises 16, 20
Students will get an improper fraction after they substitute the given number for the variable in each problem. Remind students of the meaning of a fraction. The fraction bar indicates division, so they should divide to rewrite each of these improper fractions as a whole number.

Step **4-1**

Expressions with Parentheses

Objective Students will evaluate numerical expressions that contain parentheses.

Vocabulary Parentheses, group

Professional Development

Math Background

- A numerical expression is a mathematical phrase that contains numbers and at least one operation.
- To evaluate a numerical expression that contains parentheses, do the calculation in the parentheses first.

Name ______________________ Step **4-1**

Expressions with Parentheses

The pet store had 12 angel fish. Ava bought 4 and her sister, Salma, bought 3. How many angel fish did the store have left after the sisters bought their fish?

1. Fill in the blanks to solve the problem one way.

(number of fish Ava bought; number of fish left after Ava; number of fish left after Ava; number of fish Salma bought; number of fish left)

12 − __4__ = __8__   __8__ − 3 = __5__

2. Fill in the blanks to solve the problem another way.

(number of fish Ava bought; number of fish Salma bought; number of fish sisters bought; number of fish left)

12 − (__4__ + __3__) = 12 − __7__ = __5__

3. The store had __5__ fish left after the sisters bought their fish.

To find the value of an expression, do what is in parentheses first.

4. (15 − 10) − 2 = __5__ − 2 = __3__

5. 15 − (10 − 2) = 15 − __8__ = __7__

6. Where would you place the parentheses to make the number sentence below true? Use your answers to 4 and 5 above to help.

15 − (10 − 2) = 7

Interactive Learning

1 Concept Development

Use with Exercises 1–3.

Purpose

You know how to add, subtract, multiply, and divide. Today you will learn how to evaluate a numerical expression that contains more than one operation.

Pose the Problem

The pet store had 12 angel fish. Ava bought 4, and her sister, Salma, bought 3. How many angel fish did the store have left after the sisters bought their fish? Ask students to share their ideas. Students should recognize that more than one operation is needed to solve the problem.

Model

After Ava bought her fish, how many did the pet store have left? [8] ***How do you know?*** [12 − 4 = 8] ***Then Salma bought some fish. How many were left?*** [5] ***How did you figure that out?*** [8 − 3 = 5] Have students complete Exercise 1.

Name ______________________

Step 4-1

Expressions with Parentheses (continued)

Find the value of each expression.

7. 10 − (4 + 2) 4

8. 6 + (12 − 4) 14

9. (5 + 5) − 5 5

10. (13 + 12) + 10 35

11. (15 − 5) + 8 18

12. 14 − (9 − 5) 10

13. 12 − (10 − 8) 10

14. 18 − (12 + 5) 1

15. (10 − 6) − (3 − 1) 2

16. (12 − 6) + (30 − 15) 21

17. (12 + 8) + (15 + 5) 40

18. (18 + 12) − (7 + 13) 10

Circle the number sentence that is true.

19. (16 − 7) + 6 = 3 OR (16 − (7 + 6) = 3)

20. ((20 − 8) − 5 = 7) OR 20 − (8 − 5) = 7

21. (100 − 50) + 15 = 35 OR (100 − (50 + 15) = 35)

Place parentheses to make the number sentence true.

22. 32 − (18 − 6) = 20

23. 20 − (6 + 8) = 6

24. 75 − (25 + 25) = 25

25. (30 − 27) − 2 = 1

26. (24 − 4) + 19 = 39

27. 15 − (4 + 8) = 3

28. Reasoning Carlos had $15 before he spent $4 on lunch and $5 on a kite.

Write an expression with parentheses. 15 − (4 + 5)

Use the expression to find how much money Carlos had left. Carlos had $6 left.

There's a different way to solve the problem. How many fish in all did the sisters buy? [7] *How did you figure that out?* [4 + 3 = 7] *After they bought the fish, how many did the pet store have left?* [5] *Explain how you got that answer.* [12 − 7 = 5]

In the second solution, you began by adding the number of fish the sisters bought. Then you subtracted that total from the number of fish the pet store started with. We can show that all in one numerical expression. Write 12 − (4 + 3) on the board. *The parentheses tell you how to group the numbers. The 4 and the 3 are grouped together. The sum 4 + 3 needs to be figured out first.*

When there are parentheses in a numerical expression, complete the operation inside the parentheses first. Then do the other operation. Show the following on the board as students complete Exercises 2 and 3.

12 − (4 + 3) = 12 − 7 = 5

2 Guided Practice

Use with Exercises 4–6.

Remind students that they should do the operation inside the parentheses first.

Exercises 4 and 5
Be sure to point out that even though these exercises have the same numbers and subtraction signs, they have different answers. The way the parentheses group the numbers affects the final answer.

Exercise 6
Error Intervention

If students have trouble deciding where to put the parentheses,

then have them try both possibilities. *Suppose you put the parentheses around 15 − 10. What is the value of the expression in parentheses?* [5] *What is the value of the left side of the equation?* [3] *If you put the parentheses around 10 − 2, what is the value of the expression in parentheses?* [8] *What is the value of the left side of the equation?* [7]

ELL Use Vocabulary

To check understanding, ask a student to repeat and complete this sentence: *To find the value of a numerical expression, first do the operation inside the _____.* [Parentheses]

Quick Check Formative Assessment

What is the value of 22 − (3 + 7)? [12]

3 Independent Practice

Use with Exercises 7–28.

Remind students that the parentheses tell them where to begin.

Exercises 15–18
Explain that when there are two pairs of parentheses, students should first do the operation inside the parentheses on the left, then do the operation inside the parentheses on the right, and finish by doing the remaining operation.

Step **4-3**

Properties of Operations

Objective Students will identify properties of operations and use them to give missing numbers in equations.

Vocabulary Commutative Property of Addition, Associative Property of Addition, Identity Property of Addition, Commutative Property of Multiplication, Associative Property of Multiplication, Identity Property of Multiplication, Zero Property of Multiplication

Math Background

- Two numbers can be added or multiplied in any order.
- Three addends or factors can be grouped in any order.
- You can add 0 to any number, or multiply it by 1, and the result is that number.
- The product of zero and any number is zero.

Name ______________________ Step **4-3**

Properties of Operations

1. Fill in the blanks to complete the table and summarize the properties of addition and multiplication.

Property	Example	Generalization for Any Numbers *a*, *b*, and *c*
Commutative Property of Addition	12 + 4 = 4 + __12__	*a* + *b* = *b* + __*a*__
Associative Property of Addition	(7 + 3) + 8 = 7 + (3 + __8__) __10__ + 8 = 7 + __11__	(*a* + *b*) + *c* = *a* + (*b* + __*c*__)
Identity Property of Addition	5 + 0 = __5__ 0 + 71 = __71__	*a* + 0 = __*a*__ and 0 + *a* = __*a*__
Commutative Property of Multiplication	5 × 8 = 8 × __5__	*a* × *b* = *b* × __*a*__
Associative Property of Multiplication	(6 × 2) × 4 = 6 × (__2__ × 4) __12__ × 4 = 6 × __8__	(*a* × *b*) × *c* = *a* × (*b* × __*c*__)
Identity Property of Multiplication	17 × 1 = __17__ 1 × 6 = __6__	*a* × 1 = __*a*__ and 1 × *a* = __*a*__
Zero Property of Multiplication	34 × 0 = __0__ 0 × 98 = __0__	*a* × 0 = __0__ and 0 × *a* = __0__

2. Tell which property is used.

(5 × 7) × 20 = (7 × 5) × 20

__Commutative__ Property of __Multiplication__

(7 × 5) × 20 = 7 × (5 × 20)

__Associative__ Property of __Multiplication__

36 Properties of Operations

Interactive Learning 1

Concept Development

Use with Exercise 1.

Purpose

You have learned how to write and evaluate numerical expressions. Today you will use properties of numbers to write equivalent expressions.

Pose the Problem

When you add two numbers, can you switch the order of the addends? Does it always work? Ask students to share their ideas and give examples.

Model

Mathematical properties are true for all numbers. You can use properties to write equivalent expressions. The Commutative Property of Addition states that the order in which any numbers are added does not change the sum. Start with the expression 12 + 4. If you switch the order of the addends, what is the new expression? [4 + 12] *Are the two expressions equivalent?* [Yes] *How do you know?* [Sample answer: They are both equal to 16.] Help students find the missing numbers and variables in Exercise 1 as you explain each property in words.

Name ______________________

Step **4-3**

Properties of Operations (continued)

Find each n. Name the property that you used.

3. $3 \times 6 = 6 \times n$
$n = 3$, Commutative Property of Multiplication

4. $n \times 5 = 0$
$n = 0$, Zero Property of Multiplication

5. $365 \times n = 365$
$n = 1$, Identity Property of Multiplication

6. $(3 \times 2) \times n = 3 \times (2 \times 10)$
$n = 10$, Associative Property of Multiplication

7. $5 \times 6 \times 4 \times 0 = n$
$n = 0$, Zero Property of Multiplication

8. $n + 45 = 45$
$n = 0$, Identity Property of Addition

9. $17 + 62 = 62 + n$
$n = 17$, Commutative Property of Addition

10. $21 + (n + 14) = (21 + 50) + 14$
$n = 50$, Associative Property of Addition

11. $3 \times (14 - 14) = n$
$n = 0$, Zero Property of Multiplication

12. $6 + (9 - n) = 6$
$n = 9$, Identity Property of Addition

13. **Reasoning** Katie says she is thinking of two numbers whose product is 0. John claims that he knows one number for certain. Is he right? How does he know?

Yes, the number zero; Zero Property of Multiplication

Use the Properties of Operations to Complete.

14. $10 + \underline{0} = 10$

15. $(10 \times 6) \times 2 = \underline{10} \times (6 \times 2)$

16. $(8 + 2) + 6 = (2 + \underline{8}) + 6$

17. $14 + 16 = \underline{16} + 14$

18. $c \times d = d \times \underline{c}$

19. $(q \times r) \times s = q \times (\underline{r} \times s)$

The Associative Property of Addition states that the way addends are grouped does not change the sum.

The Identity Property of Addition states that the sum of any number and zero is that number.

The Commutative Property of Multiplication states that the order in which factors are multiplied does not change the product.

The Associative Property of Multiplication states that the way factors are grouped does not change the product.

The Identity Property of Multiplication states that the product of any number and one is that number.

The Zero Property of Multiplication states that the product of any number and zero is zero.

2 Guided Practice

Use with Exercises 2–13.

Remind students that the Commutative Properties involve the *order* of the numbers being added or multiplied, while the Associative Properties involve the *grouping* of the numbers being added or multiplied.

Exercises 4 and 8
Error Intervention

If students confuse the Identity Property of Addition and the Zero Property of Multiplication,

then say: *Adding zero and multiplying by zero give completely different results.* Give examples to illustrate that adding zero does not change the value of a number, but multiplying by zero always gives a product of zero.

ELL Use Vocabulary

To check understanding, ask a student to repeat and complete this sentence: *The _____ Property of Multiplication states that the product of any number and 1 is always that number.* [Identity]

Quick Check Formative Assessment

Find the value of n and name the property that you used.
$13 \times (n \times 8) = (13 \times 5) \times 8$
[5; Associative Property of Multiplication]

3 Independent Practice

Use with Exercises 14–19.

Remind students to refer to the seven properties given in Exercise 1. You might want to suggest verbal clues to help students remember the names. For example, the Identity Properties produce the *identical* number. The Associative Properties change which group the middle number *associates* with.

Step **4-4**

More Variables and Expressions

Objective Students will identify properties of operations and use them to give missing numbers in equations.

Vocabulary Algebraic expression, order of operations

Math Background

- An algebraic expression is a mathematical phrase that contains variables and at least one operation.
- The value of an algebraic expression can be found by replacing the variables with given numbers and doing the calculations following the order of operations.

Name ______________________ Step **4-4**

More Variables and Expressions

To evaluate an expression, substitute the known value for the variable. Then use the order of operations to simplify.

1. Find $3n - 5$, when $n = 7$.

$3 \times$ <u>7</u> $- 5$	Put 7 in place of *n*.
$=$ <u>21</u> $- 5$	Use the order of operations, multiply first.
$=$ <u>16</u>	Subtract.

2. Find $3k - \frac{k}{4}$, when $k = 8$.

$3 \times$ <u>8</u> $- \frac{8}{4}$	Put 8 in place of *k*.
$=$ <u>24</u> $-$ <u>2</u>	Multiply and divide first.
$=$ <u>22</u>	Subtract.

3. Find $4y + 2z$, when $y = 5$ and $z = 7$.

$4 \times$ <u>5</u> $+ 2 \times$ <u>7</u>	Put 5 in place of *y* and 7 in place of *z*.
$=$ <u>20</u> $+$ <u>14</u>	Multiply first.
$=$ <u>34</u>	Add.

4. Find $(3a - b) \div c$, when $a = 10$, $b = 6$, and $c = 2$.

$(3 \times$ <u>10</u> $-$ <u>6</u> $) \div$ <u>2</u>	Put 10 in place of *a*, 6 in place of *b*, and 2 in place of *c*.
$= ($ <u>30</u> $-$ <u>6</u> $) \div$ <u>2</u>	Use the order of operations, do parentheses first. Inside the parentheses, multiply first.
$=$ <u>24</u> $\div$ <u>2</u>	Subtract inside the parentheses.
$=$ <u>12</u>	Divide.

Interactive Learning

1 Concept Development

Use with Exercises 1–4.

Purpose

You have learned how to find the value of an expression containing a variable when you are given the value of the variable. Today you will evaluate expressions that have more than one operation. Some have more than one variable.

Pose the Problem

Harriet bought fabric that cost $3 per yard. She had a coupon for $5 off her total purchase. What did she pay, before tax, for 7 yards of fabric? Ask students to discuss their ideas.

Model

An algebraic expression can be used to represent this situation. Let n *stand for the number of yards Harriet bought. You have to multiply 3 by the number of yards. Why?* [Each yard cost $3.] Write $3 \times n$ on the board. *How much does she save with her coupon?* [$5] So subtract 5. Revise the expression on the board to show $3 \times n - 5$.

Name ______________________________ Step 4-4

More Variables and Expressions (continued)

Evaluate each expression for $x = 3$.

5. $\left(\frac{x}{3}\right) + 15$ **16**

6. $24 - (2x)$ **18**

7. $(3x) + 5$ **14**

8. $(4x) - 12$ **0**

9. $(5x) - \left(\frac{15}{x}\right)$ **10**

10. $35 + \left(\frac{21}{x}\right)$ **42**

11. $(19 + x) \div 11$ **2**

12. $(6x) + x - 12$ **9**

13. $5x \div 3$ **5**

Evaluate each expression for $a = 9$, $b = 2$, and $c = 0$.

14. $(a + 7b) + c$ **23**

15. $13c + a$ **9**

16. $(a + b) \times 3$ **33**

17. $12b - 14c$ **24**

18. $(a + b + c) \times 2$ **22**

19. $(11 + a) \div b$ **10**

20. $c \times (b + c)$ **0**

21. $4a - 5b$ **26**

22. $(a - b - c) \times 4$ **28**

23. $7b - 12c$ **14**

24. $(2a + b) \div 5$ **4**

25. $a \times (b - c)$ **18**

Use the data at the right to answer Exercises 26–28.

Veggie Pizza House		
Size	**Pizza**	**Beverages**
small	$5.00	$1
large	$8.00	$2

26. The cost of x small pizzas with y small beverages is given by the expression $5x + y$. How much do 3 small pizzas and 2 small beverages cost? **$17**

27. The cost of x large pizzas with y large beverages is given by the expression $8x + 2y$. How much do 2 large pizzas with 3 large beverages cost? **$22**

28. Micka purchases 4 small pizzas and 3 large beverages. Romano purchases 3 large pizzas and 4 small beverages. Who spent more money? **Romano**

More Variables and Expressions 39

When an expression contains variables, the times sign can be confused with an x, so here is another way to write this expression. Write $3n - 5$ on the board.

How many yards of fabric did Harriet buy? [7] *So we need to evaluate this expression when n = 7.* Go through the steps at the board as students complete Exercise 1. *Remember to follow the order of operations.*

$3n - 5$

$= 3 \times 7 - 5$

$= 21 - 5$

$= 16$

How much did Harriet pay? [$16]

Guide students through each step in Exercises 2–4.

2 Guided Practice

Use with Exercises 5–19.

Remind students to write the steps as they evaluate each expression. They may use another sheet of paper.

Suggest to students that if certain letters such as *x*, *t*, *l*, *z*, or *q* are used as variables, they use cursive letters to avoid confusion with operators or numbers.

Exercises 5, 9, and 10
Remind students that the fraction bar indicates division.

Exercises 16 and 18
Error Intervention

If students confuse the times sign with the variable *x*,

then say: *The coefficient goes in front of the variable.* Point to the *x* in Exercise 13 and the times symbol in Exercise 16 so students can see the difference.

ELL Use Vocabulary

To check understanding, ask a student to repeat and complete this sentence: *When you evaluate an expression that contains more than one operation, you must follow the ____.* [Order of operations]

Quick Check Formative Assessment

Evaluate 2e + 6f for e = 3 and f = 8. [54]

3 Independent Practice

Use with Exercises 20–28.

Remind students to follow the order of operations after they replace the variables with the given numbers.

Exercises 26–27
Remind students that their answer should include a dollar sign. For Exercise 26, you might want to explain that *y* is the same as 1*y*. 1*y* represents the cost of the small beverage, $1, times the number of small beverages, *y*.

Step **5-1**

Properties of Equality

Objective Students will use the properties of equality to balance equations.

Vocabulary Equation, Addition Property of Equality, Subtraction Property of Equality, Multiplication Property of Equality, Division Property of Equality

Materials Counters, half-sheets of paper

Math Background

- Adding the same number to or subtracting it from both sides of an equation does not change the equality.
- Multiplying or dividing both sides of an equation by the same nonzero number does not change the equality.

Name ______________________ Step **5-1**

Properties of Equality

1. Show $4 + 3 = 7$ by putting counters on the half-sheets of paper as shown.

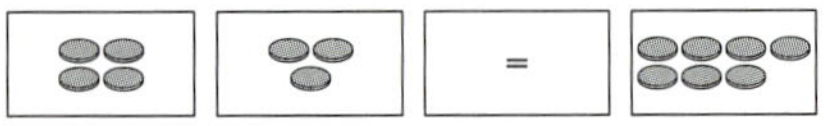

2. Take away 2 counters from each side of the equal sign.

Are the sides still equal? __yes__

3. So, $(4 + 3) - 2 = 7 -$ __2__.

Remember: Equals subtracted from equals are equal.

4. Make sure your counters show $4 + 1 = 5$.

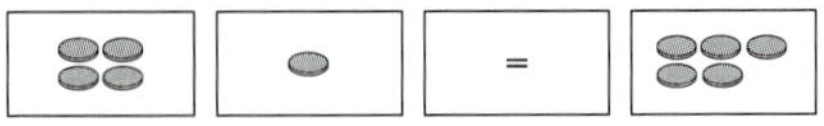

5. Add 3 counters to each side of the equal sign.

Are the two sides still equal? __yes__

6. So $(4 + 1) +$ __3__ $= 5 + 3$

Remember: Equals added to equals are equal.

7. Show $3 \times 2 = 6$ by putting counters on the half-sheets of paper as shown.

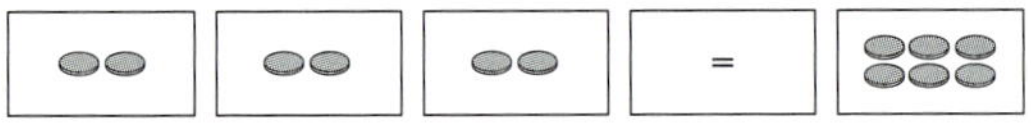

1 Concept Development

Use with Exercises 1–6.

Purpose

You already know how to write and evaluate expressions. Today you will be learning that two equal expressions can be used to write an equation.

Pose the Problem

How can you keep an equation balanced?

Model

Distribute 14 counters and 4 half-sheets of paper per student. Draw 4 rectangles on the board. *Last week Jane borrowed 4 books from the library.* Draw 4 circles in the first rectangle. *This week she checked out 3 more books.* Draw 3 circles in the second rectangle and an equal sign in the third rectangle. *How many books is this in all?* [7] Draw 7 circles in the fourth rectangle. *What equation does the model show?* [4 + 3 = 7] Have students show this model using half-sheets of paper and counters for Exercise 1.

Name ______________________ Step 5-1

Properties of Equality (continued)

8. Divide each side of the equal sign by 3. Are the two sides still equal? yes

9. So, (3 × 2) ÷ 3 = 6 ÷ 3.

Remember: Equals divided by equals are equal.

10. Show 3 + 1 = 4 with counters and paper.

11. Multiply each side by 2. Are the two sides still equal? yes

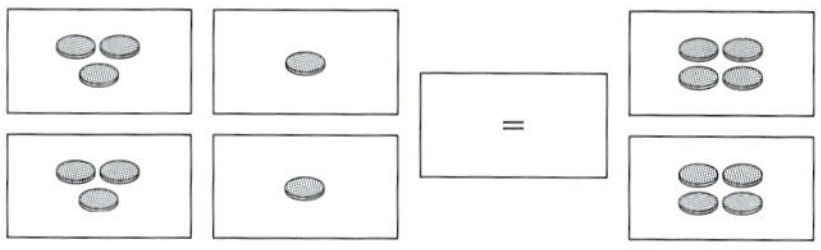

12. So, 2 × (3 + 1) = 2 × 4.

Remember: Equals multiplied by equals are equal.

Answer each question. Tell why or why not.

13. You know 48 ÷ 12 = 4. Does (48 ÷ 12) × 2 = 4 × 2?

Yes; Each side is multiplied by 2.

14. You know 16 + 18 = 34. Does (16 + 18) − 3 = 34 + 3?

No; 3 is subtracted from the left side, but added to the right side.

15. You know 6 × 4 = 24. Does (6 × 4) ÷ 2 = 24 ÷ 2?

Yes; Each side is divided by 2.

The next day Jane returned two of the library books she had borrowed. How can you show this in the equation but still keep the equation balanced? [Subtract 2 from both sides of the equation.] *The Subtraction Property of Equality states that if the same amount is subtracted from each side of an equation, the sides are still equal. So subtracting 2 from each side of the equation shows how many books Jane still has.* Have students complete Exercises 2 and 3.

Now use your counters to model Exercise 4 and then complete Exercises 5 and 6. Allow time for students to work. *The equation in Exercise 6 is still balanced because of the Addition Property of Equality. The same amount was added to both sides of the equation.*

2 Guided Practice

Use with Exercises 7–12.

Point out to students that there are also properties of equality for multiplication and division. *The Multiplication Property of Equality and the Division Property of Equality state that both sides of an equation can be multiplied or divided by the same nonzero number without changing the equality.*

Have students continue to use counters and half-sheets of paper to model the equations. Each student will need 16 counters and 7 half-sheets of paper.

Exercise 8

Error Intervention

If students have difficulty understanding why the sides are still equal,

then remind them that the Division Property of Equality lets you divide each side of an equation by the same nonzero number.

ELL Use Vocabulary

To check understanding, have a student repeat and complete this sentence: *The ________ tells you that if both sides of an equation are multiplied by the same nonzero number, the sides are still equal.* [Multiplication Property of Equality]

Quick Check Formative Assessment

Does 5 + 2 − 3 = 5 + 2 + 3? Explain. [No; the same operation was not done to both sides of the equation.]

3 Independent Practice

Use with Exercises 13–15.

Remind students to use the order of operations and complete the computations in parentheses first.

Step 5-2

Solving Addition and Subtraction Equations

Objective Students will solve one-step addition and subtraction equations.

Vocabulary Addition Property of Equality, Subtraction Property of Equality

Materials Counters, half-sheets of paper

Professional Development

Math Background

- Solving an equation involves finding the value of an unknown that makes the equation true.
- There is more than one way to solve an equation.

Name ______________________ Step 5-2

Solving Addition and Subtraction Equations

1. Show $x + 5 = 8$ with counters and paper as shown below.
Use a blank sheet of paper for x.

	+	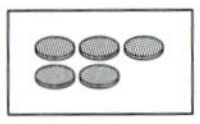	=	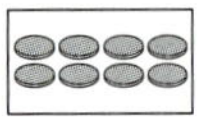

2. Equals subtracted from equals are equal.
Take away 5 counters from each side of the equal sign.
What is left? $x =$ **3**

3. Does the value of x you found in Exercise 2 make the equation $x + 5 = 8$ true? **yes**

4. Fill in the blanks to show what you did.

$x + 5 = 8$

$x + 5 - 5 = 8 -$ **5** Subtract 5 from both sides.

$x =$ **3** Subtract.

5. What is $5 - 2 + 2$? **5** What is $8 - 2 + 2$? **8**

What is $6 - 2 + 2$? **6** What is $y - 2 + 2$? **y**

6. Show $y - 2 = 6$ with counters and paper as shown below.

	−	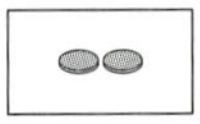	=	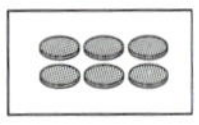

7. Equals added to equals are equal.
Add 2 counters to each side of the equal sign.
What is the result? $y =$ **8**

8. Does the value of y you found in Exercise 7 make the equation $y - 2 = 6$ true? **yes**

9. Reasoning Explain what you would add to both sides to solve $k - 19 = 36$.

Add 19 to both sides of the equation.

Interactive Learning

1 Concept Development

Use with Exercise 1–4.

Purpose

You already know that in an equation, both sides are balanced. Today you will learn how to use addition and subtraction to solve equations.

Pose the Problem

At 9:00, some students were in the classroom. A few minutes later, 5 more students came into the classroom, and there were 8 students in all. How many students were in the classroom at 9:00? Allow students to share their ideas on how to solve.

Model

One way to solve this problem is to write an equation. Draw 5 rectangles on the board. *The first rectangle will be the number of students in the classroom at 9:00. What operation shows that more students came into the classroom?* [Addition.] Write + in the second rectangle. *How many students joined the others?* [5] Write 5 in the third rectangle. *What other information is given?*

Name ______________________

Step 5-2

Solving Addition and Subtraction Equations (continued)

Solve each equation.

10. $w + 5 = 10$	**11.** $n - 17 = 5$	**12.** $77 = m + 8$
$w = 5$	$n = 22$	$69 = m$
13. $49 = a - 21$	**14.** $y - 27 = 27$	**15.** $0 = w - 10$
$70 = a$	$y = 54$	$10 = w$
16. $m + 41 = 52$	**17.** $x - 74 = 100$	**18.** $323 = a + 11$
$m = 11$	$x = 174$	$312 = a$
19. $12 = n - 14$	**20.** $y + 54 = 98$	**21.** $k - 40 = 51$
$26 = n$	$y = 44$	$k = 91$
22. $159 = n - 12$	**23.** $a - 159 = 12$	**24.** $205 = a + 148$
$171 = n$	$a = 171$	$57 = a$
25. $w + 37 = 98$	**26.** $35 = x - 149$	**27.** $y - 84 = 31$
$w = 61$	$184 = x$	$y = 115$
28. $178 = a + 167$	**29.** $19 = n - 67$	**30.** $m - 248 = 16$
$11 = a$	$86 = n$	$m = 264$
31. $w + 156 = 208$	**32.** $n - 110 = 400$	**33.** $177 = x - 45$
$w = 52$	$n = 510$	$222 = x$

34. Reasoning To solve the equation $x + 14 = 30$, Guido added 14 to both sides of the equation and got a solution of $x = 44$. Do you agree with Guido? If not, why?

No; Guido should have subtracted 14 from both sides. $x = 16$

[8 students in all] Write = in the fourth rectangle and 8 in the last rectangle. Below the rectangles write the equation $x + 5 = 8$. *The equation $x + 5 = 8$ shows this problem.*

Distribute 13 counters and 5 half-sheets of paper per student and have them make the model as shown in Exercise 1. *The amounts on both sides of the equation are equal, but there is an addition on the left side of the equation. What operation undoes addition?* [Subtraction] *The **Subtraction Property of Equality** states that if the same amount is subtracted from each side of an equation, the sides are still equal. How do you decide what number to subtract from both sides?* [5 was added, so subtract 5.] Have students complete Exercises 2 through 4.

2 Guided Practice

Use with Exercises 5–9.

Have students continue to use counters and half-sheets of paper to model the equation. Distribute 10 counters and 5 half-sheets of paper per student. *Look at the equation and the model in Exercise 6. How can you undo subtracting 2?* [By adding 2] *The **Addition Property of Equality** states that the same amount can be added to each side of an equation without changing the equality.*

Exercise 9

Error Intervention

If students have difficulty determining what number to add to solve the equation,

then ask: *What is being done on the left side of the equation?* [19 is subtracted from some number.] *What operation undoes subtraction?* [Addition] *What number is added to undo subtracting 19?* [19]

ELL Use Vocabulary

To check understanding, have a student repeat and complete this sentence: *The ________ states that we can add the same amount to both sides of an equation and the equation is still balanced.* [Addition Property of Equality]

Quick Check — Formative Assessment

What is the value of k in the equation $k + 16 = 25$? [$k = 9$]

3 Independent Practice

Use with Exercises 10–34.

Remind students that adding and subtracting the same number to both sides of an equation does not change the equality. You may wish to have students work in pairs to check their solutions.

Step 5-3

Solving Multiplication and Division Equations

Objective Students will solve one-step multiplication and division equations.

Vocabulary Multiplication Property of Equality, Division Property of Equality

Materials Counters, half-sheets of paper

Math Background

- Solving an equation involves finding the value of an unknown that makes the equation true.
- There is more than one way to solve an equation.

Name ____________________ Step **5-3**

Solving Multiplication and Division Equations

1. Show $2x = 16$ with counters and paper as shown below. Use a blank sheet of paper for each x.

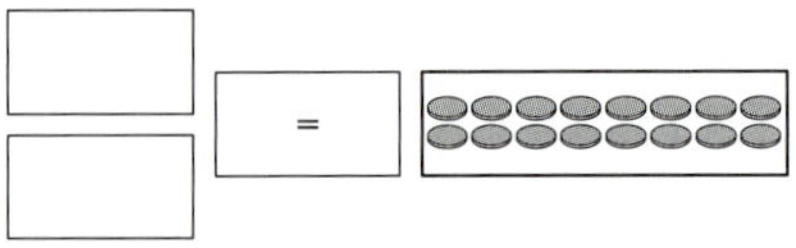

2. Equals divided by equals are equal. Divide each side of the equal sign into 2 equal parts.

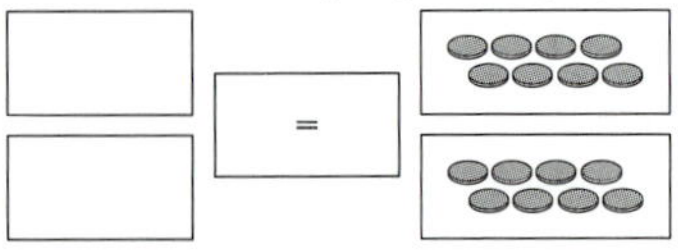

3. Remove all but one blank sheet of paper and one group of counters from each side. What is left? $x =$ 8

4. Fill in the blanks to show what you did.

$2x = 16$

$\frac{2x}{2} = \frac{16}{2}$ Divide both sides by 2.

$x =$ 8

5. Does the value of x that you found in Exercise 4 make the equation $2x = 16$ true? yes

6. Fill in the blanks to solve $\frac{n}{9} = 6$.

$\frac{n}{9} = 6$

$9 \times \frac{n}{9} =$ 9 $\times 6$ Multiply both sides by 9.

$n =$ 54

7. Does the value of n that you found in Exercise 6 make the equation $\frac{n}{9} = 6$ true? yes

1 Concept Development

Interactive Learning

Use with Exercises 1–5.

Purpose

You already know how to solve addition and subtraction equations. Today you will learn how to use multiplication and division to solve equations.

Pose the Problem

David has twice as many video games as Emma. David has 16 video games. How many video games does Emma have? Allow time for students to share their ideas.

Model

How many video games does David have? [16] ***What other information is given in the problem?*** [David has twice as many video games as Emma.] ***What do we need to find?*** [The number of video games Emma has] ***Use the variable x to represent the number of video games Emma has. What expression shows the number of video games David has compared to Emma?*** [2x]

Name ______________________

Step 5-3

Solving Multiplication and Division Equations (continued)

Fill in the blanks to solve each equation.

8. $7c = 350$

$\frac{7c}{\boxed{7}} = \frac{350}{\boxed{7}}$

$c =$ 50

9. $\frac{h}{5} = 15$

5 $\times \frac{h}{5} =$ 5 $\times 15$

$h =$ 75

10. Reasoning Why can you multiply both sides of $\frac{m}{2} = 11$ by 2 and still have a true equation?

Sample answer: Equals multiplied by equals are equal.

Solve each equation.

11. $9a = 36$ $a = 4$	**12.** $\frac{m}{5} = 6$ $m = 30$	**13.** $6x = 48$ $x = 8$
14. $20b = 40$ $b = 2$	**15.** $35y = 140$ $y = 4$	**16.** $\frac{z}{18} = 4$ $z = 72$
17. $12n = 72$ $n = 6$	**18.** $\frac{c}{4} = 21$ $c = 84$	**19.** $\frac{t}{10} = 18$ $t = 180$
20. $50r = 100$ $r = 2$	**21.** $36s = 144$ $s = 4$	**22.** $\frac{v}{24} = 12$ $v = 288$

23. Reasoning To solve an equation such as $8p = 96$, you divide both sides of the equation by 8. Why do you divide instead of multiply?

Sample answer: Since p is multiplied by 8, do the inverse operation and divide by 8 to find the value of p.

Solving Multiplication and Division Equations **45**

Distribute 16 counters and 5 half-sheets of paper per student. Write $2x = 16$ on the board. *This equation shows that 16 is the same value as 2 times the number of video games, x, that Emma has. Use counters and pieces of paper to make the model that's shown in Exercise 1.*

To solve the equation $2x = 16$, you must undo multiplying by 2. So, divide by 2. From the Division Property of Equality, you know that if you divide both sides of the equation by the same nonzero number, the equation stays balanced. Use another piece of paper and move your counters so they match the drawing in Exercise 2. Allow time for students to separate their counters into 2 groups before having them complete Exercise 3. *Fill in the blanks in Exercise 4 to show the steps you used to solve the equation.*

How can you check that your solution is correct? Have students share their ideas before completing Exercise 5.

2 Guided Practice

Use with Exercises 6–10.

Remind students that to solve an equation, they must find the value for the variable that makes the equation true.

Exercises 6 and 7

Error Intervention

If students have trouble understanding why both sides of the equation can be multiplied by 9 without changing the equality,

then remind them of the Multiplication Property of Equality. *Does the equality change when each side of an equation is multiplied by the same nonzero number?* [No.]

ELL Use Vocabulary

To check understanding, ask a student to repeat and complete this sentence: *The sides of an equation stay balanced if you divide both by the same nonzero number because of the ______.* [Division Property of Equality]

Quick Check Formative Assessment

Solve the equation: $\frac{w}{35} = 4$ [$w = 140$]

3 Independent Practice

Use with Exercises 11–23.

Exercises 11–22

Remind students that multiplying or dividing both sides of an equation by the same nonzero number does not change the equality.

For Exercise 23, remind students to think about inverse operations. *What operation undoes multiplication?* [Division]

Step 5-4

Solving Equations with Whole Numbers

Objective Students will use all operations to solve one-step equations.

Vocabulary Inverse operations, solution

Materials Equation Tables (Teaching Tool 12)

Professional Development Math Background

- To solve a one-step equation, use the inverse of the operation that is performed on the variable in the equation.
- Addition and subtraction have an inverse relationship.
- Multiplication and division have an inverse relationship.

Teaching Tool 12

Name__________

Equation Tables

Example: $12p = 48$

	Expression on Left	Inverse Operation	Equal Sign	Expression on Right	Inverse Operation
Equation	$12p$		=	48	
Inverse	$12p$	$\div 12$	=	48	$\div 12$
Answer	p		=	4	

	Expression on Left	Inverse Operation	Equal Sign	Expression on Right	Inverse Operation
Equation			=		
Inverse			=		
Answer			=		

	Expression on Left	Inverse Operation	Equal Sign	Expression on Right	Inverse Operation
Equation			=		
Inverse			=		
Answer			=		

	Expression on Left	Inverse Operation	Equal Sign	Expression on Right	Inverse Operation
Equation			=		
Inverse			=		
Answer			=		

	Expression on Left	Inverse Operation	Equal Sign	Expression on Right	Inverse Operation
Equation			=		
Inverse			=		
Answer			=		

M14

Name __________ Step 5-4

Solving Equations with Whole Numbers

Addition and subtraction have an inverse relationship. If a number is added to a variable, you subtract that number from both sides of the equation to get the variable alone.

1. In the equation $m + 9 = 45$, what number is added to the variable? **9**
2. To solve $m + 9 = 45$, should you add or subtract 9 from both sides of the equation? **subtract**
3. Fill in the blanks to solve the equation and check the solution.

$m + 9 = 45$ | **Check** $m + 9 = 45$

$m + 9 - 9 = 45 - $ **9** | **36** $+ 9 = 45$

$m =$ **36** | Does the solution check? **yes**

If a number is subtracted from a variable, you add that number to both sides of the equation to get the variable alone.

4. In the equation $x - 18 = 54$, what number is subtracted from the variable? **18**
5. So, to solve $x - 18 = 54$, should you add or subtract 18 from both sides of the equation? **add**
6. Fill in the blanks to solve the equation and check the solution.

$x - 18 = 54$ | **Check** $x - 18 = 54$

$x - 18 +$ **18** $= 54 +$ **18** | **72** $- 18 = 54$

$x =$ **72** | Does the solution check? **yes**

7. In the equation $5k = 105$, by what number is the variable multiplied? **5**
8. To solve $5k = 105$, do you multiply or divide both sides of the equation by 5? **divide**
9. Fill in the blanks to solve the equation and check the solution.

$5k = 105$ | **Check** $5k = 105$

$5k \div$ **5** $= 105 \div$ **5** | $5 \times$ **21** $= 105$

$k =$ **21** | Does the solution check? **yes**

Interactive Learning 1 Concept Development

Use with Teaching Tool 12.

Purpose

You already know how to solve equations using addition and subtraction or multiplication and division. Today you will be learning how to decide which operation to use to solve equations.

Pose the Problem

Before an amusement park opened, several people formed a line at the front gate. Sixteen more people got in line. How many people were in line ahead of them if there were 89 people in all waiting in line? Invite volunteers to share their ideas on how to solve this problem.

Model

Distribute copies of Equation Tables (Teaching Tool 12) and draw one of the tables on the board. *One way to solve the problem is to write an equation. What information do we know?* [After 16 people join a line, 89 people are in line.] *What are we trying to find?* [How many people were in the original line]

Name ______________________

Step 5-4

Solving Equations with Whole Numbers (continued)

Multiplication and division have an inverse relationship. If a variable is multiplied by a number, you divide both sides of the equation by that number to get the variable alone.

10. In the equation $m \div 4 = 18$, the variable is divided by what number? 4

11. To solve $m \div 4 = 18$, do you multiply or divide both sides of the equation by 4? multiply

12. Fill in the blanks to solve the equation and check the solution.

$\frac{m}{4} = 18$

$\frac{m}{4} \times$ 4 $= 18 \times$ 4

$m =$ 72

Check $\frac{m}{4} = 18$

$\frac{72}{4} = 18$

Does the solution check? yes

13. Reasoning Explain what operation you use on both sides of the equation to solve $15p = 105$. Solve the equation.

$p = 7$; Sample answer: Divide both sides of the equation by 15. Since p is multiplied by 15, use the inverse operation to get p alone.

Solve each equation. Check your answer.

14. $x - 21 = 40$ $x = 61$

15. $30 + y = 51$ $y = 21$

16. $7g = 28$ $g = 4$

17. $n \div 6 = 14$ $n = 84$

18. $28 = r - 11$ $r = 39$

19. $63 + x = 127$ $x = 64$

20. $9y = 81$ $y = 9$

21. $\frac{x}{8} = 10$ $x = 80$

22. Jill was born in 1958 and Bob was born in 1977. Solve the equation $1958 + y = 1977$ to find out how many years older Jill is than Bob. 19 years

Let p represent the number of people in the original line. So we need to find the solution for p + 16 = 89. Write the equation on the board above the table. As you point to the top row of the table, ask *What expression is on the left side of the equation?* [$p + 16$] *What value is on the right?* [89] Complete the top row of the table on the board and have students copy it.

What is the inverse operation of adding 16? [Subtracting 16] Below the first equation, write $p + 16 = 89$ a second time allowing space immediately to the left of the equal sign to write $- 16$. *The Subtraction Property of Equality tells us the equality does not change if the same number is subtracted from both sides of the equation.* Write $- 16$ in the space allowed and to the right of 89. *Compute 89 − 16 to find the solution.* Write $p = 73$ in the bottom row and have students copy it. *The solution p = 73 means 73 people formed the original line at the front gate. How can you check that your solution is correct?* [Substitute 73 for p and see if both sides of the equation have the same value.] *Is 73 + 16 equal to 89?* [Yes.] *So the solution p = 73 is correct.*

2 Guided Practice

Use with Exercises 1–13.

Remind students to check their work by substituting their solution for the variable and see if both sides of the equation have the same value.

Error Intervention

If students do not perform the same operation to both sides of the equation,

then suggest they circle the intermediate step to show what they are doing to both sides of each equation.

ELL Use Vocabulary

To check understanding, have a student repeat and complete this sentence: *The value for the variable that makes an equation true is the ________.* [Solution]

Quick Check Formative Assessment

Solve 6x = 132. [$x = 22$]

3 Independent Practice

Use with Exercises 14–22.

Remind students that equations stay balanced because of the properties of equality for operations. Explain to students that the same variable can be used for different equations. For example, in Exercises 15 and 20, the same variable, y, is used, but the value will be different for each .

Exercise 22
Remind students that there can be more than one equation that describes a situation. For example, solving the equation $1977 - 1958 = y$ is another way to find the difference in Jill's and Bob's ages. Note that $1977 - 1958$ is the same computation that is done to solve the equation $1958 + y = 1977$.

Step 5-5

Solving Equations with Decimals

Objective Students will solve one-step equations with decimals.

Vocabulary Inverse operations

Materials Equation Tables (Teaching Tool 12)

Math Background

- Solving an equation involves finding the value of an unknown that makes the equation true.
- To solve a one-step equation, use the inverse of the operation that is performed on the variable in the equation.

Step 5-5

Name ____________________

Solving Equations with Decimals

Carlita hiked 2.1 miles on the Chipmunk Trail on Friday. On Saturday, she hiked the Squirrel Trail. If she hiked 3.7 miles in all, use the equation $2.1 + x = 3.7$ to find how many miles she hiked on the Squirrel Trail.

1. What operation should you do to both sides of the equation $21 + x = 37$ to get x alone? subtract 21
2. What operation should you do to both sides of the equation $2.1 + x = 3.7$ to get x alone? subtract 2.1
3. Fill in the blanks to solve the equation and check the solution.

$2.1 + x = 3.7$
$2.1 + x - \underline{2.1} = 3.7 - \underline{2.1}$
$x = 1.6$

Check $2.1 + x = 3.7$
$2.1 + \underline{1.6} = 3.7$
Does this solution check? yes

4. How many miles did Carlita hike on the Squirrel Trail? 1.6 miles

Fill in the blanks to solve each equation and check the solution.

5. $x - 1.1 = 1.4$
$x - 1.1 + \underline{1.1} = 1.4 + \underline{1.1}$
$x = \underline{2.5}$

Check $x - 1.1 = 1.4$
$\underline{2.5} - 1.1 = 1.4$
Does this solution check? yes

6. $3.5y = 7$
$\frac{3.5y}{3.5} = \frac{7}{3.5}$
$y = \underline{2}$

Check $3.5y = 7$
$3.5 \times \underline{2} = 7$
Does this solution check? yes

7. $4.2 = \frac{z}{6}$
$4.2 \times \underline{6} = \frac{z}{6} \times \underline{6}$
$\underline{25.2} = z$

Check $4.2 = \frac{z}{6}$
$4.2 = \frac{25.2}{6}$
Does this solution check? yes

Teaching Tool 12

Name ____________________

Equation Tables

Example: $12p = 48$

	Expression on Left	Inverse Operation	Equal Sign	Expression on Right	Inverse Operation
Equation	$12p$		=	48	
Inverse	$12p$	÷ 12	=	48	÷ 12
Answer	p		=	4	

	Expression on Left	Inverse Operation	Equal Sign	Expression on Right	Inverse Operation
Equation			=		
Inverse			=		
Answer			=		

	Expression on Left	Inverse Operation	Equal Sign	Expression on Right	Inverse Operation
Equation			=		
Inverse			=		
Answer			=		

	Expression on Left	Inverse Operation	Equal Sign	Expression on Right	Inverse Operation
Equation			=		
Inverse			=		
Answer			=		

	Expression on Left	Inverse Operation	Equal Sign	Expression on Right	Inverse Operation
Equation			=		
Inverse			=		
Answer			=		

M14

Interactive Learning 1 Concept Development

Use with Teaching Tool 12.

Purpose

You already know how to solve equations with whole numbers. Today you will learn how to solve equations with decimals.

Pose the Problem

Carlita hiked 2.1 miles on the Chipmunk Trail on Friday. On Saturday she hiked the Squirrel Trail. How many miles did she hike on the Squirrel Trail if she hiked 3.7 miles in all? Have students share their ideas on solution methods.

Model

Distribute copies of Equation Tables (Teaching Tool 12), and draw one of the tables on the board.

What information do you know? [Carlita walked 2.1 miles on Chipmunk Trail and 3.7 miles in all] *What equation can you write to describe this information?* [$2.1 + x = 3.7$] *How is this equation similar to the equation $21 + x = 37$?* [The same digits are used in the numbers but the decimal points have moved.]

Name ______________________________

Step 5-5

Solving Equations with Decimals (continued)

8. **Reasoning** To solve an equation such as $k + 4.6 = 9.2$, you subtract 4.6 from both sides of the equation. Why do you subtract instead of add to find the solution?

Sample answer: Since 4.6 is added to *k*, do the inverse and subtract 4.6 to get *k* alone.

Solve each equation and check your answer.

9. $x + 3.7 = 6.4$ — $x = 2.7$
10. $x - 6.9 = 12.4$ — $x = 19.3$
11. $6.2y = 31$ — $y = 5$
12. $\frac{a}{4} = 5.2$ — $a = 20.8$
13. $x - 4.1 = 3.4$ — $x = 7.5$
14. $3.6 = \frac{w}{9}$ — $w = 32.4$
15. $3x = 6.3$ — $x = 2.1$
16. $x + 5 = 5.5$ — $x = 0.5$
17. $2.1 + x = 4.5$ — $x = 2.4$
18. $x - 7.3 = 2.4$ — $x = 9.7$

19. Ryan bought 5 boxes of cereal and spent \$9.45. Solve the equation $5b = 9.45$ to find the cost of each box. $b =$ **\$1.89**

20. **Reasoning** When a variable is divided by a number, should you add, subtract, multiply, or divide both sides of the equation to get the variable alone? Why?

Multiply both sides of the equation by the number because multiplying by the number is the inverse of dividing by it.

What would you do to solve 21 + x = 37? [Subtract 21 from both sides of the equation.] *Why do you subtract 21?* [To undo adding 21 to the unknown number, use the inverse operation.] *So how does this help you solve 2.1 + x = 3.7?* [You do the same thing but with different numbers.] Write the steps shown below to solve $2.1 + x = 3.7$ on the board as students complete Exercises 2 through 4.

$$2.1 + x = 3.7$$

$$2.1 + x - 2.1 = 3.7 - 2.1$$

$$x = 1.6$$

Carlita hiked 1.6 miles on the Squirrel Trail.

2 Guided Practice

Use with Exercise 5–8.

Remind students that addition and subtraction have an inverse relationship, and that multiplication and division have an inverse relationship.

Error Intervention

If students have difficulty solving addition or subtraction equations correctly,

then remind them to line up the decimals points before they add or subtract.

ELL Use Vocabulary

To check understanding, have a student repeat and complete this sentence: *To get the variable alone on one side of an equation, use the ________ to undo what has been done.* [Inverse operation]

Quick Check Formative Assessment

Solve 3n = 42.9. What operation do you use? [Division; 14.3]

3 Independent Practice

Use with Exercises 9–20.

Remind students that a whole number can be written with a decimal point and a zero in the tenths column.

Some students may have difficulty keeping digits properly aligned for computations. Suggest that they turn lined paper and use the columns to write the problems.

Step 5-6

Draw a Picture and Write an Equation

Objective Students will draw pictures or diagrams and use them to write equations and solve problems.

Vocabulary Equation

Materials Problem-Solving Recording Sheet (Teaching Tool 14)

Math Background

- Information can often be shown in a picture and used to understand and solve the problem.
- Some problems can be solved by writing and solving an equation.

Name ______________________ Step 5-6

Draw a Picture and Write an Equation

Rachel has 128 pictures to put in a photo album. Each page in the album holds 8 pictures. How many pages does Rachel need to use?

Solve by answering 1 to 7.

Answer 1 and 2 to **understand** the problem.

1. What do you know from reading the problem?

   Rachel has __128__ pictures to put in a photo album.

   Each page holds __8__ pictures.

2. What do you need to find?

   How many pages does Rachel need to use?

Answer 3 to 6 to **plan and solve** the problem.

You can solve the problem by drawing a picture and writing a number sentence.

3. Complete the picture below to show what you know.

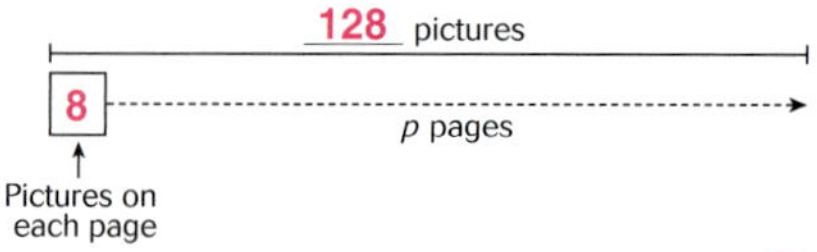

4. Write an equation to solve. __$8p = 128$__
5. What do you get for the value of p? __16__
6. How many pages does Rachel need to use? __16__

Answer 7 to **look back** at your solution.

7. **Reasoning** Explain how to check your solution.

   Substitute 16 for p, multiply 8×16 to be sure the product is 128, the value on the right.

50 Draw a Picture and Write an Equation

Name ______________________ Teaching Tool 14

Problem-Solving Recording Sheet

Problem:

Find? | **Know?** | **Strategies?**

Show the Problem
- ☐ Draw a Picture
- ☐ Make an Organized List
- ☐ Make a Table
- ☐ Make a Graph
- ☐ Act It Out/Use Objects

- ☐ Look for a Pattern
- ☐ Try, Check, Revise
- ☐ Write an Equation
- ☐ Use Reasoning
- ☐ Work Backwards
- ☐ Solve a Simpler Problem

Show the Problem? | **Solution?**

Answer? | **Check? Reasonable?**

M16

1 Concept Development

Use with Teaching Tool 14.

Purpose

You have solved addition, subtraction, multiplication, and division equations. Today you will draw pictures to help write and solve equations.

Pose the Problem

Nicole saved $27 each month for 3 months. How much had she saved at the end of the third month? Allow time for students to discuss the problem.

Model

Distribute copies of the Problem-Solving Recording Sheet (Teaching Tool 14). Write the above problem on the board and have students copy it in the top box. *What do you know?* [Nicole saved $27 each month for 3 months.] *What do you need to find?* [The total amount saved] Have students complete the *Find?* and *Know?* boxes on the recording sheet. Point out that the boxes on the recording sheet provide a step-by-step guide for solving problems.

Name ____________________

Draw a Picture and Write an Equation (continued)

Sample equations are given.

Write an equation and solve each problem.

8. There are 234 people invited to a charity banquet. Each table will seat 9 people. How many tables are needed to seat everyone?

Equation: $9t = 234$ Solution: 26 tables

9. Jon has a rock collection. The rocks are stored in cases that hold 16 rocks each. He has 176 rocks in his collection. How many cases can Jon completely fill?

Equation: $176 \div 16 = c$ Solution: 11 cases

10. Maria is 165.1 cm tall. She is 2.3 cm shorter than her aunt. How tall is her aunt?

Equation: $a - 2.3 = 165.1$ Solution: 167.4 cm

11. A book and a $2.75 magazine cost $14.50 together. How much does the book cost?

Equation: $b + 2.75 = 14.50$ Solution: $11.75

12. Phillip paid $18.75 for a soccer ball on sale. What was the price before the sale?

Sale!
$2.50 off

Equation: $p - 2.50 = 18.75$ or $18.75 + 2.50 = p$ Solution: $21.25

13. Tammy earns $8 per hour. She earned $480 last month. How many hours did she work?

Equation: $480 \div 8 = t$ Solution: 60 hours

We are going to draw a picture and write an equation to solve this problem. Draw a rectangle and a line above it for a bar diagram. Have students draw the same picture in the *Show the Problem?* box as you discuss each part of the diagram. *We can show the information we know in a diagram. What does the line segment above the bar represent?* [The whole amount or total Nicole saved]

Let's use the variable s to represent the total she saved. Write *s* on the line. *The sections of the bar represent the number of equal groups. How many sections should the bar have? Why?* [3; Nicole saved the same amount for 3 months.] *What number is written in each section? Why?* [$27; she saved $27 each month.]

What equation represents the information shown in the diagram? [$s \div 3 = 27$] *How can you solve the equation?* [Multiply both sides by 3.] *Why?* [You use the inverse operation of dividing by 3.] *What is the solution?* [$s = \$81$] *So at the end of the third month, Nicole had saved $81.* Have students complete the recording sheet.

2 Guided Practice

Use with Exercises 1–7.

Exercises 4 and 5

Error Intervention

If students have difficulty deciding which Property of Equality to use to solve,

then ask: *What operation is used with the variable?* [Multiply by 8.] *What is the inverse operation?* [Divide by 8.]

ELL Use Vocabulary

To check understanding, have a student repeat and complete this sentence: *A number sentence that shows two expressions having the same value is an _____.* [Equation]

Quick Check Formative Assessment

The town library has 6 times as many biographies as animal books. It has 594 biographies. How many animal books does it have? Draw a picture and write an equation to solve. [$6n = 594$, $n = 99$ books; Check students' drawings.]

3 Independent Practice

Use with Exercises 8–13.

Remind students that their drawings can help them choose the operation to use in the equation.

Point out that there may be more than one equation to represent a problem, but the solution will be the same. Checking the solution helps the students know if they have used the right information and if their answer is reasonable.

TEACHING TOOLS

Name ________________________________

Individual Record Form

Test	Items	Number Correct	Notes
Program Placement Test			
Book A	1–12		
Book B	13–24		
Book C	25–36		
Book A Topic Tests			
Topic 1	1–6		
Topic 2	1–6		
Topic 3	1–6		
Topic 4	1–6		
Book B Topic Tests			
Topic 1	1–6		
Topic 2	1–6		
Topic 3	1–6		
Topic 4	1–6		
Book C Topic Tests			
Topic 1	1–6		
Topic 2	1–6		
Topic 3	1–6		
Topic 4	1–6		
Topic 5	1–6		
Program Exit Test			
Book A	1–12		
Book B	13–24		
Book C	25–36		

Name ______________________________________

Student Progress Report

Date ____________________

Dear family,

Your child has just completed Topic ______ in Book ______ of our math program.

Teacher Comments:

____

____

____

____

____

____

- -

Name of student: ____________________________

I have received and reviewed this progress report for my child.

____

Parent/Guardian Signature

Parent/Guardian Comments:

____

____

Name______________________________

Bubble Answer Sheet

1.	Ⓐ	Ⓑ	Ⓒ	Ⓓ
2.	Ⓐ	Ⓑ	Ⓒ	Ⓓ
3.	Ⓐ	Ⓑ	Ⓒ	Ⓓ
4.	Ⓐ	Ⓑ	Ⓒ	Ⓓ
5.	Ⓐ	Ⓑ	Ⓒ	Ⓓ
6.	Ⓐ	Ⓑ	Ⓒ	Ⓓ
7.	Ⓐ	Ⓑ	Ⓒ	Ⓓ
8.	Ⓐ	Ⓑ	Ⓒ	Ⓓ
9.	Ⓐ	Ⓑ	Ⓒ	Ⓓ
10.	Ⓐ	Ⓑ	Ⓒ	Ⓓ
11.	Ⓐ	Ⓑ	Ⓒ	Ⓓ
12.	Ⓐ	Ⓑ	Ⓒ	Ⓓ
13.	Ⓐ	Ⓑ	Ⓒ	Ⓓ
14.	Ⓐ	Ⓑ	Ⓒ	Ⓓ
15.	Ⓐ	Ⓑ	Ⓒ	Ⓓ
16.	Ⓐ	Ⓑ	Ⓒ	Ⓓ
17.	Ⓐ	Ⓑ	Ⓒ	Ⓓ
18.	Ⓐ	Ⓑ	Ⓒ	Ⓓ
19.	Ⓐ	Ⓑ	Ⓒ	Ⓓ
20.	Ⓐ	Ⓑ	Ⓒ	Ⓓ
21.	Ⓐ	Ⓑ	Ⓒ	Ⓓ
22.	Ⓐ	Ⓑ	Ⓒ	Ⓓ
23.	Ⓐ	Ⓑ	Ⓒ	Ⓓ
24.	Ⓐ	Ⓑ	Ⓒ	Ⓓ
25.	Ⓐ	Ⓑ	Ⓒ	Ⓓ
26.	Ⓐ	Ⓑ	Ⓒ	Ⓓ
27.	Ⓐ	Ⓑ	Ⓒ	Ⓓ
28.	Ⓐ	Ⓑ	Ⓒ	Ⓓ
29.	Ⓐ	Ⓑ	Ⓒ	Ⓓ
30.	Ⓐ	Ⓑ	Ⓒ	Ⓓ
31.	Ⓐ	Ⓑ	Ⓒ	Ⓓ
32.	Ⓐ	Ⓑ	Ⓒ	Ⓓ
33.	Ⓐ	Ⓑ	Ⓒ	Ⓓ
34.	Ⓐ	Ⓑ	Ⓒ	Ⓓ
35.	Ⓐ	Ⓑ	Ⓒ	Ⓓ
36.	Ⓐ	Ⓑ	Ⓒ	Ⓓ

Name ______________________________

Multiplication Charts

A

	Thous	Hunds	Tens	Ones
×				

A

	Thous	Hunds	Tens	Ones
×				

B

	Thous	Hunds	Tens	Ones
×				
+				

B

	Thous	Hunds	Tens	Ones
×				
+				

C

	Ten Thous	Thous	Hunds	Tens	Ones
×					
+					

C

	Ten Thous	Thous	Hunds	Tens	Ones
×					
+					

Name________________________________

Fraction Models: Strips

1

$\frac{1}{2}$	

$\frac{1}{3}$		

$\frac{1}{4}$			

$\frac{1}{5}$				

$\frac{1}{6}$					

$\frac{1}{8}$							

$\frac{1}{10}$									

$\frac{1}{12}$											

Name______________________________________

Fraction Models: Circles

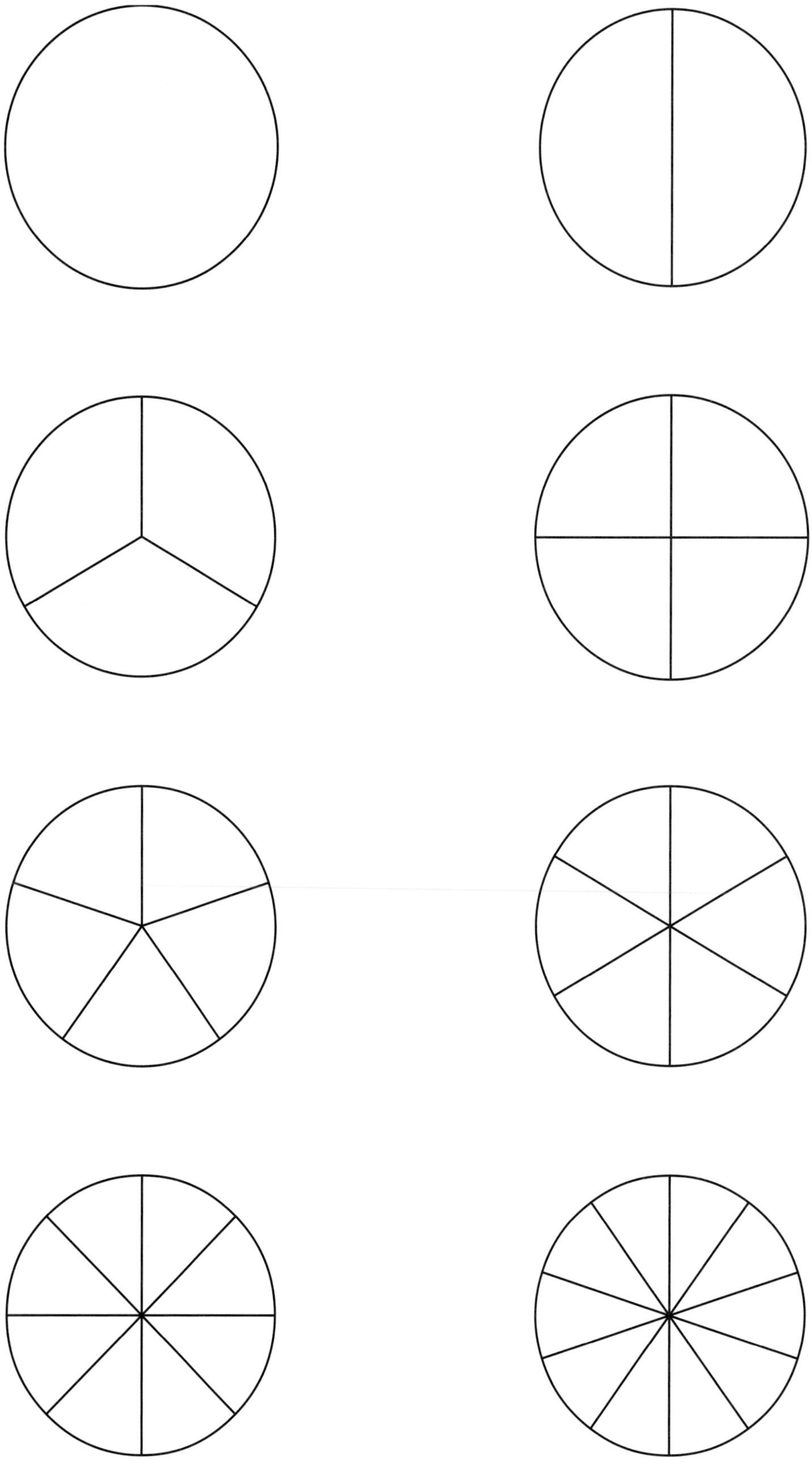

Name_______________________________________

Decimal Place-Value Chart

ONES				DECIMALS		
hundreds	tens	ones		tenths	hundredths	thousandths
			.			
			.			
			.			
			.			
			.			
			.			
			.			
			.			
			.			
			.			
			.			
			.			
			.			
			.			
			.			
			.			
			.			
			.			

Name____

Decimal Models

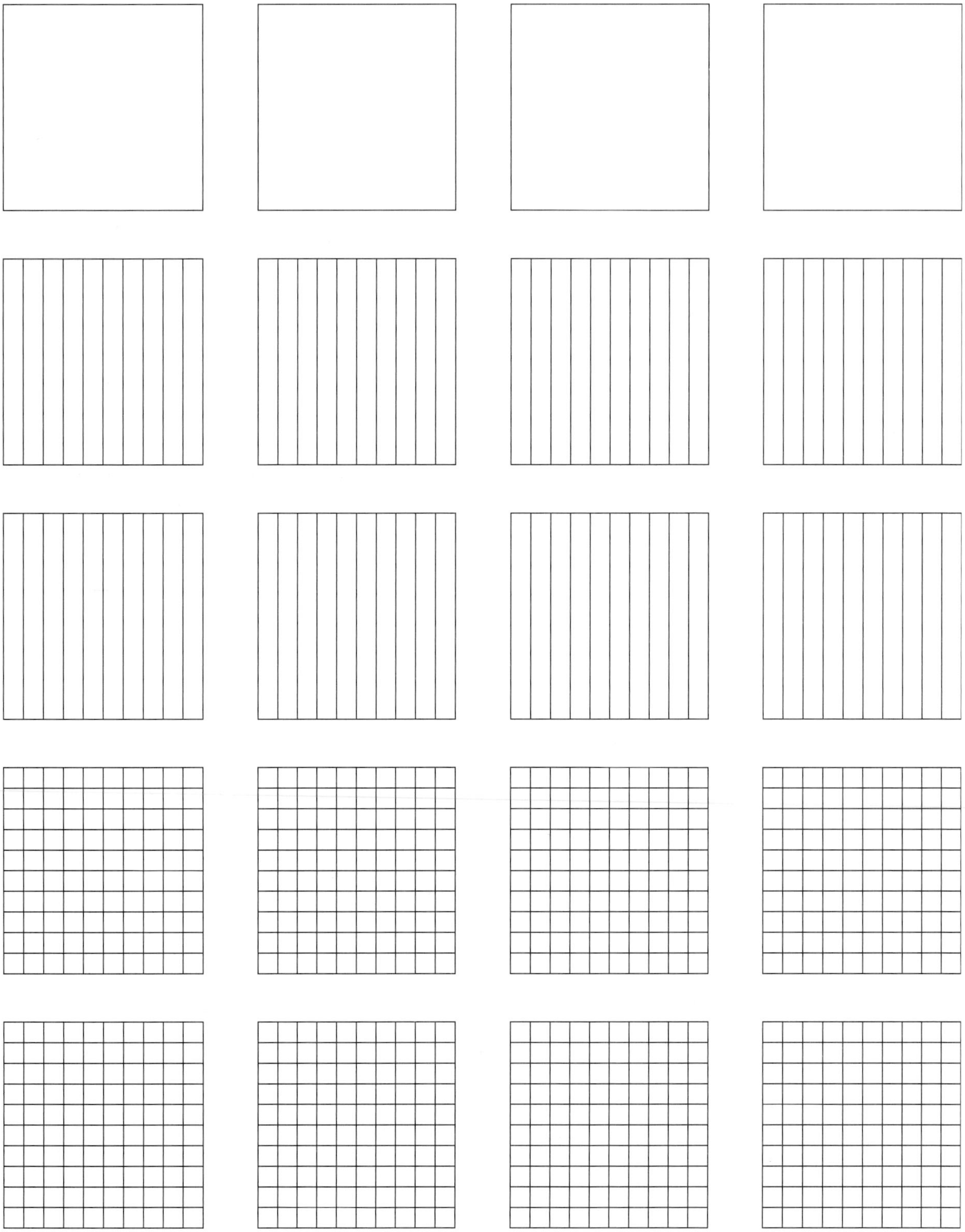

Teaching Tool
9

Name______________________________

Addition/Subtraction Templates

A

Tens	Ones

A

Tens	Ones

A

Tens	Ones

B

Tens	Ones	.	Tenths	Hundredths

B

Tens	Ones	.	Tenths	Hundredths

C

Hundreds	Tens	Ones	.	Tenths	Hundredths	Thousandths

C

Hundreds	Tens	Ones	.	Tenths	Hundredths	Thousandths

Name________________________________

Centimeter Grid Paper

Name ______________________________

Division Templates

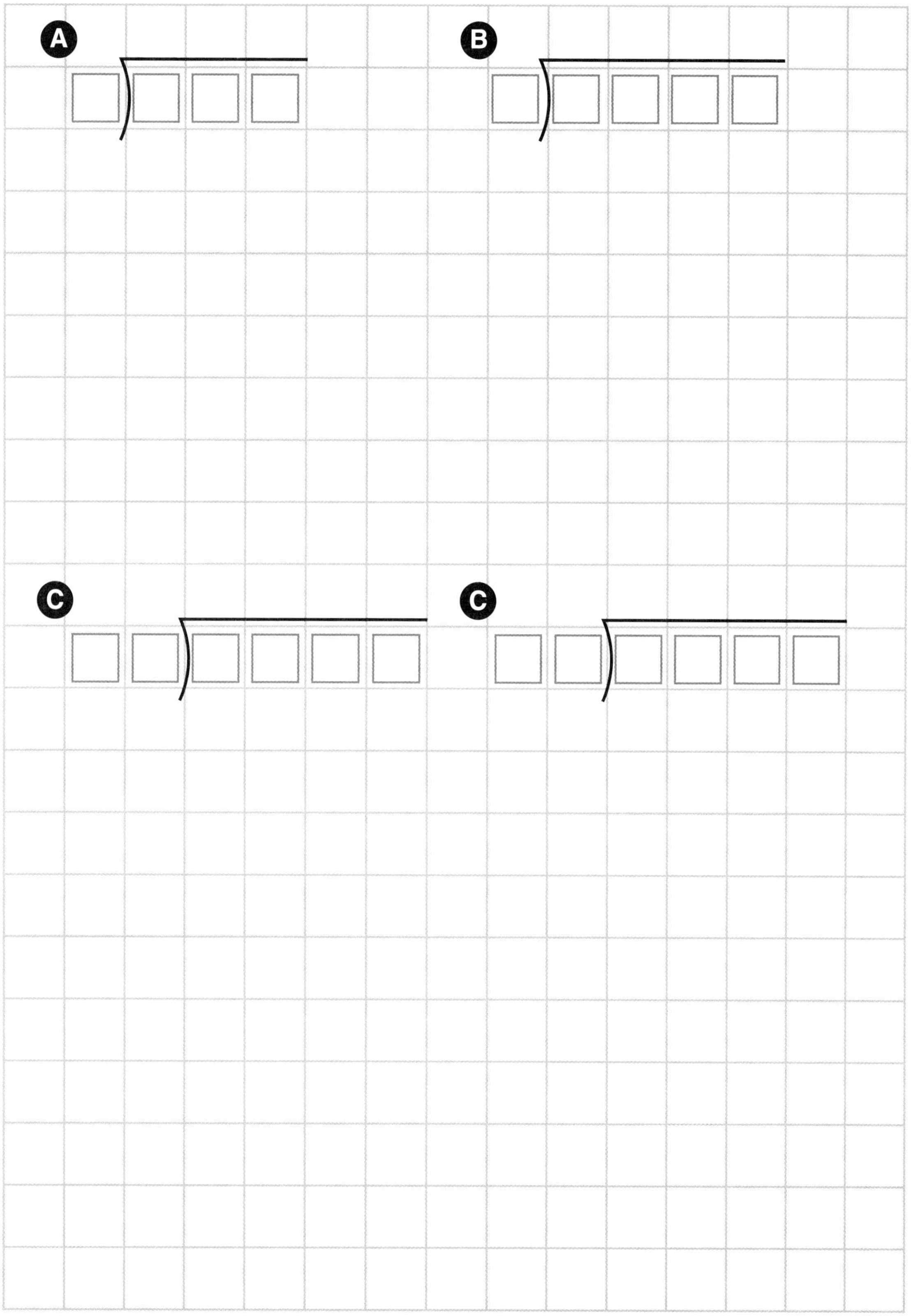

Name______________________________________

Equation Tables

Example: $12p = 48$

	Expression on Left	Inverse Operation	Equal Sign	Expression on Right	Inverse Operation
Equation	$12p$		=	48	
Inverse	$12p$	÷ 12	=	48	÷ 12
Answer	p		=	4	

	Expression on Left	Inverse Operation	Equal Sign	Expression on Right	Inverse Operation
Equation			=		
Inverse			=		
Answer			=		

	Expression on Left	Inverse Operation	Equal Sign	Expression on Right	Inverse Operation
Equation			=		
Inverse			=		
Answer			=		

	Expression on Left	Inverse Operation	Equal Sign	Expression on Right	Inverse Operation
Equation			=		
Inverse			=		
Answer			=		

	Expression on Left	Inverse Operation	Equal Sign	Expression on Right	Inverse Operation
Equation			=		
Inverse			=		
Answer			=		

Teaching Tool
13

Name ______________________________

Function Tables

Rule: ______________________

Rule: ______________________

Rule: ______________________

Rule: ______________________

Name____

Book A: Number and Operations 1

1. $\begin{array}{r} 37 \\ \times\ 24 \\ \hline \end{array}$

A 162

B 828

C 888

D 1,212

2. 6,300 ÷ 70 =

A 90

B 80

C 9

D 8

3. $46\overline{)351}$

A 6 R75

B 7 R29

C 7 R31

D 7 R39

4. What fraction of the figure is shaded?

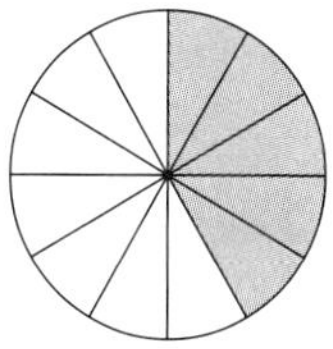

A $\frac{12}{5}$

B $\frac{5}{7}$

C $\frac{7}{12}$

D $\frac{5}{12}$

5. Which is the missing number?

$\frac{2}{3} = \frac{\square}{18}$

A 15

B 12

C 9

D 6

6. Which mixed number is equivalent to $\frac{13}{5}$?

A $1\frac{5}{8}$

B $2\frac{3}{5}$

C $3\frac{2}{5}$

D $13\frac{3}{5}$

Name______________________________

7. Which is $\frac{40}{48}$ in simplest form?

A $\frac{5}{12}$

B $\frac{20}{24}$

C $\frac{10}{12}$

D $\frac{5}{6}$

8. Which decimal describes the shaded square?

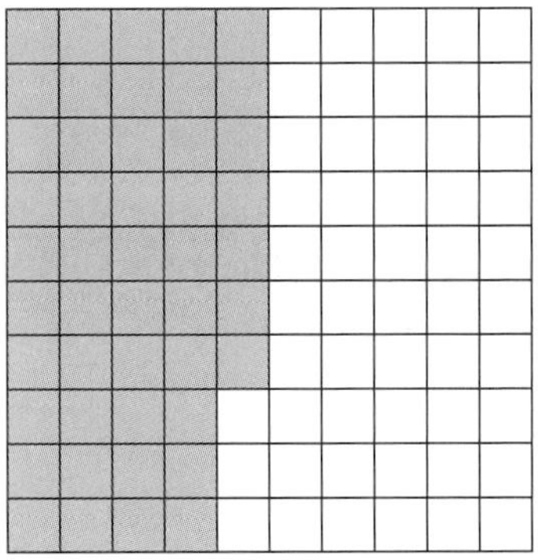

A 470

B 4.7

C 0.47

D 0.047

9. Multiply. Simplify if possible.

$\frac{2}{3} \times \frac{9}{10} =$

A $\frac{3}{10}$

B $\frac{3}{5}$

C $\frac{20}{27}$

D $1\frac{7}{20}$

10. How many thirds are in 12?

A 3

B 4

C 12

D 36

11. $\begin{array}{r} 15.3 \\ \times\ 0.32 \\ \hline \end{array}$

A 48.96

B 7.65

C 4.896

D 0.4765

12. $5.76 \div 1.8 =$

A 0.32

B 2.12

C 3.2

D 21.2

Name________________________________

Book B: Number and Operations 2

13. $\begin{array}{r} 52 \\ \times\ \ 3 \\ \hline \end{array}$

A 166

B 156

C 155

D 85

14. Jake packed 4 boxes of books for a used book sale. There were 78 books in each box. How many books did Jake pack?

A 112 books

B 282 books

C 292 books

D 312 books

15. $38\overline{)250}$

A 6 R22

B 6 R32

C 8 R6

D 60 R22

16. $23\overline{)726}$

A 36

B 35 R21

C 35 R1

D 31 R13

17.

1							
$\frac{1}{4}$		$\frac{1}{4}$		$\frac{1}{4}$			
$\frac{1}{8}$	$\frac{1}{8}$	$\frac{1}{8}$	$\frac{1}{8}$	$\frac{1}{8}$	$\frac{1}{8}$		

Which is the missing number?

$\frac{3}{4} = \frac{\square}{8}$

A 2 **C** 4

B 3 **D** 6

18.

1									
$\frac{1}{5}$		$\frac{1}{5}$		$\frac{1}{5}$		$\frac{1}{5}$			
$\frac{1}{10}$	$\frac{1}{10}$	$\frac{1}{10}$	$\frac{1}{10}$	$\frac{1}{10}$	$\frac{1}{10}$	$\frac{1}{10}$	$\frac{1}{10}$		

Which is the missing number?

$\frac{4}{5} = \frac{\square}{10}$

A 8

B 7

C 5

D 2

Name________________________________

19. Which is the greatest common factor of 15 and 40?

A 120

B 10

C 5

D 3

20. Which is $\frac{30}{80}$ in simplest form?

A $\frac{3}{10}$

B $\frac{3}{8}$

C $\frac{15}{40}$

D $\frac{3}{4}$

21. Which pair of ratios forms a proportion?

A $\frac{2}{3}, \frac{1}{15}$

B $\frac{3}{8}, \frac{2}{7}$

C $\frac{12}{20}, \frac{6}{10}$

D $\frac{12}{16}, \frac{3}{8}$

22. Solve the proportion.

$$\frac{\$21}{9\ pounds} = \frac{\$70}{x\ pounds}$$

A $x = 30$

B $x = 33$

C $x = 49$

D $x = 58$

23. Which of the following is a unit rate?

A 180 pages in 5 hours

B 2,000 cars in 1 hour

C $16 for 8 people

D 180 seats in 12 rows

24. Jenna rode her bicycle at an average speed of 7 meters per second. How many meters did Jenna ride in 16 seconds? Use the formula *distance* = *rate* × *time*.

A 9 meters

B 23 meters

C 112 meters

D 122 meters

Name________________________________

Book C: Algebra

25. $\begin{array}{r} 46 \\ +\ 34 \\ \hline \end{array}$

A 90

B 80

C 71

D 70

26. On Monday, Luis received 51 text messages. He received 23 text messages on Tuesday. How many more text messages did Luis receive on Monday than on Tuesday?

A 28 more text messages

B 32 more text messages

C 38 more text messages

D 74 more text messages

27. $\begin{array}{r} 2.8 \\ +\ 5.6 \\ \hline \end{array}$

A 84.0

B 8.4

C 7.4

D 0.84

28. $\begin{array}{r} 7.37 \\ -\ 4.88 \\ \hline \end{array}$

A 3.59

B 3.49

C 2.49

D 2.41

29. $\begin{array}{r} 63 \\ \times\ 4 \\ \hline \end{array}$

A 112

B 242

C 247

D 252

30. $\begin{array}{r} 326 \\ \times\ 4 \\ \hline \end{array}$

A 1,304

B 1,290

C 1,284

D 804

Name________________________________

Program Placement Test

31. $4\overline{)196}$

A 39

B 48

C 49

D 409

32. Ms. Rivera bought 216 water bottles for the school picnic. The water bottles came in cases of 24. How many cases did Ms. Rivera buy?

A 8 cases

B 9 cases

C 10 cases

D 12 cases

33. Evaluate $25 - 2d$ for $d = 5$.

A 235

B 115

C 15

D 0

34. Find the value of $6 \times 4 - 1$.

A 31

B 23

C 18

D 12

35. Solve $x - 25 = 42$.

A $x = 17$

B $x = 23$

C $x = 27$

D $x = 67$

36. Solve $5.4 = j + 2.5$

A $j = 7.9$

B $j = 3.9$

C $j = 3.1$

D $j = 2.9$

Name________________________________

Topic 1: Multiplying and Dividing Whole Numbers

1. $\begin{array}{r} 45 \\ \times\ 29 \\ \hline \end{array}$

A 495

B 1,205

C 1,224

D 1,305

2. A laptop costs $436. How much will it cost to order a laptop for each of the 53 sixth-graders at Edison School?

A $24,108

B $23,108

C $23,008

D $13,108

3. Which number is divisible by 3?

A 211

B 234

C 248

D 271

4. 7,200 ÷ 90 =

A 80

B 60

C 8

D 6

5. $32\overline{)853}$

A 25 R53

B 26

C 26 R21

D 27

6. $26\overline{)216}$

A 9

B 8 R8

C 8

D 7 R34

Name______________________________

Topic 2: Fraction Meanings and Concepts

1. What fraction of the circle is shaded?

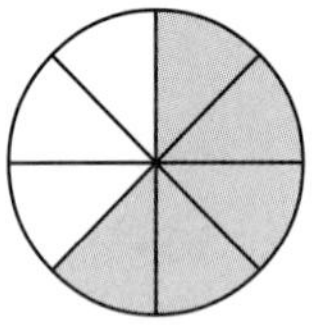

A $\frac{8}{5}$

B $\frac{5}{8}$

C $\frac{3}{6}$

D $\frac{3}{8}$

2. Which is the missing number?

$\frac{3}{10} = \frac{■}{20}$

A 2

B 5

C 6

D 12

3. Which mixed number is equivalent to $\frac{23}{4}$?

A $5\frac{3}{4}$

B $5\frac{1}{3}$

C $3\frac{4}{5}$

D $2\frac{3}{4}$

4. Which improper fraction is equivalent to $2\frac{5}{8}$?

A $\frac{8}{21}$

B $\frac{16}{8}$

C $\frac{21}{8}$

D $\frac{18}{5}$

5. Which is the greatest common factor of 24 and 32?

A 96

B 8

C 4

D 2

6. Which is $\frac{24}{32}$ in simplest form?

A $\frac{1}{8}$

B $\frac{12}{16}$

C $\frac{6}{8}$

D $\frac{3}{4}$

Name ______________________________

Topic 3: Multiplying and Dividing Fractions and Mixed Numbers

1. Multiply. Simplify, if possible.
$\frac{4}{9} \times \frac{3}{4} =$

A $1\frac{11}{16}$

B $\frac{16}{27}$

C $\frac{1}{3}$

D $\frac{8}{27}$

2. There are 20 students in Jenny's class. If $\frac{2}{5}$ of the students are boys, how many boys are there in Jenny's class?

A 4 boys

B 8 boys

C 10 boys

D 50 boys

3. Multiply. Simplify, if possible.
$1\frac{2}{5} \times 2\frac{3}{4} =$

A $3\frac{17}{20}$

B $2\frac{3}{10}$

C $1\frac{27}{28}$

D $\frac{28}{55}$

4. How many sixths are there in 3?

A 2

B 9

C 12

D 18

5. Divide. Simplify, if possible.
$\frac{3}{8} \div \frac{3}{5} =$

A $\frac{9}{40}$

B $\frac{5}{8}$

C $\frac{15}{24}$

D $\frac{8}{11}$

6. Divide. Simplify, if possible.
$3\frac{1}{2} \div 1\frac{5}{6} =$

A $6\frac{5}{12}$

B $3\frac{3}{5}$

C $1\frac{10}{11}$

D $\frac{11}{21}$

Name________________________________

Topic 4: Multiplying and Dividing Decimals

1. What is the value of the 3 in 94.23?

A 0.03

B 3

C 0.3

D 0.23

2. Which is $\frac{47}{100}$ written as a decimal?

A 0.047

B 0.47

C 4.7

D 470

3. A bottle of nail polish holds 0.45 ounce. How many ounces would 7 of these bottles hold?

A 0.315 ounce

B 3.15 ounces

C 31.5 ounces

D 315 ounces

4. $\begin{array}{r} 12.6 \\ \times\ 0.32 \\ \hline \end{array}$

A 0.710

B 3.922

C 4.032

D 40.32

5. $5\overline{)7.25}$

A 1.05

B 1.45

C 14.5

D 145

6. $0.64 \div 1.6 =$

A 0.04

B 0.3

C 0.4

D 4

Name________________________________

Topic 1: Multiplication and Division

1. $\begin{array}{r} 64 \\ \times \ 7 \\ \hline \end{array}$

A 448

B 452

C 474

D 481

2. $43\overline{)605}$

A 15 R6

B 14 R3

C 13 R8

D 12 R3

3. The grocery has 19.2 pounds of rice. If the rice is divided equally into 8 bags, how many pounds of rice will be in each bag?

A 1.2 pounds

B 1.5 pounds

C 2.2 pounds

D 2.4 pounds

4. $3.33 \div 3.7 =$

A 9.0

B 0.9

C 0.8

D 0.09

5. Solve $8b = 48$.

A $b = 40$

B $b = 12$

C $b = 6$

D $b = 4$

6. Solve $\frac{c}{18} = 4$.

A $c = 72$

B $c = 22$

C $c = 14$

D $c = 6$

Name______________________________

Topic 2: Fractions

1. 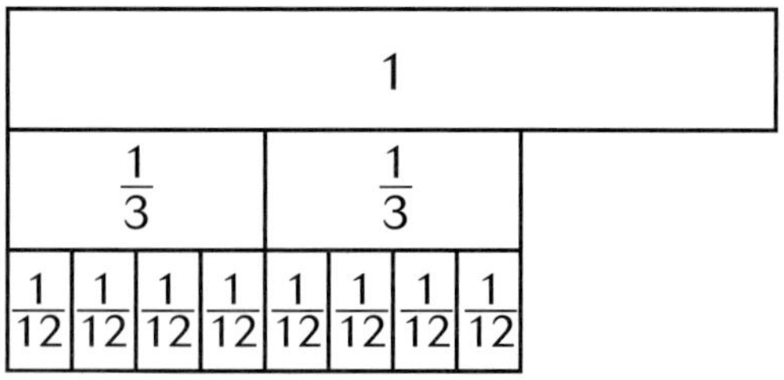

What is the missing number?

$\frac{2}{3} = \frac{\blacksquare}{12}$

A 6

B 8

C 9

D 11

2. Which is the greatest common factor of 18 and 30?

A 18

B 9

C 6

D 3

3. Which is $\frac{21}{28}$ in simplest form?

A $\frac{3}{4}$

B $\frac{1}{2}$

C $\frac{3}{8}$

D $\frac{1}{4}$

4. Multiply. Simplify, if possible.

$\frac{1}{2} \times \frac{3}{8} =$

A $3\frac{1}{16}$

B $1\frac{1}{8}$

C $\frac{3}{4}$

D $\frac{3}{16}$

5. $\frac{5}{6} \times 42 =$

A 54

B 38

C 35

D 26

6. Divide. Simplify, if possible.

$\frac{2}{3} \div \frac{5}{8}$

A $\frac{5}{12}$

B $\frac{1}{2}$

C $\frac{15}{16}$

D $1\frac{1}{15}$

Name____________________________________

Topic 3: Ratios and Proportions

1. Which is the ratio of Is to Ps in the word MISSISSIPPI?

A 4:4

B 2:4

C 4:2

D 3:2

2. In which row below is the ratio of Xs to Os 3 to 4?

A O O O X X X O

B O O X O O X

C X X O X X O O

D O O X X O X O X

3. Which pair of ratios forms a proportion?

A $\frac{2}{4}, \frac{7}{12}$

B $\frac{3}{4}, \frac{8}{9}$

C $\frac{8}{14}, \frac{5}{7}$

D $\frac{6}{8}, \frac{18}{24}$

4. Solve the proportion.

$\frac{23 \text{ seats}}{\text{bus}} = \frac{x \text{ seats}}{4 \text{ buses}}$

A $x = 96$

B $x = 92$

C $x = 72$

D $x = 5\frac{3}{4}$

5. Find the value of the missing number, c, in the proportion.

$\frac{3}{5} = \frac{c}{20}$

A $c = 30$

B $c = 22\frac{1}{2}$

C $c = 18$

D $c = 12$

6. The rectangles shown below are similar. Find the value of t.

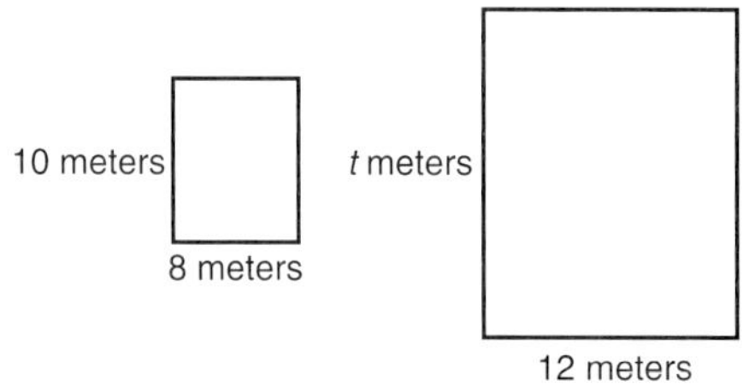

A $t = 15$

B $t = 9$

C $t = 8$

D $t = 7$

Name____________________

Topic 4: Rates

1. Which of the following is a unit rate?

A 280 kilometers in 4 hours

B $14 for 1 jacket

C 24 apples in 3 bags

D 4 pints in 2 quarts

2. There are 36 slices of bread in 3 loaves. What is the unit rate?

A 18 slices per loaf

B 16 slices per loaf

C 12 slices per loaf

D 9 slices per loaf

3. Bananas at Zeke's Produce are $6 for 3 pounds. Which store has a better buy for bananas than Zeke's?

A Store A: $9 for 5 pounds

B Store B: $8 for 3 pounds

C Store C: $5 for 2 pounds

D Store D: $3 for 1.2 pounds

4. Alonso's bakery can make 48 banana-nut muffins each hour. How many of these muffins can the bakery make in 4 hours?

A 12 muffins

B 52 muffins

C 96 muffins

D 192 muffins

5. A train traveled at an average speed of 75 miles per hour for 6 hours. Use the formula *distance* = *rate* × *time* to find how far the train traveled.

A 300 miles

B 450 miles

C 500 miles

D 600 miles

6. Cindy biked for 5 hours at an average speed of 8 kilometers per hour. Use the formula *distance* = *rate* × *time* to find the distance Cindy traveled.

A 4 kilometers

B 8 kilometers

C 13 kilometers

D 40 kilometers

Name________________________________

Topic 1: Addition and Subtraction

1. $\begin{array}{r} 56 \\ +\ 28 \\ \hline \end{array}$

A 111

B 84

C 82

D 74

2. $\begin{array}{r} 43 \\ -\ 17 \\ \hline \end{array}$

A 60

B 36

C 34

D 26

3. $\begin{array}{r} 0.63 \\ +\ 2.98 \\ \hline \end{array}$

A 2.61

B 3.51

C 3.61

D 361

4. $\begin{array}{r} 9.23 \\ -\ 2.71 \\ \hline \end{array}$

A 65.2

B 7.52

C 6.52

D 6.32

5. Andy is 1.388 meters tall, and Raul is 1.723 meters tall. How much taller is Raul than Andy?

A 0.335 meter

B 0.445 meter

C 3.35 meters

D 3.111 meters

6. Sandy has a string that is 1.282 meters long. Haley has a string that is 1.126 meters long. Which is the total length of the strings when laid end-to-end?

A 1.286 meters

B 1.308 meters

C 2.408 meters

D 2.562 meters

Name________________________________

Topic 2: Multiplication and Division

1. $\begin{array}{r} 32 \\ \times \quad 4 \\ \hline \end{array}$

A 8

B 36

C 78

D 128

2. $\begin{array}{r} 273 \\ \times \quad 5 \\ \hline \end{array}$

A 1,365

B 1,355

C 1,055

D 765

3. $8\overline{)432}$

A 504

B 54

C 53 R8

D 52

4. $41\overline{)897}$

A 2 R77

B 19 R18

C 21 R26

D 21 R36

5. A bag of shredded cheese weighs 1.25 pounds. What is the weight of 7 of these bags of cheese?

A 875 pounds

B 87.5 pounds

C 8.75 pounds

D 0.875 pound

6. $8\overline{)26.56}$

A 33.2

B 3.32

C 3.032

D 0.332

Name________________________________

Topic 3: Variables and Algebraic Expressions

1. What is a rule for the table?

Number of Packages	Number of Markers
1	4
2	8
5	20
7	28

A Add 3.

B Divide by 2.

C Subtract 15.

D Multiply by 4.

2. If r stands for the input, what is a rule for the table?

Input	Output
9	3
16	10
17	11
21	15

A $r + 7$

B $r - 9$

C $r - 6$

D $r + 6$

3. If n stands for the input, what is a rule for the table?

Input	Output
3	8
6	11
7	12

A $n + 5$

B $n - 8$

C $n - 5$

D $n + 3$

4. If n stands for the input, what is a rule for the table?

Input	Output
18	2
45	5
72	8

A $n \times 2$ **C** $n \times 9$

B $n \div 5$ **D** $n \div 9$

5. Evaluate $x \div 3$ for $x = 24$.

A 8 **C** 27

B 21 **D** 72

6. Evaluate $23 - f - 2$ for $f = 5$.

A 20 **C** 15

B 16 **D** 13

Name________________________________

Topic 4: Equivalent Expressions

1. Find the value of $27 - (6 + 9)$.

A 42

B 30

C 14

D 12

2. Find the value of $20 - 4 \times 2 + 3$.

A 0

B 9

C 15

D 35

3. Use the properties of operations to find the value of n.

$8 + (6 \times 12) = 8 + (n \times 12)$

A $n = 80$

B $n = 72$

C $n = 8$

D $n = 6$

4. Use the properties of operations to find the value of q.

$(4 + 7) \times 8 = (4 + 7) \times q$

A $q = 8$

B $q = 9$

C $q = 11$

D $q = 88$

5. Evaluate $6x - 3$ for $x = 4$.

A 61

B 27

C 21

D 7

6. Evaluate $5c + 2d$ for $c = 3$ and $d = 7$.

A 17

B 29

C 41

D 80

Name________________________________

Topic 5: Equations

1. You know $36 \div 6 = 6$. Which of the following is **NOT** true?

A $36 \div 6 + 12 = 6 + 12$

B $36 \div 6 - 3 = 6 - 3$

C $36 \div 6 \times 4 = 6 \times 4$

D $36 \div 6 \times 7 = 6 + 7$

2. You know $8 \times 10 = 80$. Which of the following is **NOT** true?

A $8 \times 10 - 7 = 80 - 7$

B $8 \times 10 + 5 = 80 - 5$

C $8 \times 10 \times 3 = 80 \times 3$

D $8 \times 10 \div 2 = 80 \div 2$

3. Solve $w + 25 = 66$.

A $w = 1{,}650$

B $w = 91$

C $w = 41$

D $w = 31$

4. Solve $16b = 80$.

A $b = 5$

B $b = 74$

C $b = 96$

D $b = 1{,}280$

5. Solve $42 = m - 14$.

A $m = 3$

B $m = 28$

C $m = 56$

D $m = 588$

6. Solve $y \div 6 = 4.2$.

A $y = 25.2$

B $y = 10.2$

C $y = 2.2$

D $y = 0.7$

Name____

Book A: Number and Operations 1

1. $\begin{array}{r} 36 \\ \times\ 17 \\ \hline \end{array}$

A 288

B 594

C 612

D 1,012

2. 4,900 ÷ 70 =

A 7

B 9

C 70

D 90

3. $87\overline{)750}$

A 7 R41

B 8 R54

C 8 R64

D 9 R33

4. What fraction of the circle is shaded?

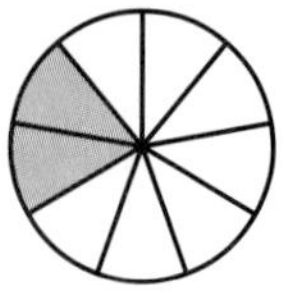

A $\frac{2}{9}$

B $\frac{2}{7}$

C $\frac{7}{9}$

D $\frac{9}{2}$

5. Which is the missing number?
$\frac{5}{8} = \frac{\blacksquare}{24}$

A 3

B 10

C 12

D 15

6. Which mixed number is equivalent to $\frac{32}{5}$?

A $6\frac{2}{5}$

B $5\frac{2}{5}$

C $3\frac{2}{5}$

D $2\frac{6}{5}$

Name ______________________________

7. Which is $\frac{30}{36}$ in simplest form?

A $\frac{0}{6}$

B $\frac{2}{3}$

C $\frac{15}{18}$

D $\frac{5}{6}$

8. Which is equivalent to $\frac{84}{100}$?

A 840

B 8.4

C 0.84

D 0.084

9. Multiply. Simplify, if possible.

$\frac{5}{12} \times \frac{8}{15} =$

A $\frac{2}{9}$

B $\frac{1}{3}$

C $\frac{13}{27}$

D $\frac{25}{32}$

10. How many fourths are in 8?

A 64

B 32

C 16

D 2

11.

$$\begin{array}{r} 14.7 \\ \times\ 0.28 \\ \hline \end{array}$$

A 41.16

B 41.6

C 4.216

D 4.116

12. $5.6 \div 1.4 =$

A 4

B 0.4

C 0.22

D 0.04

Name

Book B: Number and Operations 2

13. $\begin{array}{r} 85 \\ \times \ 3 \\ \hline \end{array}$

A 245

B 255

C 265

D 291

14. A shuttle bus has seats for 57 people. How many people can ride the bus in 9 trips?

A 4,563 people

B 513 people

C 506 people

D 486 people

15. $37\overline{)810}$

A 201 R33

B 26 R11

C 21 R33

D 21 R23

16. $34\overline{)772}$

A 21 R58

B 22 R24

C 23

D 24 R22

17.

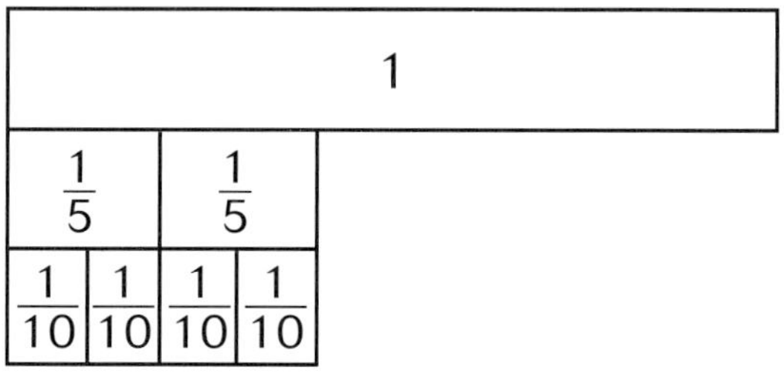

Which is the missing number?

$\frac{2}{5} = \frac{\square}{10}$

A 1

B 2

C 4

D 5

18.

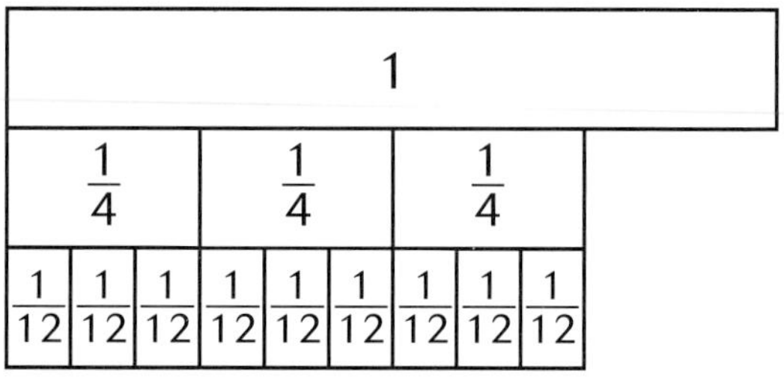

Which is the missing number?

$\frac{3}{4} = \frac{\square}{12}$

A 6

B 9

C 10

D 11

Name________________________________

19. Which is the greatest common factor of 27 and 12?

A 324

B 9

C 3

D 1

20. Which is $\frac{12}{16}$ in simplest form?

A $\frac{2}{3}$

B $\frac{3}{4}$

C $\frac{6}{8}$

D $\frac{7}{8}$

21. Which pair of ratios forms a proportion?

A $\frac{4}{18}, \frac{2}{9}$

B $\frac{8}{14}, \frac{5}{7}$

C $\frac{9}{10}, \frac{20}{18}$

D $\frac{3}{8}, \frac{15}{45}$

22. Solve the proportion.

$$\frac{56 \text{ pages}}{4 \text{ hours}} = \frac{x \text{ pages}}{6 \text{ hours}}$$

A $x = 96$

B $x = 84$

C $x = 20$

D $x = 2\frac{1}{3}$

23. There are 24 barrettes in 6 packages. Which is the unit rate?

A 144 barrettes per package

B 18 barrettes per package

C 6 barrettes per package

D 4 barrettes per package

24. Lorna hiked for 5 hours at an average speed of 3 miles per hour. How far did Lorna hike? Use the formula *distance* = *rate* × *time*.

A 53 miles

B 35 miles

C 15 miles

D 8 miles

PROGRAM PLACEMENT TEST

Program Placement Test

Name________________________

Book A: Number and Operations 1

1. $\begin{array}{r} 37 \\ \times\ 24 \\ \hline \end{array}$

- **A** 162
- **B** 828
- **(C)** 888
- **D** 1,212

2. 6,300 ÷ 70 =

- **(A)** 90
- **B** 80
- **C** 9
- **D** 8

3. $46\overline{)351}$

- **A** 6 R75
- **(B)** 7 R29
- **C** 7 R31
- **D** 7 R39

4. What fraction of the figure is shaded?

- **A** $\frac{12}{5}$
- **B** $\frac{5}{7}$
- **C** $\frac{7}{12}$
- **(D)** $\frac{5}{12}$

5. Which is the missing number?

$\frac{2}{3} = \frac{■}{18}$

- **A** 15
- **(B)** 12
- **C** 9
- **D** 6

6. Which mixed number is equivalent to $\frac{13}{5}$?

- **A** $1\frac{5}{8}$
- **(B)** $2\frac{3}{5}$
- **C** $3\frac{2}{5}$
- **D** $13\frac{3}{5}$

page M19

Program Placement Test

Name________________________

7. Which is $\frac{40}{48}$ in simplest form?

- **A** $\frac{5}{12}$
- **B** $\frac{20}{24}$
- **C** $\frac{10}{12}$
- **(D)** $\frac{5}{6}$

8. Which decimal describes the shaded square?

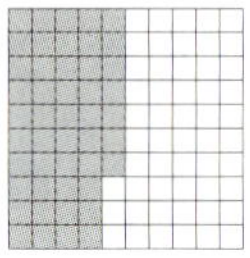

- **A** 470
- **B** 4.7
- **(C)** 0.47
- **D** 0.047

9. Multiply. Simplify if possible.

$\frac{2}{3} \times \frac{9}{10} =$

- **A** $\frac{3}{10}$
- **(B)** $\frac{3}{5}$
- **C** $\frac{20}{27}$
- **D** $1\frac{7}{20}$

10. How many thirds are in 12?

- **A** 3
- **B** 4
- **C** 12
- **(D)** 36

11. $\begin{array}{r} 15.3 \\ \times\ 0.32 \\ \hline \end{array}$

- **A** 48.96
- **B** 7.65
- **(C)** 4.896
- **D** 0.4765

12. 5.76 ÷ 1.8 =

- **A** 0.32
- **B** 2.12
- **(C)** 3.2
- **D** 21.2

page M20

Program Placement Test

Name________________________

Book B: Number and Operations 2

13. $\begin{array}{r} 52 \\ \times\ 3 \\ \hline \end{array}$

- **A** 166
- **(B)** 156
- **C** 155
- **D** 85

14. Jake packed 4 boxes of books for a used book sale. There were 78 books in each box. How many books did Jake pack?

- **A** 112 books
- **B** 282 books
- **C** 292 books
- **(D)** 312 books

15. $38\overline{)250}$

- **(A)** 6 R22
- **B** 6 R32
- **C** 8 R6
- **D** 60 R22

16. $23\overline{)726}$

- **A** 36
- **B** 35 R21
- **C** 35 R1
- **(D)** 31 R13

17.

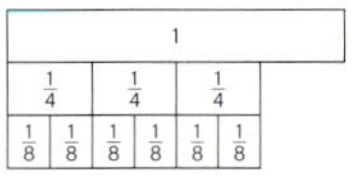

Which is the missing number?

$\frac{3}{4} = \frac{■}{8}$

- **A** 2
- **B** 3
- **C** 4
- **(D)** 6

18.

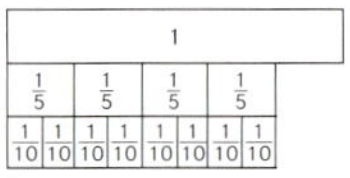

Which is the missing number?

$\frac{4}{5} = \frac{■}{10}$

- **(A)** 8
- **B** 7
- **C** 5
- **D** 2

page M21

Program Placement Test

Name________________________

19. Which is the greatest common factor of 15 and 40?

- **A** 120
- **B** 10
- **(C)** 5
- **D** 3

20. Which is $\frac{30}{80}$ in simplest form?

- **A** $\frac{3}{10}$
- **(B)** $\frac{3}{8}$
- **C** $\frac{15}{40}$
- **D** $\frac{3}{4}$

21. Which pair of ratios forms a proportion?

- **A** $\frac{2}{3}, \frac{1}{15}$
- **B** $\frac{3}{8}, \frac{2}{7}$
- **(C)** $\frac{12}{20}, \frac{6}{10}$
- **D** $\frac{12}{16}, \frac{3}{8}$

22. Solve the proportion.

$\frac{\$21}{9\ pounds} = \frac{\$70}{x\ pounds}$

- **(A)** $x = 30$
- **B** $x = 33$
- **C** $x = 49$
- **D** $x = 58$

23. Which of the following is a unit rate?

- **A** 180 pages in 5 hours
- **(B)** 2,000 cars in 1 hour
- **C** $16 for 8 people
- **D** 180 seats in 12 rows

24. Jenna rode her bicycle at an average speed of 7 meters per second. How many meters did Jenna ride in 16 seconds? Use the formula *distance = rate × time.*

- **A** 9 meters
- **B** 23 meters
- **(C)** 112 meters
- **D** 122 meters

page M22

Name

Program Placement Test

Book C: Algebra

25. $\begin{array}{r} 46 \\ +\ 34 \\ \hline \end{array}$

A 90

B 80

C 71

D 70

26. On Monday, Luis received 51 text messages. He received 23 text messages on Tuesday. How many more text messages did Luis receive on Monday than on Tuesday?

A 28 more text messages

B 32 more text messages

C 38 more text messages

D 74 more text messages

27. $\begin{array}{r} 2.8 \\ +\ 5.6 \\ \hline \end{array}$

A 84.0

B 8.4

C 7.4

D 0.84

28. $\begin{array}{r} 7.37 \\ -\ 4.88 \\ \hline \end{array}$

A 3.59

B 3.49

C 2.49

D 2.41

29. $\begin{array}{r} 63 \\ \times\ 4 \\ \hline \end{array}$

A 112

B 242

C 247

D 252

30. $\begin{array}{r} 326 \\ \times\ 4 \\ \hline \end{array}$

A 1,304

B 1,290

C 1,284

D 804

M23

page M23

Name

Program Placement Test

31. $4\overline{)196}$

A 39

B 48

C 49

D 409

32. Ms. Rivera bought 216 water bottles for the school picnic. The water bottles came in cases of 24. How many cases did Ms. Rivera buy?

A 8 cases

B 9 cases

C 10 cases

D 12 cases

33. Evaluate $25 - 2d$ for $d = 5$.

A 235

B 115

C 15

D 0

34. Find the value of $6 \times 4 - 1$.

A 31

B 23

C 18

D 12

35. Solve $x - 25 = 42$.

A $x = 17$

B $x = 23$

C $x = 27$

D $x = 67$

36. Solve $5.4 = j + 2.5$

A $j = 7.9$

B $j = 3.9$

C $j = 3.1$

D $j = 2.9$

M24

page M24

TOPIC TESTS

Book A
Topic 1 Test

Name______________________

Topic 1: Multiplying and Dividing Whole Numbers

1. $\begin{array}{r} 45 \\ \times\ 29 \\ \hline \end{array}$

   A 495
   B 1,205
   C 1,224
   D 1,305 (circled)

2. A laptop costs $436. How much will it cost to order a laptop for each of the 53 sixth-graders at Edison School?

   A $24,108
   B $23,108 (circled)
   C $23,008
   D $13,108

3. Which number is divisible by 3?

   A 211
   B 234 (circled)
   C 248
   D 271

4. 7,200 ÷ 90 =

   A 80 (circled)
   B 60
   C 8
   D 6

5. $32\overline{)853}$

   A 25 R53
   B 26
   C 26 R21 (circled)
   D 27

6. $26\overline{)216}$

   A 9
   B 8 R8 (circled)
   C 8
   D 7 R34

M25

page M25

Book A
Topic 2 Test

Name______________________

Topic 2: Fraction Meanings and Concepts

1. What fraction of the circle is shaded?

   A $\frac{8}{5}$
   B $\frac{5}{8}$ (circled)
   C $\frac{3}{6}$
   D $\frac{3}{8}$

2. Which is the missing number?
   $\frac{3}{10} = \frac{\blacksquare}{20}$

   A 2
   B 5
   C 6 (circled)
   D 12

3. Which mixed number is equivalent to $\frac{23}{4}$?

   A $5\frac{3}{4}$ (circled)
   B $5\frac{1}{3}$
   C $3\frac{4}{5}$
   D $2\frac{3}{4}$

4. Which improper fraction is equivalent to $2\frac{5}{8}$?

   A $\frac{8}{21}$
   B $\frac{16}{8}$
   C $\frac{21}{8}$ (circled)
   D $\frac{18}{5}$

5. Which is the greatest common factor of 24 and 32?

   A 96
   B 8 (circled)
   C 4
   D 2

6. Which is $\frac{24}{32}$ in simplest form?

   A $\frac{1}{8}$
   B $\frac{12}{16}$
   C $\frac{6}{8}$
   D $\frac{3}{4}$ (circled)

M26

page M26

Book A
Topic 3 Test

Name______________________

Topic 3: Multiplying and Dividing Fractions and Mixed Numbers

1. Multiply. Simplify, if possible.
   $\frac{4}{9} \times \frac{3}{4} =$

   A $1\frac{11}{16}$
   B $\frac{16}{27}$
   C $\frac{1}{3}$ (circled)
   D $\frac{8}{27}$

2. There are 20 students in Jenny's class. If $\frac{2}{5}$ of the students are boys, how many boys are there in Jenny's class?

   A 4 boys
   B 8 boys (circled)
   C 10 boys
   D 50 boys

3. Multiply. Simplify, if possible.
   $1\frac{2}{5} \times 2\frac{3}{4} =$

   A $3\frac{17}{20}$ (circled)
   B $2\frac{3}{10}$
   C $1\frac{27}{28}$
   D $\frac{28}{55}$

4. How many sixths are there in 3?

   A 2
   B 9
   C 12
   D 18 (circled)

5. Divide. Simplify, if possible.
   $\frac{3}{8} \div \frac{3}{5} =$

   A $\frac{9}{40}$
   B $\frac{5}{8}$ (circled)
   C $\frac{15}{24}$
   D $\frac{8}{11}$

6. Divide. Simplify, if possible.
   $3\frac{1}{2} \div 1\frac{5}{6} =$

   A $6\frac{5}{12}$
   B $3\frac{3}{5}$
   C $1\frac{10}{11}$ (circled)
   D $\frac{11}{21}$

M27

page M27

Book A
Topic 4 Test

Name______________________

Topic 4: Multiplying and Dividing Decimals

1. What is the value of the 3 in 94.23?

   A 0.03 (circled)
   B 3
   C 0.3
   D 0.23

2. Which is $\frac{47}{100}$ written as a decimal?

   A 0.047
   B 0.47 (circled)
   C 4.7
   D 470

3. A bottle of nail polish holds 0.45 ounce. How many ounces would 7 of these bottles hold?

   A 0.315 ounce
   B 3.15 ounces (circled)
   C 31.5 ounces
   D 315 ounces

4. $\begin{array}{r} 12.6 \\ \times\ 0.32 \\ \hline \end{array}$

   A 0.710
   B 3.922
   C 4.032 (circled)
   D 40.32

5. $5\overline{)7.25}$

   A 1.05
   B 1.45 (circled)
   C 14.5
   D 145

6. 0.64 ÷ 1.6 =

   A 0.04
   B 0.3
   C 0.4 (circled)
   D 4

M28

page M28

Name________________________

Book B
Topic 1 Test

Topic 1: Multiplication and Division

1. 64×7

   (A) 448
   B 452
   C 474
   D 481

2. $43\overline{)605}$

   A 15 R6
   (B) 14 R3
   C 13 R8
   D 12 R3

3. The grocery has 19.2 pounds of rice. If the rice is divided equally into 8 bags, how many pounds of rice will be in each bag?

   A 1.2 pounds
   B 1.5 pounds
   C 2.2 pounds
   (D) 2.4 pounds

4. $3.33 \div 3.7 =$

   A 9.0
   (B) 0.9
   C 0.8
   D 0.09

5. Solve $8b = 48$.

   A $b = 40$
   B $b = 12$
   (C) $b = 6$
   D $b = 4$

6. Solve $\frac{c}{18} = 4$.

   (A) $c = 72$
   B $c = 22$
   C $c = 14$
   D $c = 6$

page M29

Name________________________

Book B
Topic 2 Test

Topic 2: Fractions

1. 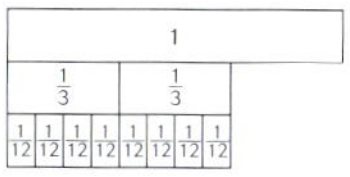

   What is the missing number?
   $\frac{2}{3} = \frac{\square}{12}$

   A 6
   (B) 8
   C 9
   D 11

2. Which is the greatest common factor of 18 and 30?

   A 18
   B 9
   (C) 6
   D 3

3. Which is $\frac{21}{28}$ in simplest form?

   (A) $\frac{3}{4}$
   B $\frac{1}{2}$
   C $\frac{3}{8}$
   D $\frac{1}{4}$

4. Multiply. Simplify, if possible.
   $\frac{1}{2} \times \frac{3}{8} =$

   A $3\frac{1}{16}$
   B $1\frac{1}{8}$
   C $\frac{3}{4}$
   (D) $\frac{3}{16}$

5. $\frac{5}{6} \times 42 =$

   A 54
   B 38
   (C) 35
   D 26

6. Divide. Simplify, if possible.
   $\frac{2}{3} \div \frac{5}{8}$

   A $\frac{5}{12}$
   B $\frac{1}{2}$
   C $\frac{15}{16}$
   (D) $1\frac{1}{15}$

page M30

Name________________________

Book B
Topic 3 Test

Topic 3: Ratios and Proportions

1. Which is the ratio of Is to Ps in the word MISSISSIPPI?

   A 4:4
   B 2:4
   (C) 4:2
   D 3:2

2. In which row below is the ratio of Xs to Os 3 to 4?

   (A) O O O X X X O
   B O O X O O X
   C X X O X X O O
   D O O X X O X O X

3. Which pair of ratios forms a proportion?

   A $\frac{2}{4}, \frac{7}{12}$
   B $\frac{3}{4}, \frac{8}{9}$
   C $\frac{8}{14}, \frac{5}{7}$
   (D) $\frac{6}{8}, \frac{18}{24}$

4. Solve the proportion.
   $\frac{23 \text{ seats}}{\text{bus}} = \frac{x \text{ seats}}{4 \text{ buses}}$

   A $x = 96$
   (B) $x = 92$
   C $x = 72$
   D $x = 5\frac{3}{4}$

5. Find the value of the missing number, c, in the proportion.
   $\frac{3}{5} = \frac{c}{20}$

   A $c = 30$
   B $c = 22\frac{1}{2}$
   C $c = 18$
   (D) $c = 12$

6. The rectangles shown below are similar. Find the value of t.

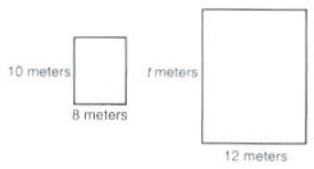

   (A) $t = 15$
   B $t = 9$
   C $t = 8$
   D $t = 7$

page M31

Name________________________

Book B
Topic 4 Test

Topic 4: Rates

1. Which of the following is a unit rate?

   A 280 kilometers in 4 hours
   (B) $14 for 1 jacket
   C 24 apples in 3 bags
   D 4 pints in 2 quarts

2. There are 36 slices of bread in 3 loaves. What is the unit rate?

   A 18 slices per loaf
   B 16 slices per loaf
   (C) 12 slices per loaf
   D 9 slices per loaf

3. Bananas at Zeke's Produce are $6 for 3 pounds. Which store has a better buy for bananas than Zeke's?

   (A) Store A: $9 for 5 pounds
   B Store B: $8 for 3 pounds
   C Store C: $5 for 2 pounds
   D Store D: $3 for 1.2 pounds

4. Alonso's bakery can make 48 banana-nut muffins each hour. How many of these muffins can the bakery make in 4 hours?

   A 12 muffins
   B 52 muffins
   C 96 muffins
   (D) 192 muffins

5. A train traveled at an average speed of 75 miles per hour for 6 hours. Use the formula *distance* = *rate* × *time* to find how far the train traveled.

   A 300 miles
   (B) 450 miles
   C 500 miles
   D 600 miles

6. Cindy biked for 5 hours at an average speed of 8 kilometers per hour. Use the formula *distance* = *rate* × *time* to find the distance Cindy traveled.

   A 4 kilometers
   B 8 kilometers
   C 13 kilometers
   (D) 40 kilometers

page M32

TOPIC TESTS

Book C
Topic 1 Test

Name________________________

Topic 1: Addition and Subtraction

1. 56 + 28

A 111
(B) 84
C 82
D 74

2. 43 − 17

A 60
B 36
C 34
(D) 26

3. 0.63 + 2.98

A 2.61
B 3.51
(C) 3.61
D 361

4. 9.23 − 2.71

A 65.2
B 7.52
(C) 6.52
D 6.32

5. Andy is 1.388 meters tall, and Raul is 1.723 meters tall. How much taller is Raul than Andy?

(A) 0.335 meter
B 0.445 meter
C 3.35 meters
D 3.111 meters

6. Sandy has a string that is 1.282 meters long. Haley has a string that is 1.126 meters long. Which is the total length of the strings when laid end-to-end?

A 1.286 meters
B 1.308 meters
(C) 2.408 meters
D 2.562 meters

M33

page M33

Book C
Topic 2 Test

Name________________________

Topic 2: Multiplication and Division

1. 32 × 4

A 8
B 36
C 78
(D) 128

2. 273 × 5

(A) 1,365
B 1,355
C 1,055
D 765

3. 8)432

A 504
(B) 54
C 53 R8
D 52

4. 41)897

A 2 R77
B 19 R18
C 21 R26
(D) 21 R36

5. A bag of shredded cheese weighs 1.25 pounds. What is the weight of 7 of these bags of cheese?

A 875 pounds
B 87.5 pounds
(C) 8.75 pounds
D 0.875 pound

6. 8)26.56

A 33.2
(B) 3.32
C 3.032
D 0.332

M34

page M34

Book C
Topic 3 Test

Name________________________

Topic 3: Variables and Algebraic Expressions

1. What is a rule for the table?

Number of Packages	Number of Markers
1	4
2	8
5	20
7	28

A Add 3.
B Divide by 2.
C Subtract 15.
(D) Multiply by 4.

2. If r stands for the input, what is a rule for the table?

Input	Output
9	3
16	10
17	11
21	15

A $r + 7$
B $r - 9$
(C) $r - 6$
D $r + 6$

3. If n stands for the input, what is a rule for the table?

Input	Output
3	8
6	11
7	12

(A) $n + 5$
B $n - 8$
C $n - 5$
D $n + 3$

4. If n stands for the input, what is a rule for the table?

Input	Output
18	2
45	5
72	8

A $n \times 2$
C $n \times 9$
B $n \div 5$
(D) $n \div 9$

5. Evaluate $x \div 3$ for $x = 24$.

(A) 8
C 27
B 21
D 72

6. Evaluate $23 - f - 2$ for $f = 5$.

A 20
C 15
(B) 16
D 13

M35

page M35

Book C
Topic 4 Test

Name________________________

Topic 4: Equivalent Expressions

1. Find the value of $27 - (6 + 9)$.

A 42
B 30
C 14
(D) 12

2. Find the value of $20 - 4 \times 2 + 3$.

A 0
B 9
(C) 15
D 35

3. Use the properties of operations to find the value of n.
$8 + (6 \times 12) = 8 + (n \times 12)$

A $n = 80$
B $n = 72$
C $n = 8$
(D) $n = 6$

4. Use the properties of operations to find the value of q.
$(4 + 7) \times 8 = (4 + 7) \times q$

(A) $q = 8$
B $q = 9$
C $q = 11$
D $q = 88$

5. Evaluate $6x - 3$ for $x = 4$.

A 61
B 27
(C) 21
D 7

6. Evaluate $5c + 2d$ for $c = 3$ and $d = 7$.

A 17
(B) 29
C 41
D 80

M36

page M36

Name________________________

Book C
Topic 5 Test

Topic 5: Equations

1. You know 36 ÷ 6 = 6. Which of the following is **NOT** true?

A 36 ÷ 6 + 12 = 6 + 12

B 36 ÷ 6 − 3 = 6 − 3

C 36 ÷ 6 × 4 = 6 × 4

D 36 ÷ 6 × 7 = 6 + 7

2. You know 8 × 10 = 80. Which of the following is **NOT** true?

A 8 × 10 − 7 = 80 − 7

B 8 × 10 + 5 = 80 − 5

C 8 × 10 × 3 = 80 × 3

D 8 × 10 ÷ 2 = 80 ÷ 2

3. Solve $w + 25 = 66$.

A $w = 1{,}650$

B $w = 91$

C $w = 41$

D $w = 31$

4. Solve $16b = 80$.

A $b = 5$

B $b = 74$

C $b = 96$

D $b = 1{,}280$

5. Solve $42 = m - 14$.

A $m = 3$

B $m = 28$

C $m = 56$

D $m = 588$

6. Solve $y \div 6 = 4.2$.

A $y = 25.2$

B $y = 10.2$

C $y = 2.2$

D $y = 0.7$

M37

page M37

PROGRAM EXIT TEST

Program Exit Test

Name________________________

Book A: Number and Operations 1

1. 36 $\times$ 17

   A 288
   B 594
   (C) 612
   D 1,012

2. 4,900 ÷ 70 =

   A 7
   B 9
   (C) 70
   D 90

3. $87\overline{)750}$

   A 7 R41
   (B) 8 R54
   C 8 R64
   D 9 R33

4. What fraction of the circle is shaded?

   (A) $\frac{2}{9}$
   B $\frac{2}{7}$
   C $\frac{7}{9}$
   D $\frac{9}{2}$

5. Which is the missing number?
   $\frac{5}{8} = \frac{■}{24}$

   A 3
   B 10
   C 12
   (D) 15

6. Which mixed number is equivalent to $\frac{32}{5}$?

   (A) $6\frac{2}{5}$
   B $5\frac{2}{5}$
   C $3\frac{2}{5}$
   D $2\frac{6}{5}$

M38

page M38

Program Exit Test

Name________________________

7. Which is $\frac{30}{36}$ in simplest form?

   A $\frac{0}{6}$
   B $\frac{2}{3}$
   C $\frac{15}{18}$
   (D) $\frac{5}{6}$

8. Which is equivalent to $\frac{84}{100}$?

   A 840
   B 8.4
   (C) 0.84
   D 0.084

9. Multiply. Simplify, if possible.
   $\frac{5}{12} \times \frac{8}{15} =$

   (A) $\frac{2}{9}$
   B $\frac{1}{3}$
   C $\frac{13}{27}$
   D $\frac{25}{32}$

10. How many fourths are in 8?

   A 64
   (B) 32
   C 16
   D 2

11. 14.7 $\times$ 0.28

   A 41.16
   B 41.6
   C 4.216
   (D) 4.116

12. 5.6 ÷ 1.4 =

   (A) 4
   B 0.4
   C 0.22
   D 0.04

M39

page M39

Program Exit Test

Name________________________

Book B: Number and Operations 2

13. 85 $\times$ 3

   A 245
   (B) 255
   C 265
   D 291

14. A shuttle bus has seats for 57 people. How many people can ride the bus in 9 trips?

   A 4,563 people
   (B) 513 people
   C 506 people
   D 486 people

15. $37\overline{)810}$

   A 201 R33
   B 26 R11
   (C) 21 R33
   D 21 R23

16. $34\overline{)772}$

   A 21 R58
   (B) 22 R24
   C 23
   D 24 R22

17.

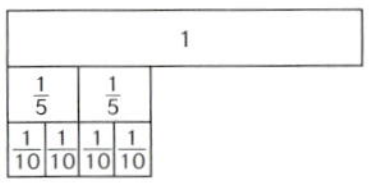

   Which is the missing number?
   $\frac{2}{5} = \frac{■}{10}$

   A 1
   B 2
   (C) 4
   D 5

18.

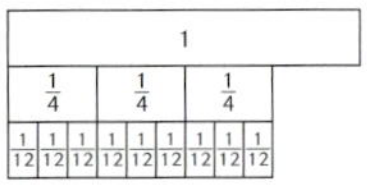

   Which is the missing number?
   $\frac{3}{4} = \frac{■}{12}$

   A 6
   (B) 9
   C 10
   D 11

M40

page M40

Program Exit Test

Name________________________

19. Which is the greatest common factor of 27 and 12?

   A 324
   B 9
   (C) 3
   D 1

20. Which is $\frac{12}{16}$ in simplest form?

   A $\frac{2}{3}$
   (B) $\frac{3}{4}$
   C $\frac{6}{8}$
   D $\frac{7}{8}$

21. Which pair of ratios forms a proportion?

   (A) $\frac{4}{18}, \frac{2}{9}$
   B $\frac{8}{14}, \frac{5}{7}$
   C $\frac{9}{10}, \frac{20}{18}$
   D $\frac{3}{8}, \frac{15}{45}$

22. Solve the proportion.
   $\frac{56 \text{ pages}}{4 \text{ hours}} = \frac{x \text{ pages}}{6 \text{ hours}}$

   A $x = 96$
   (B) $x = 84$
   C $x = 20$
   D $x = 2\frac{1}{3}$

23. There are 24 barrettes in 6 packages. Which is the unit rate?

   A 144 barrettes per package
   B 18 barrettes per package
   C 6 barrettes per package
   (D) 4 barrettes per package

24. Lorna hiked for 5 hours at an average speed of 3 miles per hour. How far did Lorna hike? Use the formula *distance* = *rate* × *time*.

   A 53 miles
   B 35 miles
   (C) 15 miles
   D 8 miles

M41

page M41

Name____________________ Program Exit Test

Book C: Algebra

25. $44 + 37$

A 83
(**B**) 81
C 76
D 61

26. There are 56 students in sixth grade at Riley School. If 28 of the students are girls, how many are boys?

A 46
B 38
C 32
(**D**) 28

27. $0.67 + 1.29$

(**A**) 1.96
B 1.89
C 1.38
D 0.62

28. $8.65 - 3.82$

A 6.44
B 5.23
C 4.92
(**D**) 4.83

29. 76×8

A 548
B 568
C 604
(**D**) 608

30. 183×7

A 1,417
(**B**) 1,281
C 1,101
D 813

M42

page M42

Name____________________ Program Exit Test

31. $7\overline{)371}$

A 503
(**B**) 53
C 51
D 50

32. A bakery has 513 muffins to put on trays. Each tray holds 27 muffins. How many trays will the bakery fill?

A 17 trays
(**B**) 19 trays
C 24 trays
D 29 trays

33. Evaluate $11 - f + 3$ for $f = 5$.

(**A**) 9
B 8
C 6
D 3

34. Find the value of $30 - 5 \times 2 + 4$.

A 0
B 16
(**C**) 24
D 54

35. Solve $m + 18 = 35$.

A $m = 53$
B $m = 24$
(**C**) $m = 17$
D $m = 6$

36. Solve $4.2 = 3h$.

(**A**) $h = 1.4$
B $h = 1.26$
C $h = 1.2$
D $h = 0.14$

M43

page M43

RESEARCH BIBLIOGRAPHY

Lester, Frank K., Jr., and Randall I. Charles, eds. 2003. *Teaching Mathematics through Problem Solving: Prekindergarten–Grade 6*. Reston, VA: National Council of Teachers of Mathematics.

Fuchs, Lynn S., and Douglas Fuchs. 2001. Principles for the Prevention and Intervention of Mathematics Difficulties. *Learning Disabilities Research & Practice* 16 (2): 85–95.

Gersten, R., S. Beckmann, B. Clarke, A. Foegen, L. Marsh, J. R. Star, and B. Witzel. 2009. *Assisting Students Struggling with Mathematics: Response to Intervention (RtI) for Elementary and Middle Schools* (NCEE 2009-4060). Washington, DC: National Center for Education Evaluation and Regional Assistance, Institute of Education Sciences, U.S. Department of Education. Retrieved from http://ies.ed.gov/ncee/wwc/publications/practiceguides/.

Mack, N. K. 1990. Learning Fractions with Understanding: Building on Informal Knowledge. *Journal for Research in Mathematics Education* 21 (1): 16–32.

Mathematics Learning Study Committee. 2001. *Adding It Up: Helping Children Learn Mathematics.* Edited by J. Kilpatrick, J. Swafford, and B. Findell. Washington, D.C.: National Academy Press.

National Council of Teachers of Mathematics. 2000. *Principles and Standards for School Mathematics*. Reston, VA: National Council of Teachers of Mathematics.

Paris, S. G., and A. E. Cunningham. 1996. "Children becoming students." In D. C. Berliner & R. C. Calfee, eds. *Handbook of Educational Psychology*. New York: Macmillan.